Ni___ _____ __ ___ is the author of over a hundred and fifty books including *A Brief History of Robin Hood*, *A Brief Guide to James Bond*, *A Brief History of Sherlock Holmes*, *A Brief Guide to Jeeves and Wooster*, *A Brief Guide to J. R. R. Tolkien*, *Jack the Ripper's Secret Confession*, *House of Horrors*, *The Mammoth Book of the Mafia*, *Against Their Will* and a forthcoming biography of Agatha Christie's one-time rival John Creasey.

Recent titles in the series

A Brief Guide to Star Trek
Brian J. Robb

A Brief Guide to James Bond
Nigel Cawthorne

A Brief Guide to Jane Austen
Charles Jennings

A Brief Guide to Secret Religions
David Barrett

A Brief History of Angels and Demons
Sarah Bartlett

A Brief History of Bad Medicine
Robert Youngston

A Brief History of France
Cecil Jenkins

A Brief History of Slavery
Jeremy Black

A Brief History of Sherlock Holmes
Nigel Cawthorne

A Brief Guide to J. R. R. Tolkien
Nigel Cawthorne

A Brief Guide to Jane Austen
Charles Jennings

A Brief Guide to C. S. Lewis
Paul Simpson

A Brief History of the Private Life of Elizabeth II
Michael Patterson

A Brief Guide to Jeeves and Wooster
Nigel Cawthorne

A Brief History of Superheroes
Brian J. Robb

A Brief History of the Spy
Paul Simpson

A Brief Guide to Oz
Paul Simpson

A BRIEF GUIDE TO

AGATHA CHRISTIE

Nigel Cawthorne

ROBINSON

RUNNING PRESS
PHILADELPHIA · LONDON

Constable & Robinson Ltd
55–56 Russell Square
London WC1B 4HP
www.constablerobinson.com

First published in the UK by Robinson,
An imprint of Constable & Robinson Ltd, 2014

A copy of the British Library Cataloguing in
Publication data is available from the British Library

ISBN 978-1-47211-057-2 (paperback)
ISBN 978-1-47211-069-5 (ebook)

1 3 5 7 9 10 8 6 4 2

First published in the United States in 2013 by Running Press Book Publishers,
A Member of the Perseus Books Group

Books published by Running Press are available at special discounts for bulk purchases
in the United States by corporations, institutions, and other organizations. For more
information, please contact the Special Markets Department at the Perseus Books
Group, 2300 Chestnut Street, Suite 200, Philadelphia, PA 19103, or call (800) 810-4145,
ext. 5000, or email special.markets@perseusbooks.com.

US ISBN 978-0-7624-5473-0
US Library of Congress Control Number: 2014931617

9 8 7 6 5 4 3 2 1
Digit on the right indicates the number of this printing

Running Press Book Publishers
2300 Chestnut Street
Philadelphia, PA 19103-4371

Visit us on the web!
www.runningpress.com

Typeset by TW Typesetting, Plymouth, Devon

Printed and bound in the UK

CONTENTS

INTRODUCTION

No one is really sure just how many books Agatha Christie has sold, or in how many languages. However, it is thought that she is the number-three bestseller worldwide behind the Bible and Shakespeare. Though her books are largely set in parochial England, she has a following around the world. This may well be because she was free from the pretensions that plague other authors.

'I regard my work as of no importance,' she said. 'I've simply been out to entertain.'

Asked where she got her ideas from, she would say that she went to Harrods, or the Army & Navy Store, or Marks & Spencer. The real answer was from her own head. However, she was steeped in literature and culture. Her antecedents are as much Shakespeare, Webster, Tennyson and Wagner as Sir Arthur Conan Doyle and Edgar Allan Poe. She also travelled widely and, through her second husband archaeologist Sir Max Mallowan and his colleagues, knew a great deal about the ancient world.

Although she died nearly forty years ago, she is as popular as she ever was, with the long-running TV series *Poirot* and *Miss Marple* airing on both sides of the Atlantic. While the world these two much-loved characters inhabit may appear cosy and middle class, it is heaving with forgery, blackmail, adultery and murder. It is also awash with drugs – first with cocaine and morphine, later heroin and, latterly, marijuana. Then there were the guns. Largely these were brought back from the wars but, as we see in *The Seven Dials Mystery* of 1924, it was still a time when you could pop into Harrods to buy a pistol.

Readers should be warned of the casual racism of the era. The books abound with slighting remarks about Jews, 'dagos', 'Chinks', black people and foreigners. However, one must remember that Agatha Christie began writing during the era of Modernism. Indeed she was some eight years younger than Virginia Woolf and James Joyce. So we should now view these racial slights in a Post-Modernist light and grow up about the N word. Yes, she called a book *Ten Little Niggers*. The word comes up in other books too. It was offensive then and remains so. But we cannot whitewash the past, if you will excuse the pun. And it was not as if Christie was particularly racist herself. In *Hickory, Dickory, Death*, written in 1955, Poirot's secretary Miss Lemon says: 'Half the nurses in our hospitals seem to be black nowadays . . . and I understand much pleasanter and more attentive than the English ones.'

What's more, Christie is positively revolutionary in some eyes. In the 1970s, the communist Tupamaros guerrillas in Uruguay adopted Miss Marple as their honorary leader. Inmates of the Buchenwald concentration camps used to perform her plays in the face of the horrors there. Some say that it is the extraordinary simplicity of her characters that appeals. Others say that everyone wants the whole world to be like an English village.

During her lifetime, Christie was pilloried by some intellectuals. But her work has endured, while those of her critics have remained resolutely unheeded. True, the genteel world of country houses and the grand tour between the wars that she portrays is comforting. But her subject matter is life and, more particularly, death. Her characters are motivated by real emotions and the stage they are set upon is just as relevant as Elizabethan England or ancient Greece.

Agatha Christie is, of course, the Queen of Crime, the Duchess of Death. Her books are largely whodunnits, so I have taken great pains not to give away the endings. But if you want to spoil them for yourself, you can look up the plots on Wikipedia.

Nigel Cawthorne

I

AGATHA CHRISTIE

Although Agatha Christie's stories were written between the First World War and her death in 1976, they seem to bask in the glorious certainties of the Edwardian era, and the home of all the murder and mayhem she unleashed on the world was the innocent Devon seaside resort of Torquay. Indeed, Agatha Mary Clarissa Miller was born on 15 September 1890 when Queen Victoria was still firmly on the throne and the sun never set on the British Empire. She recalled as her childhood reality 'ladies, their shirts looped up and held in one hand . . . playing croquet, or, with straw boater-hats on their heads . . . playing tennis'. But elsewhere in the gardens of her family home, Ashfield in Barton Road, was a wood where enchantment lay.

Agatha's father, Frederick Alvah Miller, was an American of independent means. Once a suitor of Brooklyn heiress Jenny Jerome, Winston Churchill's mother, he spent most of his life playing whist in the yacht club, returning by taxi for lunch and to dress for dinner. He was president of the local cricket club and staged amateur theatricals.

Her mother, Clarissa 'Clara' Margaret Boehmer, was brought up by her Aunt Margaret, the second wife of Frederick's father, in the north of England. Eight years her senior, cousin Fred would visit on his way from his home in New York, where he was on the Social Register, to the south of France. They married in 1878 when Fred was thirty-two and Clara twenty-four. The marriage was a happy one.

Their first child, Margaret Frary Miller, was born in Torquay, where they had taken furnished lodgings. Their second child, Louis Montant, was born during a visit to New York in 1880. They had intended to live in America, however, after returning to England, Fred was called back to New York on business. While he was away, Clara used a small inheritance to buy Ashfield, a large house in Torquay, then a fashionable south-coast resort.

Fred insisted that they live there for a year at most, but Clara was a forceful woman and they were still there when Agatha was born ten years later. Clara was also a serious, high-minded woman who flirted with a series of religions, but they lived the life of the moneyed classes. They went out to dine several times a week. Five-course dinners at home were provided by the cook, Jane, while a chef and butler were hired when they entertained.

The older children were sent away to boarding school, but Agatha's upbringing was overseen by 'Nursie', then by a series of parlour maids, while Jane taught her how to make cakes. This entourage was ruled over by Clara, who seemed to possess second sight. Agatha's older sister Madge once said that she did not even dare think when Clara was in the room. And Agatha herself learned to be secretive. When asked why she had not reported a parlour maid seen tasting soup from the tureen before dinner, she said pompously: 'I don't care for parting with information.'

When her parents travelled together, Agatha would stay with her 'Auntie-Grannie' Margaret in the west London suburb of Ealing. There she would become acquainted with her mother's widowed mother Mary Ann, who then lived in Bayswater and would take her shopping at the Army & Navy stores in Victoria. She also got to know her uncles, one of whom worked for the Army & Navy. Another worked for the Home Office, while a third was with his regiment in India. Their gossip was full of the characters that would later inhabit Agatha's literary output.

Agatha's education – such as it was – took place at home. However, her father had an extensive library, well stocked with American books and children's adventure stories, as well as dictionaries, atlases and encyclopaedias. Agatha learned to write at the age of six and, thanks to her father, quickly mastered arithmetic, along with the basic principles of physics and chemistry. But apart from music tuition, she had no formal education. However, she was a voracious reader, relishing particularly the detective stories *The Woman in White* and *The Moonstone* by Wilkie Collins, Edgar Allan Poe's *The Murders in the Rue Morgue*, Sir Arthur Conan Doyle's tales of Sherlock Holmes, the stories of French writer Maurice Leblanc concerning the gentleman-thief Arsène Lupin and Dickens' *Bleak House* with Inspector Bucket. She read Alexandre Dumas in French, particularly enjoying *The Count of Monte Cristo*.

Agatha mixed with other children at dance classes, but otherwise her childhood companions were her pets, along with a number of imaginary friends. She even made up a make-believe school full of imaginary girls and had adventures with a whole dynasty of invented kings and queens.

She was still a child when her father's business affairs ran into trouble. To save money, the family often rented out Ashfield and spent the time in hotels in France and Italy. The language was no problem. After Nursie retired, Clara took on a French governess who spoke no English. Beset with money worries, Fred grew ill and died at the age of fifty-five. Agatha was just eleven.

By then, Agatha's older sister had married and her brother was in the army. Agatha and her mother would spend the evenings reading aloud Scott, Thackeray and Dickens. But Agatha grew concerned about her mother's health and slept in Fred's dressing room, next to Clara's bedroom, in case her mother needed reviving in the night. They would spend the Christmas holiday at Madge's new home, Cheadle Hall, a Georgian building, and the Gothic revival Abney Hall in Manchester, home of Madge's in-laws. Madge's brothers-in-law included a professional actor in London and an actor-manager who owned a theatre in Manchester. Agatha's Christmas treat involved a visit to the pantomime.

At home, Agatha had absorbed a great deal of literature and mastering riddles, codes and word games. Then, at the age of thirteen she was sent to Miss Guyer's Girls' School in Torquay, two days a week. There she was taught algebra, grammar and spelling. Used to engaging with only those things that interested her, the discipline of formal lessons did not suit Miss Miller. However, she began to develop a circle of friends, including the five Huxley sisters who shocked polite society in Torquay because they did not wear gloves. Through them, Agatha got a part in a production of *The Yeomen of the Guard*, singing the role of Colonel Fairfax. While with the Lucy family, she went swimming in the ladies' bathing cove.

At fifteen Agatha was sent to a succession of finishing schools in Paris. When she returned, her mother could not afford for her to come out in London or New York, so took her to Cairo, then safely under British administration, where she could meet suitable young men at balls, the races and polo matches. They stayed at the Gezirah Palace Hotel and she attended some fifty dances. With long, blonde hair that had to be piled on top of her head, she was tall and attractive, but painfully shy. One dance partner remarked that, while she could dance beautifully, her mother 'had better try and teach her to talk'. Nevertheless she made new friends, accompanying them on expeditions to see the sights or picnic in the desert. She would be swathed in muslin to keep off the sun and corseted in whalebone, while temptation was kept at bay by chaperones.

Back in England, the friends she made in Egypt invited her to stay at their country houses to attend hunt balls, race meetings and regattas. She played tennis and croquet, went riding and out for fast drives down narrow country lanes in the latest automobiles. The impresario Charles Cochran and his wife invited Agatha to stay with them in London and she continued the family tradition, putting on amateur theatricals.

As well as contributing to sketches, Agatha began writing poetry. At the age of eleven, she had had a poem about the new tram service published in the local paper. Later she began earning a guinea a poem sending work to the *Poetry Review*. Some of her early poems were published in *The Road of Dreams* in 1924. She set some to music, but in public performance, her nerve failed her. Although she trained as a singer in Paris and continued her musical studies in London, her shyness put paid to any thought she had of being a professional singer or pianist.

Before she married, Agatha's sister Madge had published a series of stories in *Vanity Fair*. Bored, while recovering from influenza, Agatha followed her example and wrote the 6,000-word story 'The House of Beauty'. A supernatural tale, it was revised and published as 'The House of Dreams' in *Sovereign Magazine* in January 1926, though it did not appear in any of her collections until 1997.

Next she wrote 'The Call of Wings', which appeared in the UK in *The Hound of Death and Other Short Stories* in 1933 and in the US in *The Golden Ball and Other Short Stories* in 1971. This grisly story about a séance was rewritten many years later as *The Sittaford Mystery*. A fourth story has not survived, while her fifth paranormal tale 'The Little Lonely God', appeared as 'The Lonely God' in *Royal Magazine* in July 1926. For the time being, though, the short stories she sent out to magazines under the names 'Mac Miller', 'Nathaniel Miller' and 'Sydney West' – West being the maiden name of her great-aunt Margaret – were promptly returned.

One of Sydney West's other stories, 'The Choice', echoes a story written by Agatha's mother called 'Mrs Jordan's Ghost'. In it, a ghost turns up every time a piece of music is played, a device that Christie would use later.

Undaunted by her rejections, Agatha wrote a novel set in Cairo called *Snow Upon the Desert*. She sent it out under the pen-name 'Monosylaba'. It was returned. Clara now suggested that she consult their neighbour, author Eden Phillpotts – Agatha had attended dance classes with his daughter, Adelaide. His reaction was encouraging and he gave helpful advice. He also introduced her to his literary agent Hughes Massie, but he too rejected the novel.

Agatha was inspired by another psychic story, *The Flaw in the Crystal* by May Sinclair, to write 'Vision'. But this also showed the influence of the detective story *The Mystery of the Yellow Room* by Gaston Leroux. However, she put it aside and sent the story 'Being So Very Wilful' to Phillpotts, who again was encouraging and constructive.

Meanwhile Agatha had met Bolton Fletcher, a colonel in the Lancers. He proposed. He was fifteen years older than Agatha and Clara insisted that she wait six months before she gave her decision. When the moratorium was up, Agatha said no. Her engagement to childhood friend Wilfred Pirie similarly failed to blossom when he bored her with his talk of spiritualism and theosophy. There was also a romantic correspondence with Reginald Lucy, the older brother of the Lucy sisters with whom Agatha went rollerskating and picnicking on Dartmoor. Apart from her brother-in-law, they were the only people who got away with calling her 'Aggie'. Agatha was now in her twenties in an age where a woman's only prospect was to marry well. Her mother and elder sister began to worry. However, at a dance, she met Archibald Christie, a second lieutenant stationed in Exeter. Born in India, where his father had been a judge, Archie had ambitions to join the newly formed Royal Flying Corps. At twenty-three, he was just a year older than Agatha.

Tall and attractive, he fell for Agatha instantly and, shortly after, appeared at Ashfield on a motorbike. Agatha was playing badminton and trying out the latest dance steps at the Mellors' opposite and had to be summoned home by phone. He stayed for supper.

After several irreproachable dates, Archie announced that he had been accepted by the RFC and was being posted to Farnborough. He asked Agatha to marry him. She said that she had an understanding with Reggie Lucy. Archie brushed this aside, but Clara urged caution. They could hardly marry on a subaltern's pay. But the romance continued, with Agatha both excited and appalled at Archie's daredevil escapades. She, too, took to the air, paying £5 for a short flight at an air exhibition. Although thrilled, she wrote begging Archie to give up flying. He refused.

Several attempts were made to break off the engagement. As it dragged on Agatha's family fortunes continued to decline. An attempt was made to sell off the family plot in Greenwood Cemetery in Brooklyn. Then in August 1914 the war came and the RFC was sent to France.

Archie quickly proved himself in action and rose through the ranks. Determined to do her bit, Agatha joined the Voluntary Air Detachment at the local hospital. Tending to the wounded, she shared the horrors of the war. When they met at the end of the year, both had changed. Agatha had become more serious; Archie more flippant. She was now determined to marry; he was against it, fearing that he would leave a young widow with a baby on the way. This led to a row. Archie capitulated. They married, despite his mother's objections, by special licence on Christmas Eve, 1914. Their one-day honeymoon was spent in the Grand Hotel, Torquay, after informing Clara and Madge of their nuptials. On Boxing Day, he returned to France; she to the hospital. They were separated for six months.

Great-aunt Margaret, whose sight was failing, moved into Ashfield, bringing her heavy Victorian mahogany furniture. One of Agatha's duties was to read her the newspaper reports of the latest murder trials. Fearing Germany's blockade of Britain, they began hoarding food. This attracted pests and the house fell to ruin.

After an attempt to move to Paris to be nearer Archie, Agatha went to work in the hospital's dispensary. Studying to qualify as an apothecary, she learned about poisons. The pharmacist, who Christie found unnervingly incompetent, carried a lump of curare in his pocket, saying that it was interesting stuff.

'Taken by mouth, it does no harm at all. Enter the bloodstream, it paralyses and kills you,' he would say.

Agatha continued writing and in the poem 'In the Dispensary', published in *The Road of Dreams* in 1924, she reveals her fascination for poisons, writing: 'Here is menace and murder and sudden death/in these phials of green and blue.'

Her interest in detective stories continued and, after discussing Leroux's *The Mystery of the Yellow Room*, Madge challenged her to write one. The key, she decided, was not to have an unusual murder for an unusual motive – 'that did not appeal to me artistically,' she said – but rather to construct a riddle.

'The whole point of a good detective story,' she wrote in her *Autobiography*, 'was that it must be somebody obvious, but at the same time, for some reason, you would then find that it was not obvious, that he could not possibly have done it. Though really, of course, he had done it.'

It is a trick she uses repeatedly, initially concentrating the suspicions so firmly on one character that the reader discounts them. The murderer is not at the scene of the crime or appears to be the intended victim. They might be a policeman or a child, physically incapacitated – or even, famously, the narrator of the stories. In some way, Agatha Christie makes the reader eliminate the most obvious suspect. Neither did she believe in giving characters exotic motivations. Her characters are all driven by normal human emotions.

Then she needed a memorable detective, a singular character of a type that had not been used before. At the time, Torquay was awash with Belgian refugees, so Christie came up with Hercule Poirot, a retired Belgian police officer. Belgians were both seen as exotic and gallant at the time – Britain had gone to war because gallant little Belgium had been overrun by the Hun.

She wrote in longhand, typing a fair copy of each finished chapter on her sister's typewriter. But she became bogged down in the plot, which employed a lot of her knowledge of pharmacy. At her mother's suggestion she took a fortnight off and went to stay at the Moorland Hotel at Haytor on Dartmoor. There she wrote all morning, then she walked over the moors in the afternoon speaking out loud the dialogue for the next section. This was a lifelong habit that made her feel that her characters were real. Then she would sleep for twelve hours before resuming work.

Returning with the completed manuscript of *The Mysterious Affair at Styles*, she added some love interest – vital for the modern popular novel – before sending it off to be professionally typed. It was then rejected by Hodder & Stoughton and Methuen, before disappearing into the slush-pile at The Bodley Head.

Repeatedly decorated for bravery, Archie returned as a colonel in September 1918 to work in the Air Ministry. He and Agatha moved into a small flat in St John's Wood. Soon after, the Great War was over and she was expecting a baby. The following August their daughter, Rosalind Margaret Clarissa, was born. With few friends in London, they did most of their socializing in Torquay. Archie found a well-paid job in the City and, in 1919, they moved into an unfurnished four-bedroomed flat near Holland Park where they employed a nurse and a housemaid. Agatha threw herself into decorating the place.

Just before they moved, John Lane from The Bodley Head came round to discuss *The Mysterious Affair at Styles*, which she had submitted two years earlier and had long given up hope of having published. He suggested some alterations, including a major change to the ending. Instead of a courtroom scene where Poirot delivers the solution in evidence, Lane wanted the dénouement to take place in the library during a conversation between Poirot and Captain Hastings, the narrator.

Lane offered her a 10 per cent royalty on sales of over 2,000 in the UK and over 1,000 in the US. She would also get half of the sale of any serial or dramatic rights. Lane also wanted an option on her next five books which, back then, she had no plans to write.

Agatha received £25 for the book's serialisation in *The Times* newspaper's *Colonial Edition*, known as *The Weekly Times*. This ran from 27 February to 26 June 1920. That October, John Lane published the book in New York at $2, while The Bodley Head edition came out in London the following January at seven shillings and six pence (37½p). It was dedicated to Clara.

Although great-aunt Margaret had died and Agatha had moved away, Clara's fortune continued to decline. Archie thought she should sell Ashfield and move somewhere more modest. Agatha was outraged at the idea so, instead,

Archie suggested that she write another book. While she did not think that she would earn any money that way, she was touched by the faith Archie showed in her literary ability.

She did not attempt another detective story, but turned her hand to a comedy thriller about two 'young adventurers' named Tommy Beresford and Tuppence Cowley – based on herself and Archie – left rudderless by the end of the war. John Lane published *The Secret Adversary* in 1922. It earned her £50 and was again serialized in *The Weekly Times*. This brought her to the attention of Bruce Ingram, editor of the *Sketch* magazine, who commissioned a series of twelve Poirot stories. She also set to work on another Poirot novel, *The Murder on the Links*, based on a murder case that had occurred in France not long before. Masked men had broken into a hotel, killed the owner and left the wife bound and gagged. However, inconsistencies in the wife's story suggested that she had either colluded or been the murderer herself.

Meanwhile, Archie had been offered a job promoting the forthcoming Empire Exhibition and, as they travelled around South Africa, New Zealand, Australia and Canada, Agatha knocked out the stories on a small Corona typewriter, while Rosalind was left at home in the care of Clara and Madge. The trip was something of a gamble as Archie would have no secure City job to come home to.

They travelled in stately fashion on liners and staying at the best hotels. In South Africa, they learned to surf, attended a garden party at the archbishop's palace and lunched with the governor general, the Duke of Connaught. After a visit to the Cape Town Museum, Agatha enthused about the prehistoric rock carvings and all the paintings. They then found themselves in the middle of an insurrection in Pretoria that was swiftly put down. After a visit to the diamond mines at Kimberley, she went on to Rhodesia (Zimbabwe) to see the Victoria Falls.

As they sailed on to Australia, Agatha read the reviews of *The Secret Adversary* John Lane had sent. All of them were good. After a trip to Tasmania, Agatha received a letter telling her that Madge had found a producer for a play she had written, continuing the literary rivalry between the two sisters. Meanwhile, between trips out into the bush, tea parties and official luncheons, Agatha managed to keep writing.

After more official visits in New Zealand, Archie and Agatha took a holiday in Hawaii. Like the rest of the US, it was in the grip of prohibition. But then Agatha Christie both loathed the taste of alcohol and disliked its effects. She would normally quaff neat cream while others drank champagne, though she had a life-long appetite for caviar. Only once in her adult life did she eschew pure water – a sanctimonious teetotaller had come to lunch and she ostentatiously ordered a bottle of beer.

While Archie's £1,000 fee for the trip was dwindling fast, Agatha found that money was coming in from John Lane, including £47 for the Swedish-language rights to *The Mysterious Affair at Styles*. Nevertheless, by the time they reached Canada, they sustained themselves by gorging on the $1 all-you-can-eat hotel breakfast and making soup with meat extract and jugs of hot water they had sent to their room. They were also sustained with enormous meals laid on by local dignitaries they visited.

In Winnipeg, Archie came down with bronchitis and Agatha was left to nurse him. He caught up with the official party in Newfoundland while she travelled to New York to stay with her aunt. From there, they sailed home on the RMS *Majestic*, arriving in England on 1 December, having been away for ten months.

While they had been away, the tranquillity of Ashfield had been disturbed by the return of Agatha's brother Monty who had squandered his inheritance in the colonies and was suffering with an infected wound sustained in Africa during the war. He had brought with him to Torquay an African manservant named Shebani, and disturbed the neighbourhood by firing a pistol out of the window – 'to keep his eye in' he told the police. When Shebani returned to Africa, Monty was installed in a cottage on Dartmoor with a doctor's widow as housekeeper to look after him.

Archie found it difficult to fit back into life in the City. Though they could still afford a nurse for Rosalind, there was no money for a housekeeper, so Agatha did the cooking and cleaning.

The short stories she had written for the *Sketch* were published as *Poirot Investigates*. She also submitted 'Vision' to The Bodley Head. Lane rejected it, but Christie insisted that it constituted one of the five books she was under contract to provide. The next book was to be *The Man in the Brown Suit*, another thriller with a young woman as protagonist which drew heavily on her trip to South Africa.

She now became more assured in her business dealings, holding back dramatic, cinematic and foreign rights, asking for higher royalties and insisting on changes to the covers. Her work was now in demand by magazines, which strengthened her hand with The Bodley Head. The Inland Revenue also took an interest. To cope with their demands she acquired an agent – Edmund Cork, successor to Hugh Massie who was now dead. Cork would be her agent for the next fifty years.

Madge had some success with the production of her play *The Claimant* in the West End. Archie got a new job in the City and they took a large flat in Sunningdale in nascent stockbroker belt thirty miles from London, where Archie could indulge his newfound passion for golf. And when the *Evening News* acquired the serial rights to *The Man in the Brown Suit* for £500, Agatha bought a car, a bottle-nosed Austin Cowley that would be her pride and joy. Learning to drive a car that she had bought with her own money gave her a new sense of independence.

With growing confidence, she published, at her own

expense, her collection of poems, *The Road of Dreams*. It was not a success. Meanwhile, Cork negotiated a three-book deal with Collins, getting a £200 advance on each title and a generous royalty. But first Christie had to deliver one last book to The Bodley Head. This was to be *The Secret of Chimneys*. 'Chimneys', where most of the action is set, is a version of Abney Hall. It also introduces her stock policeman, Superintendent Battle.

Agatha and Archie holidayed at Cauterets in the Pyrenees where she had spent time as a child. Otherwise, life in Sunningdale was dull with Agatha finding herself increasingly a 'golf widow'. She diverted herself by writing *The Murder of Roger Ackroyd*, which used the revolutionary device of making the narrator the perpetrator of the crime. The idea had come from Madge's husband James Watt who had suggested that someday Dr Watson ought to be the murderer. Christie demurred, saying that technically it would be difficult to pull this off. But then Louis Mountbatten wrote to her, care of the *Sketch*, suggesting the same thing and even outlining the plot.

The book was published in June 1926 by Collins in the UK and Dodd, Mead & Co., who had acquired John Land & Co. in 1922, in the US. Critics attacked the book and a reader wrote a letter of complaint to *The Times*. Christie conceded that 'a lot of people say that *The Murder of Roger Ackroyd* is cheating; but if they read it carefully they will see that they are wrong. Such little lapses of time as there have to be are nicely concealed in an ambiguous sentence . . .' The narrator, Dr James Sheppard, 'took great pleasure himself in writing nothing but the truth, though not the whole truth'.

Archie and Agatha now had a house built on the Wentworth Estate, where the golf course had just been opened. They called the new house Styles. Soon after Clara died, leaving Ashfield to Agatha. It was in a poor state of repair and Agatha took on the responsibility of salvaging it.

To save money, they decided to rent out Styles with Archie staying at his club in London while Agatha occupied herself in Torquay. They planned a holiday in Italy, but during their separation Archie fell in love with Miss Nancy Neele, a golf partner and an acquaintance of Agatha's. Archie told Agatha that he no longer loved her and wanted a divorce. She was devastated, unable to eat or sleep. Her sole source of comfort seems to have been a wire-haired terrier called Peter.

Returning to Styles, they sought to bring about a reconciliation. Divorce in the 1920s was both difficult and a disgrace. However, Archie soon moved back to his club, seeing Nancy at the weekends in the company of friends to keep the scandal to a minimum. Meanwhile, Agatha was so distraught that she could not work.

On 3 December 1926, she persuaded her secretary and Rosalind's nurse Charlotte Fisher – known as Carlo – to take the day off. When Carlo returned that evening, she found the garage doors open. The maids said that Mrs Christie had driven off at around eleven o'clock that evening. At six the following morning, her car was found abandoned in some bushes at Newlands Corner, around an hour's drive away.

Before she had left Wentworth, she had removed her wedding ring and kissed Rosalind goodnight. She had also left a note for Carlo, telling her to cancel a booking she had made with a boarding house in Yorkshire where she had planned to stay with Archie. But Archie had already made other plans. He was going to stay at some friends' house in Surrey with Nancy.

Carlo called him. By the time he returned to Styles, the newspapers had got the story and the house was besieged. Archie had little time for the press or the police, but Carlo gave an interview every day to the *Daily Mail*, Agatha's favourite paper. Meanwhile, the newspapers scoured the countryside for leads.

Witnesses had seen a woman answering Agatha's description on the night she had disappeared having trouble with her car. The police presumed that she had crashed it then, in a dazed and confused state, got lost in the woods. Local streams and ponds were dragged, but nothing was found.

Other witnesses said that she had been seen with a well-dressed man of about thirty-two. The theory circulated that she had gone into hiding with a young companion. The water was further muddied when it was discovered that Archie's brother had received a letter from her, postmarked 'London SW, 9.45, December 4'. However he misplaced it and did not find it again until 8 December, five days after Agatha had disappeared. The newspapers reported that in it, Agatha had said that she was going to a spa town in Yorkshire to rest and recuperate. However, *The Times* reported that the Surrey Police had been in touch with their counterparts in Yorkshire and were convinced that she was not in that county.

Fresh theories abounded, including one that Mrs Christie had suffered some sort of psychological breakdown and was subconsciously playing out the plot from some forthcoming novel.

By the end of the week, the newspapers discovered that there had been problems in the Christie's marriage and that Agatha had been depressed since the death of her mother. On 10 December, Archie told the *Daily Mail* that Agatha had mentioned the possibility of disappearing at will. This was what he thought had happened, he said; at least he comforted himself with the thought. He dismissed the idea that his wife had committed suicide even though her books demonstrated that she was thoroughly familiar with poison.

On 12 December some 5,000 volunteers, many with dogs, made another search of the area around Newlands Corner. An aeroplane circled overheard and the local beauty spot,

Silent Pool, was dragged again and divers were brought in. The newspapers were now offering a reward for anyone who could find the missing crime writer. This brought in bogus sightings from all over the country. Reporters were now linking the Christie case to the disappearance of other young women and fellow crime writer Edgar Wallace was brought in to comment. In the *Daily Mail* he reasoned that if she was not dead of shock or exposure in the vicinity of where her car was found, she must be alive and well, probably in London, though she may have lost her memory. Dorothy L. Sayers concurred in the *Daily News*, while Sir Arthur Conan Doyle told the *Morning Post* that Christie would soon be found.

On Tuesday 14 December, Agatha Christie was spotted in the Winter Garden Ballroom of the Hydropathic Hotel in the Yorkshire spa town of Harrogate by two musicians in the dance band. They reported the matter to the West Riding Police in the hope of collecting the reward.

The Surrey Police contacted Carlo, but she could not leave Rosalind. She called Archie who took the train from King's Cross to make the identification. In the hotel, the police stationed themselves in an alcove by the lift. When Christie came downstairs for dinner, she crossed the lobby to pick up an evening paper that was carrying the story of her disappearance. Archie approached her. She held out her hand as if greeting an acquaintance.

'Hello,' she said. 'My name is Neele, Mrs Teresa Neele.'

It was the name she had used when she had checked into the hotel on 4 December. Once the identification was confirmed, she was taken by Archie to Abney Hall, where she would be safe from reporters.

Examined by doctors it seems that she could not remember anything between leaving Styles on 3 December and being greeted by Archie in the Hydropathic Hotel. What she was doing on the night she went missing has never been determined. Nor is it known how she travelled the three-and-a-half miles between Newlands Corner and Guildford, where she caught the milk train to Waterloo.

There she had cup of tea at the buffet and wrote the letter to Archie's brother. At Waterloo, she saw a poster advertising a spa in Yorkshire. She had blood on her face and her arm ached, so she assumed she was heading there for therapy.

Not only did she have money from a small cheque Carlo had cashed for her, she was also carrying a money belt – her grandmother had always advised her to carry extra cash in case of emergencies. At Whiteleys department store, she bought a cloth coat, a small travel case and some toiletries.

Then she took the train to Harrogate, reaching the Harrogate Hydro around 7 p.m. – before the story of the missing novelist had been reported in the newspapers or broadcast on the evening news. She registered with the hotel as 'Mrs Neele, of Cape Town, SA'. In the pre-Christmas season, the hotel was not full and she was given a small room with a basin and an easy chair. When the maid brought her breakfast, she covered her face as if hiding a bruise.

At Abney Hall, Agatha was persuaded to see a psychiatrist. She cavilled at this, but as she had caused so much distress and worry she reluctantly agreed and took a flat in West Kensington to be handy for Harley Street. With the aid of the psychiatrist, Agatha recalled that she had played bridge with fellow guests at the Hydro and even discussed the whereabouts of the rogue novelist. Staff noticed the similarity between their guest and the missing writer, but the management asked them to be discreet.

After a few days, she began to worry that her money would soon be exhausted, so on Saturday 11 December she put a small ad in *The Times* asking for 'friends and relatives of Theresa Neele, late of South Africa' to contact her, giving a box number. She never explained why she called herself Theresa Neele, except that she knew someone named Theresa in Torquay; Neele was the name of the woman her husband had left her for.

Because the two musicians who had identified her had gone to the police rather than the newspapers, they had not received the reward. However, Archie later gave them each a silver pencil in gratitude for their discretion.

Once the news of Agatha Christie's discovery had hit the 'stop press' column of the *Yorkshire Post*, the Hydro was mobbed by reporters. The *Daily Mail* even had a special train standing by to whisk her to London if she agreed to give them an exclusive. Archie was eventually persuaded to talk to one representative of the press, but only gave him a prepared statement about his wife's loss of memory. Most of the press were fooled when a limousine pulled up at the front entrance. But a photographer from the *Daily Mail* got the scoop when Agatha and Archie were bundled out of the back.

More reporters and photographers tried to beard them at Leeds, but the Christies were soon safe behind the gates of Abney Hall. Disturbingly, when Agatha was reunited with Rosalind she did not seem to recognize her own daughter. Meanwhile, a cynical public wrote it off as a publicity stunt, though few writers had done less to court publicity.

2

THE QUEEN OF CRIME

The controversy over *The Mystery of Roger Ackroyd* and her mysterious disappearance made Agatha Christie public property. A chronically shy person, she was an unwilling celebrity. Meanwhile, her private life was in tatters.

Uncertain about her future, she was also short of money – and unable to write. However, she put together the last twelve stories from the *Sketch* and reworked them as a novel, *The Big Four*.

By then she was living with Carlo and Rosalind in Chelsea, still believing that her marriage could be resuscitated. However, Archie believed that only marriage to Nancy would make him happy and Agatha reluctantly agreed to a divorce. She felt the shame of it intensely and, afterwards, never took communion in church again. However, she continued to write using her married name.

Encouraged by Carlo and her brother-in-law James Watt, she took Carlo and Rosalind to the Canary Islands where she forced herself to complete *The Mystery of the Blue Train*. The murder victim, heiress Ruth Kettering, has an unhappy marriage. The heroine, Katherine Grey, is another young independent woman in her thirties that Agatha enjoyed portraying. However, she did not like the book, while the critics enjoyed the return of Hercule Poirot to top form. It was dedicated to Carlo and Peter.

Rosalind was then sent to the boarding school Benenden in Kent, which later provided the backdrop for *Cat Among the Pigeons*. To pay the bills, Christie wrote the thriller *The Seven Dials Mystery*, where she resurrected Lady Eileen 'Bundle' Brent and Superintendent Battle from *The Secret of Chimneys*, and *Partners in Crime*. This was a collection of short stories featuring Tommy Beresford and Tuppence from *The Secret Adversary* – six years on and now married. They are now professional sleuths and in each story they parody the various detective teams known to readers in the 1920s.

Agatha was now the consummate writer, noting down ideas for stories on anything that came to hand. Newspapers and magazines were keen to serialize her work and money from her books came rolling in.

Then she made a new departure. As Mary Westmacott, she wrote *Giant's Bread* about a composer, Vernon Deyre, struggling to master the new forms of artistic expression that appeared after the First World War.

She then considered going to the West Indies to enjoy the sunshine there. Instead she headed for Baghdad after discovering that she could get there on the Orient Express. Agatha travelled alone, finding herself courted by numerous gentleman passengers. To escape the stifling expat community in Baghdad she travelled on to the ancient city of Ur, at the time being excavated by Leonard Woolley, who had previously worked alongside T. E. Lawrence – Lawrence of Arabia – on digs in Syria. There she was befriended by Woolley's wife Katharine, the kind of sexual tease who would appear in her future stories.

Back in London, Agatha bought a small mews cottage in Chelsea, while Edmund Cork negotiated a six-book deal with Collins, again upping the advance, increasing the royalty and holding back the foreign rights which were now in demand. She also wrote the 'Mr Quin' stories for magazines, teaming Harley Quin with the snobbish Mr Satterthwaite. A collection was published in 1930 as *The Mysterious Mr Quin* and it is said that Quin and Satterthwaite became her favourite characters. That year she also created Miss Marple in *The Murder at the Vicarage*.

Hercule Poirot had already taken to the stage in *Alibi*, which was adapted from *The Murder of Roger Ackroyd*. Charles Laughton was cast in the role. Christie thought him too fat for the part. Neither was she happy with *The Passing of Mr Quin*, a silent film based on her short story 'The Coming of Mr Quin', or the German movie *Die Abenteuer GmbH* – or 'Adventure Inc.' – based on *The Secret Adversary*. So in 1929, she sat down to write her first play, *Black Coffee*, which proved to be a success.

Returning to Ur, she found that twenty-five-year-old archaeologist Max Mallowan had joined the digging party. He had become Katharine Woolley's favourite. One of his duties became showing Agatha around. She was nearly forty, but Max was not intimidated by being around successful women. On a trip to Baghdad, they took a dip together in a salt lake. Then on the way back, their car got stuck in the desert. After they were rescued, they had to spend the night together in a police station, occupying adjacent cells. Afterwards, with the Woolleys, Max and Agatha travelled to Greece.

Although every inch an Englishman, Max Mallowan's father was Austrian; his mother was born in Paris, the daughter of an opera singer. Educated at the English public school Lancing College, he emulated Evelyn Waugh, a senior boy in his house, and became a rebel. He then read classics at New College, Oxford.

From Athens, they took the train home. However, when they alighted in Milan, it went on without them and they had to chase after it in an expensive hire car. So by the time they reached Paris to meet his mother, they were penniless.

In London, Max found a job at the British Museum, while Agatha went to Ashfield with Rosalind. They met up again at Agatha's house in Chelsea when she came to London to meet her American publishers. Soon after, he was invited to Ashfield for the weekend. After strenuous walks on Dartmoor, on the last night of his stay, he knocked on Agatha's bedroom door, sat down on the end of her bed and asked her to marry him.

She refused him. He was fifteen years her junior and a Catholic. Besides, Agatha admitted, she was 'afraid of being hurt'. After a flurry of correspondence, she changed her mind. Did she mind spending the rest of her life 'digging up the dead'? he asked, referring to his career in archaeology. 'I adore corpses and stiffs,' she replied.

Their different faiths proved no obstacle. When Max discovered that the Catholic church would not recognize his marriage, he abandoned his religion.

To avoid the attention of the press, they kept their engagement secret. The banns were read on the Isle of Skye and the wedding took place in Edinburgh. They honeymooned in Venice, before travelling down the Dalmatian coast. Arriving in Greece, they visited Delphi, then trekked around other ancient sites, leading Agatha to think, briefly, that Max was too young and fit for her.

Although Agatha became ill, Max headed on to Ur without her. She eventually took a train back to London. Max was already planning to move to a new dig at Nineveh and, when he returned to London, she had moved to Campden Hill to be on a direct tube line to the British Museum. In the meantime, they kept in touch by letter. She informed him of her latest attempts at drawing, her studies of the latest scientific and mathematical theories

– which had proved vital in the creation of *Black Coffee* – and pictures of her latest attempts at pottery. He replied with a reading list concerning his forthcoming archaeological endeavours.

In 1931, Agatha joined Dorothy L. Sayers and other crime writers in producing serials for the BBC where each writer in turn read their episode. These were *Behind the Screen* and *The Scoop*. She also contributed a chapter to the collaborative novel *The Floating Admiral* with other members of the Detection Club, set up in the 1920s to maintain the standard of crime fiction. G. K. Chesterton provided a prologue. However, these ventures did not bring in the money she could command when she wrote alone.

In 1931, she returned to the supernatural with *The Sittaford Mystery*, which begins with a séance. It also intruded into her short stories written for magazines that appeared in the collection *The Hound of Death* in 1933. She cleverly managed to write tales that appealed to both believers and sceptics.

She returned to Ur for the end of the digging season and, after visiting Persia, Agatha and Max headed back to England via the Soviet Union where she indulged her taste for caviar.

Poirot returned in *Peril at End House* and, in *The Thirteen Problems*, Miss Marple solved the mysteries posed by thirteen dinner guests who met each Tuesday night. The book was dedicated to Leonard and Katharine Woolley. With Max at Nineveh, Agatha set about *Lord Edgware Dies* (*Thirteen for Dinner* in the US) on Rhodes, but her routine there was hardly strict. She spent between 9 a.m. and 11.30 a.m. in 'violent hitting of the typewriter', finishing the end of a chapter. But she admitted that, if it was a lovely day, she would make the chapter a short one. After a swim and lunch, she would wander round the town or chat on the terrace. After tea she would do some more work, or sleep until dinner.

She now meticulously plotted her novels before she began writing and she got the idea for *Lord Edgware Dies* (*Thirteen for Dinner*) from the American actress Ruth Draper, who performed dramatic monologues on the London stage where she skilfully moved from one character to another with the use of a sparse array of props. After finishing the novel in Nineveh, Christie travelled back to London aboard the Orient Express. The journey provided a storm and a cast of characters that would appear in *Murder on the Orient Express* (*Murder in the Calais Coach* in the US).

Back in England, Agatha Christie had a miscarriage. This put paid to her attempts to start a family with Max. Besides, he got on well enough with Rosalind.

In the spring of 1933, Max managed to raise the funds for an expedition of his own. Agatha was to come along to keep a written record of their activities and make drawings of anything they discovered. In her free moments, she continued her literary output, including a new novel from Mary Westmacott, *Unfinished Portrait*, which told the tale of her first marriage in fictional form.

Bobby Jones and his friend Frankie Derwent become sleuths in *Why Didn't They Ask Evans?* After that she wrote two more collections of short stories – *The Listerdale Mystery* and *Parker Pyne Investigates* (*Mr Parker Pyne, Detective* in the US) – introducing retired civil servant Parker Pyne who Christie thought a much more realistic figure then Hercule Poirot.

When the political mood in Iraq grew hostile, Max and Agatha moved to Syria, then on to Beirut where she continued to write. In *Death in the Clouds* she moved the scene of the crime to an aeroplane with Poirot on board. Mr Satterthwaite returned in *Three Act Tragedy*, while Poirot teamed up again with Captain Hastings in *The ABC Murders*, whose plot is built around the *ABC* guide, a collected volume of British train timetables. When it was made into a movie in 1966, it was renamed *The Alphabet Murders* to prevent confusion with the ABC chain of cinemas in Britain that showed it.

Agatha bought another house in Campden Hill where Max had a library and she had a room of her own to work in. As Max was fond of Oxford, they bought a country house just outside at Wallingford. But they still spent their winters on digs in Syria where Agatha became more involved in archaeology. It featured largely in her next novel *Murder in Mesopotamia*, which was dedicated to 'my many archaeological friends in Iraq and Syria' and featured a character based on Katharine Woolley. Although Christie enjoyed the opportunities being married to an archaeologist gave her, one she did not enjoy was the quip that followed her around – the older she became, the more interesting she was to him.

Her second book of 1935, *Cards on the Table*, featured crime novelist Mrs Ariadne Oliver, a version of herself, who first appeared in the stories 'The Case of the Discontented Soldier' and 'The Case of the Rich Woman' alongside Parker Pyne. Now she became a regular foil to Hercule Poirot, except in *The Pale Horse* where she acts alone. Superintendent Battle and Colonel Race, who first appeared in *The Man in the Brown Suit*, also put in an appearance.

In *Cards on the Table*, the murder takes place during a game of contact bridge, a popular game in the 1930s, which Christie often played after dinner. It provided the 'close circle' where Christie often liked to set her murders.

Dumb Witness (*Poirot Loses a Client* in the US) is dedicated to her dog Peter, 'most faithful of friends, a dog in a thousand' and features a wire-haired terrier called Bob. It is also set in Wallingford, masquerading as Market Basing.

In 1934, Christie had published a Parker Pyne short story called 'Death on the Nile', based on her trip to Egypt with Max and Rosalind in 1933. Four years later she re-used the title in a murder mystery featuring Hercule Poirot, which she had first outlined as a play called *Moon on the Nile*. She revived the dramatization as *Murder on the Nile* in 1944, removing Poirot and changing the ending. The title was then changed to *Hidden Horizon*. Poirot reappears, portrayed by Peter Ustinov, in the film version in 1977.

A visit to the ancient city of Petra in Jordan inspired *Appointment with Death*. Again, Christie removed Poirot for the stage adaptation only for him to reappear, once more played by Peter Ustinov, in the 1988 film version. Some of the ideas she considered for *Appointment with Death* and discarded were re-used in *Evil Under the Sun* three years later.

Hercule Poirot's Christmas, published in 1938, is prefaced with the epigram from Shakespeare's *Macbeth*: 'Yet who would have thought the old man to have had so much blood in him.' It is one of Christie's many locked-room mysteries.

While Christie set about writing *Murder is Easy* (*Easy to Kill* in the US), there was a strike at the dig in Syria and the expedition moved a hundred miles to the west to the Balikh Valley. She spent autumn and spring in the desert, summer in Ashfield with Rosalind, Christmas at Abney Hall and the rest of the year divided between London and Wallingford. She was now producing two or three books a year, with Edmund Cork still handling her affairs in London and Harold Oder looking after her interests in the US.

At seventeen, Rosalind was now due to become a debutante. Having not come out herself in London and denied attendance at Buckingham Palace as a divorcee, Agatha left the arrangements to the mothers of other girls, although she was on hand in London, attending exhibitions, the opera, ballet and theatre matinees. She also attended photography classes with Rosalind, which she thought would be useful on digs.

Now Rosalind was grown up, Agatha decided to sell Ashfield. Instead she bought Greenway, a large Georgian house standing in thirty acres of Woodland ten miles from Torquay. Her next book was set in Devon with the action taking place on Burgh Island off the coast at Bigbury-on-Sea. Originally called *Ten Little Niggers* – changed to *And Then There Were None* in the US – it was based on a minstrel song that became a British nursery rhyme in which the participants disappear one by one. Due to the sensitivity of the epithet, the rhyme was later renamed 'Ten Little Indians' and all references in the books changed. She also uses the word 'Kafir' – now considered an offensive word for black people – in *The Man in the Brown Suit*. The short story 'The Regatta Mystery' was also set in nearby Dartmouth.

In the summer of 1938, Peter died and Agatha could not bear to have another dog. She then got news that the Internal Revenue Service was looking into to her tax affairs in the US and a prominent tax lawyer had to be hired. With war looming, foreign travel became inadvisable. Otherwise she carried on as normal, writing the Poirot novels *Sad Cypress* and *One, Two, Buckle My Shoe* (*The Patriotic Murders* in the US), and delivering a series of short stories to the *Strand Magazine* that would be collected as *The Labours of Hercules*. The twelve Poirot stories correspond to the labours of Hercules in Greek mythology and are comic in tone. Agatha strongly objected to the proposed cover which seemed to show Poirot naked. She also exploded when she discovered that *Crime Club News* planned to summarize the plot of *Ten Little Niggers* and put a stop to it. On another occasion Collins had to apologize to Agatha for giving away the identity of the murderer in the cover notes. Generally, though, her relations with publishers were cordial and she would make the changes they asked for – but only once they had been framed diplomatically by Cork. She usually reserved venting her spleen for the covers. After threatening to have 15,000 copies of a jacket pulped during paper rationing, she was granted prior approval of all future covers.

Life at the house in Devon became disrupted by the war and Agatha moved to London where she took a course in Air Raid Precautions and wrote the play *Akhnaton*, set in ancient Egypt, under the guidance of Egyptologist Stephen Granville, a friend of her husband's. But her endeavours were hampered by the loss of Carlo to war work.

Peril at End House was adapted for the stage and Christie began to make appearances dressed as a grande dame of the stage. When interest was expressed in staging *Ten Little Niggers*, Agatha insisted on doing the dramatization herself, though first she delivered the novel *N or M?*, another thriller featuring Tommy and Tuppence Beresford, this time set during the Second World War. Again she used a nursery rhyme – here 'Goosey, goosey, gander' – as a central device. *Collier's* magazine in the US refused to serialize the book because of its anti-Nazi stance.

Strict exchange controls brought about by America's entry into the war in December 1941 meant that her earnings in the US were withheld until the matter of her taxes was settled. Publishers were becoming more parsimonious with their advances and Christie's sales were not what they once had been. To make ends meet, she rented out her various houses.

She also began to tire of Poirot, whom she had never liked, and she began work on *Curtain*, the book where she kills him off but which would not be published until nearly thirty-five years later. Fearing that she might not survive the war when London came under heavy bombing, she wanted to give her readers a satisfactory ending to her great detective. The manuscript would languish in a bank vault for all those years as, no matter how insufferable she found Poirot, he was her main source of income and she could not kill him off while she still needed him.

In 1940, she wrote a book called *Cover Her Face* – a quote from bloodthirsty Jacobean play *The Duchess of Malfi*, which features frequently in Christie's notes. She also makes reference to Alfred, Lord Tennyson's narrative poem *Enoch Arden*, a name she gives to a character in the novel *Taken at the Flood*. After her problems with The Bodley Head early in her career, Christie liked having a manuscript in hand in case she needed quick money. This was a Miss Marple book that was eventually published as *Sleeping Murder* after her death. Its copyright was assigned to Max, while Rosalind was given the copyright of *Curtain*. Copies were sent to New York for safekeeping as Cork's office in Fleet Street had already been bombed. Meanwhile, Christie had little money coming in and the British authorities were also pushing her to pay taxes. While Max had finally found a post in the Air Ministry – he had difficulties because of his Austrian parentage – she tried to sell her Georgian house in Devon, but could not find a buyer. She had no alternative but to quickly write another Miss Marple book, *The Moving Finger*. However, the *Saturday Evening Post* found it too slow to serialize.

A little money came in from the dramatization of *Peril at End House*, but Christie then had a run in with Collins who were trying to change the terms of her contracts due to the increase in production costs.

Agatha also gave some time over to war work, spending several days a week in the dispensary at University College Hospital. The publicity helped her standing in America. She knocked out *The Body in the Library* and Hollywood began showing an interest in *N or M?* as well as *And Then There Were None*. With advances from Collins and money for an option on *N or M?*, Agatha was in funds again, especially after Cork advised her to take no notice of the assessment the Inland Revenue had made on her income which would have made her pay out nearly four times what she had received.

While Max was posted to Cairo, Agatha finished *Towards Zero*, dedicating a copy to Robert Graves, a wartime neighbour in Devon with whom she discussed her passion for

Shakespeare. *Five Little Pigs* (*Murder in Retrospect* in the US) followed, which listed among her other titles *Death on the Hill* instead of *Death on the Nile*.

Despite the promise of commissions by the *Saturday Evening Post* and *Collier's*, Agatha could not get permission to visit Max in Egypt. Meanwhile, her house in Devon had been taken over by American officers in preparation for D-Day. To console her in her loneliness, Agatha eventually got a new dog, James, though he disliked the sound of her typewriter. Otherwise she wrote long letters to Max discussing Shakespeare.

She spent as much time as she could at the theatre and began adapting *Ten Little Niggers* for the stage, finding that she had to change the ending. Fortunately, there was an alternate ending to the nursery rhyme. Then she got to work on *Murder on the Nile*.

Now with her various homes rented out or otherwise occupied, Agatha lived in rented accommodation or stayed with friends. Meanwhile, she wrote *Absent in the Spring* as Mary Westmacott. She returned to Wallingford to write *Death Comes as the End*, a murder mystery set in ancient Egypt suggested by Stephen Granville. It was based on the letters of a village landowner found by an expedition in the 1920s.

Max showed some concern about the close relationship that developed between Agatha and Granville. His wife and children were away in Canada and he was known to have a roving eye. But Agatha was now in her mid-fifties and had put on weight, though was still attractive. However, his main concern was with *Death Comes as the End*, a project of which he did not approve professionally.

After writing two plays, a novel and a detective story, along with her dispensary work and helping take care of Rosalind's baby Mathew, Agatha fell ill. She had further money troubles when both the theatre where *Ten Little Niggers* was playing and Collins' offices were bombed.

Max's meagre pay as a colonial administrator now in Libya
was little help, but he could at least indulge his passion for
archaeology.

After adapting *Appointment with Death* for the stage,
Christie wrote *Remembered Death* based on an idea from
Richard III. Collins renamed it *Sparkling Cyanide*, but it
retained its original title in the US. She wrote *The Hollow*,
then adapted *Towards Zero* for the stage.

In the autumn of 1944, news came that Rosalind's husband had been killed. That Christmas, Agatha wrote a collection of poems and stories with a religious theme. She
sent these to Cork, but they were not published until 1965
under the name *Star Over Bethlehem* by Agatha Christie Mallowan. She had always been interested in theology.
With the end of the war, Agatha could move back to Devon
and Max came home. She celebrated, recalling their time in
Syria in *Come, Tell Me How You Live* published in 1946,
again under her married name. The title is a pun – a 'tell'
is an archaeological term for an artificial mound formed
by the accumulated remains of ancient settlements in the
Middle East.

Recovering from the bomb damage, Collins managed to
compile sales figures that showed she was selling better than
they had thought and upped her advance. That summer
Sparkling Cyanide was serialized in the *Daily Express*. She
came to a settlement with the British tax authorities, and the
US and UK concluded a double-taxation treaty. Now she
could receive her US earnings – which outstripped those in
the UK, particularly after the opening of the movie *And
Then There Were None* that autumn.

The BBC wanted her for a quiz show, but she found herself unavailable. She hated such appearances. But she did
write an article on four leading crime writers – including
herself – for the Ministry of Information. It was to be published in Russian in a Moscow magazine.

There were still problems. *Collier's* wanted *The Hollow*

to be shortened for serialization. Collins wanted some changes too. With her money worries behind her, Agatha obliged. She was still working on *Appointment with Death*, while the American producer of *Towards Zero* wanted her to come to New York to make changes to her stage adaptation. However, she got no further than Rosalind's house in Wales.

Crime fiction had been at its zenith in the 1930s, but in *The New Yorker* of 14 October 1944, the critic Edmund Wilson attacked the genre with his article 'Why Do People Read Detective Stories?' In the issue of 20 June 1945, he followed up with a second article, directly attacking Christie, called 'Who Cares Who Killed Roger Ackroyd?'

Nevertheless offers were still being made for movie rights and short stories by everyone from *Good Housekeeping* to *Ellery Queen's Mystery Magazine*, while the Mutual Network ran a weekly radio series featuring Hercule Poirot. In the UK, she swept the board with cheap paperbacks.

The BBC commissioned Agatha to write a radio play to celebrate the eightieth birthday of Queen Mary, who was a fan. Her fee was given to the Southport Infirmary Children's Toys Fund. She then adapted it as a short story that was published in *Cosmopolitan* magazine in the US and *Woman's Own* in the UK. It later appeared in a volume of short stories in the US. However, it was never published in that form in the UK. American movie producers also wanted the rights. Instead, it was adapted for the stage as *The Mousetrap*, now the longest-running production in London theatres.

Meanwhile, Mary Westmacott had another outing with *The Rose and the Yew Tree*, a quote from T. S. Eliot, another fan. However, Collins did not like it because it concerned the recent, contentious, General Election. Instead, William Heinemann published it in the UK; Farrar & Rinehart in the US. Soon after, it was revealed in the American papers that Mary Westmacott was Agatha Christie. She then ran into trouble over the US serialization of *Taken at the Flood* (*There is a Tide* in the US). She was asked to rewrite it, taking Poirot out. However, after she had laboured at this, the story was published with Poirot in it in the *Toronto Star*.

Christie was also pilloried, by the Anti-Defamation League among others, for anti-Semitism in her novels, sadly not uncommon in the works of that time. She was also criticized for disparaging remarks about Catholics, although there didn't seem to be any. However, in her *Autobiography* she makes it clear she had no time for the Nazis after meeting the German director of antiquities in Baghdad in 1933. Curiously, an amateur adaptation of *Ten Little Niggers* was performed by inmates in the Buchenwald concentration camp. Agatha was touched when, later, a survivor told her that it had sustained them.

She found herself increasingly out of touch in the postwar world where it was now difficult to get servants. Restrictions on foreign exchange made it difficult to travel, though a short trip to Switzerland and the south of France was arranged when she fell ill.

Max found a new post as professor of western Asiatic archaeology at the Institute of Archaeology, now part of the University of London, which would allow him to return to the Middle East. Agatha could obtain a business allowance to go too, if she produced a book on her travels. The result was *They Came to Baghdad*. Before she left, she compiled the short-story collection *Witness for the Prosecution* for the US and wrote *Crooked House*, one of Christie's favourite novels.

The Mallowans spent five months in Baghdad while Max negotiated permission for a new dig and Agatha voraciously consumed American detective stories. She did not write for twelve months and renewed problems with the tax authorities pushed her close to bankruptcy. However, Pocket Books awarded her a 'Golden Gertrude' for sales over five million in their editions.

Penguin now took an interest in republishing her early works and the hunt was on for old editions as both Cork's and Collins' file copies had been destroyed in the Blitz. Requests came from the US for permission to adapt her work for the stage, the radio and even the television. This last medium she refused. NBC also refused to broadcast a serialization of *Crooked House* on grounds of morality.

In the UK she began her own dramatization of *The Murder in the Vicarage*. And by 1949, she was writing prolifically again, and she and Max returned to Iraq. Equipped with a new typewriter, she began a series of Miss Marple stories. These culminated with the novel *A Murder is Announced*, which Agatha had acted out in Wallingford with the help of neighbours.

Though plots came easily to her, writing was still difficult and she turned increasingly to working for the stage. Following *The Murder at the Vicarage*, she dramatized *The Hollow*. However, when *A Daughter's a Daughter*, written under the name Mary Westmacott, failed to make it to the West End, she quickly turned it into a novel.

The death of her sister Madge only redoubled her efforts and Collins celebrated her sixtieth birthday with the publication of her sixtieth book. Penguin reprinted a list they called the 'Christie million', though they had sold two-and-a-half million, while Dodd, Mead & Co. and Avon Publishing in the US started issuing reprints with *The Mysterious Affair at Styles*. But the irrepressible Agatha produced *Mrs McGinty's Dead* and *They Do It with Mirrors* (*Murder with Mirrors* in the US).

They Came to Baghdad outsold her previous books and *Ellen Queen's Mystery Magazine* named her one of the ten greatest mystery writers then active. Dashiell Hammett was disqualified as he was in jail for his supposed Communist sympathies, along with Dorothy L. Sayers, who had given up crime for religion. However, the US Post Office refused to send her trophy – a plaque hung from an antique pistol – as it could 'theoretically' be fired.

In her sixties, Agatha would still go to Max's dig in the Middle East in December or January, returning to England in March. Free from distractions, while she was away she would plan and write her books. She also recorded, preserved and photographed the finds, looked after younger members of the expedition and bought presents in the bazaar. Even in the desert, the Mallowans dressed for dinner. Though she slept in a tent, she kept a room in the expedition's house for writing.

Max's expedition made important finds, now on display in the British Museum and the Metropolitan Museum, New York. But there were hardships to endure, suffering snow, mud, thunderstorms and dust storms. However, all her other worries were taken over by Cork, who now acted as her general factotum. He had to supply a dictating machine when she fell and broke a wrist so that she could finish *A Pocketful of Rye*. In it, she returned to the nursery rhyme 'Sing a Song of Sixpence' – the title of a short story published in collection *The Listerdale Mystery* in the UK in 1934. It was followed by 'Four and Twenty Blackbirds' in *Three Blind Mice* published in the US in 1950. *A Pocketful of Rye* was serialized in the *Daily Express* and the *Chicago Tribune*. Christie's sales soared again and royalties from the book were given to the British School of Archaeology in Iraq to publish Max's book on his dig at Nimrud. Collins not only upped her royalty, they bought her a car.

Witness for the Prosecution was adapted for the stage. While it was being produced she wrote *Spider's Web* for Margaret Lockwood. Christie became a hit on the London stage, but Collins became worried that they did not have a book for 1954, however she brought back from Iraq the finished draft of *Destination Unknown* (*So Many Steps to Death* in the US).

Christie's Devon house Greenway was the setting for *Dead Man's Folly*, though she wrote the book in Wallingford. It was, of course, inhabited by Mrs Ariadne Oliver. *Hickory Dickory Dock* (*Hickory Dickory Death* in the US) was written in Iraq that year. It was the last book based on a nursery rhyme, though her notebooks are full of similar ideas. She gave the royalties to *Hickory Dickory Dock* to a trust fund for her nephews.

The Queen attended a special performance of *Witness for the Prosecution* and *The Mousetrap*, revived after clocking up a thousand performances. Meanwhile, offers for the dramatic rights on her other works were rejected. She turned down all opportunities for publicity, particularly if it meant appearing on television. Nevertheless she wrote an hour-long play, *Butter in a Lordly Dish*, for BBC radio in 1955. That year, she and Max celebrated their silver wedding.

The following year she produced *The Burden* as Mary Westmacott, and was awarded a CBE in the New Year's Honours List.

'One up for the Low-Brows,' she wrote from Baghdad where she was feted by diplomats. Then she set to work on *4.50 from Paddington*. It was published in the US under various titles and was filmed in 1961 as *Murder, She Said*, starring Margaret Rutherford as Miss Marple.

At last Agatha Christie was to visit the US again. Max had been awarded a gold medal by the University of Pennsylvania. Although by then she had paid thousands of dollars in US tax, before she could travel she first had to satisfy the authorities that she would not be a burden on the public purse. At the time, *Witness for the Prosecution* was being filmed in Hollywood and she made the long journey to visit the set. She returned to write the novel *Ordeal by Innocence*, inspired by the tale of an Arctic explorer who had heard no news for months, and the short story 'The Dressmaker's Doll', another of her spooky tales. After a holiday in Barbados and a season of West End plays, it was back to Baghdad again.

Her next play, *Verdict*, was a flop, but she began work on another, *The Unexpected Guest*, while completing the Poirot novel *Cat Among the Pigeons*. It revived her reputation on the London stage. Then on 13 April 1958, there was a huge party at the Savoy for *The Mousetrap*, which had already become the longest-running production on the British stage. A well-wisher sent her a tiny silver mouse that she kept in her handbag and stroked for good luck. However, she was not terribly proud of the play, though recognized that it was well crafted.

Her next publication was a collection of short stories, *The Adventure of the Christmas Pudding*. She would not allow 'Three Blind Mice' to be included in it in case it spoilt the play for anyone who had not seen it yet.

The political situation in Iraq became increasingly fraught and in 1958 there was a revolution. The young King Feisal, to whom Agatha had presented one of her books, was killed and in 1960 she and Max left the dig at Nimrud for the last time.

Max now devoted himself to setting up schools of archaeology in other countries and they set off for Ceylon (Sri Lanka), India, Pakistan, Nepal and Persia (Iran). Fame dogged her every step. She returned to London to see *Go Back for Murder* – a stage adaptation of *Five Little Pigs* – panned by the critics.

By 1961, Agatha Christie was the best-selling author in the English language. Her books were published in fifty languages and sold in 102 countries, twice as many as those of Graham Greene. Her agents were swamped with fan mail. She occasionally answered letters herself and was always intrigued by the mistakes readers pointed out. But, generally, she had too much to do to reply in person. She completed the novel *The Pale Horse*, in which Ariadne Oliver solves the crime without the assistance of Hercule

Poirot, and prepared *Double Sin*, a collection of short stories including 'The Dressmaker's Doll' for America, before heading back to Persia with Max.

While in London, she went to see Samuel Beckett's plays to keep herself up to date with what was happening on the stage, and wrote *Rule of Three*, a series of three playlets – *The Patient*, *Afternoon at the Seaside* and *The Rats*. However, in the 1960s the cinema became her medium with adaptations of *Witness for the Prosecution*, *Ten Little Indians*, *Murder, She Said* and *Spider's Web*, for which she wrote the screenplay. She was later asked to write a treatment of Dickens' *Bleak House*.

Agatha dedicated her next Miss Marple novel *The Mirror Crack'd from Side to Side* (*The Mirror Crack'd* in the US) – a quotation from Tennyson – to Margaret Rutherford. Then she returned to Persia and Kashmir.

Max took a fellowship at All Souls College, Oxford, and became a trustee of the British Academy and the British Museum, while Agatha remained at Wallingford to write. But she continued to visit London for meetings of the Detection Club and to attend the opera. In 1962, she went to the Bayreuth Festival in Germany, having become a fan of Wagner. Again she was besieged by fans.

An attempt was made to make a musical out of *Hickory Dickory Dock*, and there was another party at the Savoy to celebrate ten years of *The Mousetrap*.

Max and Agatha were in Persepolis while *Rule of Three* tried out in Aberdeen. Reviews were poor and it lasted only two months in London. However, in 1963, *The Mirror Crack'd from Side to Side* became a bestseller. She followed up with a Poirot novel, *The Clocks*.

Christie then had a run in with MGM. She refused to let them film *Murder on the Orient Express*, after they had filmed *After the Funeral* as *Murder at the Gallop*, substituting Miss Marple for Poirot. They did the same thing with *Mrs McGinty's Dead* – one of Agatha's favourite novels

– which they filmed as *Murder Most Foul*. Christie consoled herself by sending Miss Marple off to the West Indies in *A Caribbean Mystery*. Meanwhile, Max had finished his book *Nimrud and its Remains* and they took a trip to Upper Egypt. Collins then tried to upstage the release of *Murder Most Foul* with 'Agatha Christie Fortnight' during which they would flood the bookshops with ten million paperbacks.

MGM responded with *Murder Ahoy* which put Miss Marple on a Royal Navy training ship. It owed nothing to any Agatha Christie story. She then managed to stop the filming of *The ABC Murders* with Zero Mostel playing Poirot. After that, the contract with MGM was terminated.

Miss Marple returned to Piccadilly under the wing of Agatha in the novel *At Bertram's Hotel*. The book was serialized in America by *Good Housekeeping* but changes had to be made. It sold like hot cakes.

Christie turned down all advances from biographers, saying that her readers were interested in her books, not the author. However, she bowed to the inevitable and began marshalling her diaries so she could write an autobiography. The manuscript was finished in 1965. Meanwhile, collected editions of her work were being published.

In June 1966, she and Max visited a museum in Belgium named after Hercule Poirot. They went on to Switzerland. She returned to write *Third Girl*, which sought to embrace some of the atmosphere of Swinging London.

That autumn she accompanied Max on a speaking tour of the US. Along the way, she wrote notes for *Endless Night*, a suspense story set in Wales. She was unhappy with the 1972 movie version that spiced up the plot with sex scenes. However, the book was well received and, after another trip to Persia, she told Collins that she intended to continue writing a book a year.

In the 1967 New Year's Honours List, Max received a knighthood. That made Agatha Lady Mallowan – she had long hidden behind 'Mrs Mallowan' to preserve her privacy. However, at the Detection Club, Max always introduced himself as Agatha's husband. The couple took a second honeymoon in Yugoslavia.

Agatha was now being treated for growing deafness and Max had to be flown home from Persia after having a stroke. Nevertheless, 1968 saw the publication of *By the Pricking of My Thumbs*. Again the title was a quotation from *Macbeth*. The novel reintroduces Tommy and Tuppence Beresford after an absence of nearly three decades. The following year came *Hallowe'en Party* which pits Poirot against Mrs Oliver again.

With her eightieth birthday approaching, Agatha refused again to appear on television. However, she sat for a portrait by Austrian artist Oskar Kokoschka who consumed half a bottle of whisky at each sitting.

She was still very much in demand with the public. Even her hardback books sold forty or fifty thousand copies in the first weeks after publication. Advances had been dropped, but her royalty rates had been raised. Still she had trouble paying tax and was frequently short of money. She refused to move to a tax haven, and the problem was only sorted out when she hid behind a series of companies and trust funds. However, she still faced the prospect of huge death duties being levied on her copyright material. Booker McConnell, the conglomerate that started the Booker prize and owned 51 per cent of Glidrose Productions (which owned the rights to Ian Fleming's work) took 51 per cent – then 64 per cent – of Agatha Christie Ltd.

After a holiday on Cyprus, Agatha went to see the Oberammergau Passion Play. Then she wrote *Passenger to Frankfurt*, a spy novel. The plot had come to her after meeting Friedelind Wagner, granddaughter of the composer Richard Wagner, at Bayreuth. By skilful slight of hand, it was publicized as her eightieth book in her eightieth year. It had the largest print run for any Christie first edition and sold out 58,000 copies almost immediately. She celebrated her birthday with a picnic on the moor and presents included a gold pen.

In the New Year's Honours List for 1971, Agatha was created a Dame Commander of the British Empire. After a short visit to Paris, she gave Miss Marple another outing in *Nemesis*. It was the final Miss Marple novel and the plot surrounds the death of Jason Rafiel, last seen in *A Caribbean Mystery*.

She made notes for several plays, including one provisionally entitled 'Mousetrap II' where the victim is poisoned at a '*Mousetrap* party' in Soho. One new play, *This Mortal Coil*, toured but did not do well.

After a trip to Paris, Christie fell over in Wallingford and broke a hip, but by Christmas she was mobile enough to travel to London to be measured for her waxwork in Madame Tussaud's. She then headed for Nice. After a visit to the opera and seeing the play *Sleuth*, she put the finishing touches to *Fiddler's Three*. It did not make it to the West End.

Undaunted, she wrote the novel *Elephants Can Remember*, featuring Hercule Poirot and Ariadne Oliver, along with Mr Goby who appeared in *The Mystery of the Blue Train*, *After the Funeral* and *Third Girl*.

At eighty-one, she began getting her literary estate in order and in 1973 Collins published a collection of her *Poems* and the script of the play *Akhnaton*, which had been considered too expensive to put on even when an exhibition of the treasures of Tutankhamun in 1972 sparked new interest in ancient Egypt.

Nineteen seventy-three also saw the publication of *Postern of Fate* in the UK (1974 in the US) with another outing for Tommy and Tuppence Beresford. It was Christie's last book and, again, became a bestseller.

Her health was now failing, and in October 1974 she turned up at the royal premiere of *Murder on the Orient*

Express in a wheelchair, though she clambered to her feet to be presented to the Queen. Photographs were taken of her to promote the film in the *Sunday Times* by the Queen's brother-in-law Lord Snowdon.

Rosalind had already forbidden her to write any more books that year. Instead, the compilation *Poirot's Early Cases* came out.

Despite another fall, she went to Wimbledon for the tennis, attended the Lord Mayor's Dinner and turned up to vote in the referendum about whether Britain should stay in the European Economic Community. Apparently, she voted yes. And she made a final outing to the last *Mousetrap* party.

With the end approaching, *Curtain* was finally published, ridding her of the 'insufferable Poirot'. A new edition of *Come, Tell Me How You Live* was issued and she began to make arrangements for her funeral and her burial. Then on 12 January 1976, she died. Agatha was eighty-five.

She was buried in a private ceremony at Cholsey, near her home at Wallingford. There was a memorial service at St Martin-in-the-Fields in London. But her literary career was not yet over. In 1976, the novel *Sleeping Murder* was published. It had been written over thirty years before and kept in hand as a fitting finale for Miss Marple.

By the time she died, she had sold some 350 million copies of her books, though the number pirated behind the Iron Curtain were uncountable, and Agatha Christie Ltd was turning over more than a million pounds a year. However, her affairs were complicated and it has proved impossible to establish her true worth.

Her *Autobiography* was published in 1977. *Woman's Own* said it was 'the best thing she's ever written'. She did, of course, continue publishing, in various compilations, long after her death.

3

THE BELGIAN BRAINBOX

Already, by 1938, Agatha Christie lamented: 'Why, why, why did I ever invent this detestable, bombastic, tiresome little creature?' She complained that Poirot was 'eternally straightening things, eternally boasting, eternally twirling his moustaches and tilting his egg-shaped head'.

She could have destroyed him at any time, but the public loved him. After she killed him off in *Curtain*, written in 1940, he appears in some twenty books, not to mention plays and films before she finally published his literary obituary.

Agatha Christie was just twenty-five when she created her famous detective. She looked to certain models. There was Sherlock Holmes, but his author Sir Arthur Conan-Doyle was still alive and writing. There was Maurice Leblanc's Arsène Lupin, but was he a criminal or a detective? Then there was *The Mystery of the Yellow Room* – the immediate cause of sister Madge's challenge. The sleuth in it was a young journalist named Joseph Rouletabille, who had a head as 'round as a bullet'. He was also pitted against a professional policeman from the Sûreté named Frédéric Larsan. Rouletabille was a man of mysterious origins and Christie thought he was the 'sort of person whom I would like to invent'.

As there were a lot of Belgian refugees around at the time and, as Britain had entered the Great War over Germany's violation of Belgian neutrality, they were seen as heroic. She also needed a man who was adept at solving crimes, so she made him a retired police officer. And he must be fiercely intelligent. From his first appearance in *The Mysterious Affair at Styles*, he is tapping his forehead and talking of his 'little grey cells'.

Like Holmes he is a bachelor, brilliant and vain. And he has a faithful sidekick – and sometime chronicler who is not as bright as him – Arthur Hastings who, like Watson, was a former military man, discharged from the service after being wounded. They fall out sometimes. In *The Big Four*, Hastings asks Poirot if he is going to try to cure his 'overweening vanity' and his 'finicky tidiness'. The quotes come from notes supplied to agents of the Big Four outlining their characters and weaknesses. However, his vanity is just a ruse. It makes the English underestimate him – 'A fellow who thinks as much of himself as that cannot be worth much.'

It is thought that Poirot was born in Brussels. In *Three Act Tragedy*, he mentions that he was due to retire from the Belgian Police Force when the war came along. If he was due to retire in 1914, he must have been born around 1850.

He was injured and moved to England, 'a sad and weary refugee'. When we first meet him living near Styles Court, in Style St Mary in Essex, he appears to be in his late fifties or early sixties. Sadly, this means that when he died in *Curtain* in 1975, fifty-five years later, he would be well over a hundred. Although he appears bald and wheelchair bound in that book, it is just a charade. The story announcing his death in *The New York Times* on 6 August 1975, mistakenly says that he retired in 1904, which would have made him even older. Nevertheless, in *Third Girl*, he seems to have served in Normandy during the Second World War, though in what capacity is not revealed.

Christie thought a good name for a small man would be Hercules, but settled on Hercule. She had no idea why she settled on Poirot, though its similarity to *poireau*, the French for 'leek' has been noted. The similarity to Marie Belloc Lowndes' fictional detective Hercule Popeau, formerly of the Sûreté, and G. K. Chesterton's criminal-turned-detective Hercule Flambeau has also been noted. Nevertheless, Poirot himself was inordinately proud of his name. In *The Mystery of the Blue Train* he boasts: 'It is the name of one of the great ones of the world.'

Like Christie, Poirot guarded his privacy and gave little away about his early life in Belgium. In *The Murder of Roger Ackroyd*, Caroline Sheppard believes that she knows everything about Poirot's family, but is deceived.

However, in *Three Act Tragedy*, he mentioned that, as a boy, he was poor. His was a large family and the children had to get on in the world. So he entered the Police Force, where he made a name for himself. In 'The Affair at the Victory Ball', Hastings says that Poirot was 'formerly chief of the Belgian force'.

Even before the war, he said, he had acquired an international reputation, though he reminds Hastings of a 'bad failure' he had in the affair of the box of chocolates in Belgium in 1893. Usually boastful, in 'The Chocolate Box', Poirot admits to failing 'innumerable times', but makes excuses for himself, saying: '*La bonne chance*, it cannot always be on your side. I have been called in too late. Very often another, working towards the same goal, has arrived there first. Twice I have been struck down with illness just as I was on the point of success.'

However, all that was long behind him. In *Cards on the*

Table, set in 1937, he says that his last failure was twenty-eight years ago.

In 'The Nemean Lion', he boasts of one of his early successes, a case involving a wealthy soap manufacturer in Liege who poisoned his wife so that he could marry his secretary – a blonde. Detective Inspector James Japp of Scotland Yard certainly knew of him. Introducing Poirot to a colleague in *The Mysterious Affair at Styles*, Japp says: 'You've heard me speak of Mr Poirot? It was in 1904 he and I worked together – the Abercrombie forgery case – you remember he was run down in Brussels. Ah, those were the days Moosier. Then, do you remember "Baron" Altara? There was a pretty rogue for you! He eluded the clutches of half the police in Europe. But we nailed him in Antwerp – thanks to Mr Poirot here.'

In 'The Cornish Mystery', Poirot tells Hastings: 'I am very strong on the family life, as you know.' And in 'The King of Clubs' he says: 'Family strength is a marvellous thing.' Although he rarely mentions his father, he also says, revealingly: '. . . we, in our country, have a great tenderness, a great respect for the mother. The *mère de famille* is everything.' Plainly he was very attached to her. In *Lord Edgware Dies*, he says: 'I comprehend the mother's heart. No one comprehends it better than I, Hercule Poirot.'

In *Mrs McGinty's Dead*, he recalls playing *cache cache* – hide and seek – and *le boulanger* as a child, but 'felt no desire to talk about it or even to think about it' and, even after half a lifetime in England, he could not understand why the English constantly looked back on their childhood. Indeed, he tries to avoid house parties at Christmas saying 'In my country, Christmas is for the children.' However, when confronted by the governess Cecilia Williams in *Five Little Pigs*, he 'once again felt the years falling away and himself a meek and apprehensive little boy'.

Dr Burton, a fellow of All Souls, suspects that Poirot had never had time to study the classics – which Poirot admits, saying that he had got on very well without them. In *After the Funeral* Poirot himself laments: 'Alas, there is no proper education nowadays. Apparently one learns nothing but economics – and how to set Intelligence Tests!' He is, of course, an accomplished linguist. A native French-speaker, he had been taught to speak German, Italian and, haltingly, English – with French phrases thrown in especially when excited. In *Three Act Tragedy*, he says that he puts this on to put people off their guard.

In *Dumb Witness* (*Poirot Loses a Client*) he seems to have mastered Arabic. Hastings remarks: 'Poirot's travellings in the East, as far as I knew, consisted of one journey to Syria extended to Iraq, and which occupied perhaps a few weeks. To judge by his present conversation one would swear that he had spent most of his life in jungles and bazaars and in intimate converse with fakirs, dervishes, and mahatmas.'

There is a mention of a sister named Yvonne in an early draft of 'The Chocolate Box', and in *Cards on the Table* Poirot mentions that he has to buy Christmas presents for 'my nieces and grand-nieces'. But he finds it difficult as he does not know what to choose for young ladies as his tastes, he admits, are 'rather old-fashioned'. So he sends them silk stockings, along with fur-lined gloves, calendars and boxes of bonbons.

In *The Murder of Roger Ackroyd* Poirot claims to have an imbecile nephew 'who's quite off his crumpet', though this is a ruse so he can find out about care homes for the mentally disabled. And in *Dumb Witness*, he pretends to have an aged and obstreperous mother so that he can investigate local nurses, along with an invalid uncle and a cousin suffering from jaundice.

In *The Big Four*, Poirot invents a twin brother named Achille who lived near the town of Spa in Belgium. Unlike Hercule, he does nothing and is of a 'singularly indolent disposition'. Nevertheless, 'his abilities are hardly less than my own – which is saying a great deal'.

They look alike, although Poirot maintains Achille is not nearly so handsome and 'wears no moustaches'. Later Hastings discovers that Poirot himself has a quiet retreat in the Ardennes in a small hamlet just outside Spa. In *One, Two, Buckle My Shoe*, he says: 'Sometimes . . . I return for a short while to my own country – Belgium.' When asked about his brother in *The Labours of Hercules*, Poirot says that he had one 'only for a short space of time'. However, to impersonate his twin he had to shave off his precious moustaches.

His grandfather left Poirot a 'large turnip of a watch', which he consults in the earlier stories. Later it is replaced by a neat wristwatch.

In 'The Apples of Hesperides' it is revealed that Poirot is Catholic by birth. Brought up by nuns, he hears a convent bell tolling when in Ireland – it was a sound that he had been familiar with from early youth. He takes his religion seriously and, in *Taken at the Flood*, he goes to church to pray. In *Hallowe'en Party*, he rues going into the police force rather than studying theology. And his morality is palpable. In *Cards on the Table*, he says: 'I have a bourgeois attitude to murder. I disapprove of it.' Nevertheless, in some cases, such as *Murder on the Orient Express*, he lets the killers get away with it, provided there is some overriding morality to their actions or they are punished by the fates anyway.

Apparently, as a youth Poirot was shy and clumsy. When the young American photographer Carl Reiter in *Murder in Mesopotamia* complains of such things, Poirot says: 'We all do these things when we are young . . . The poise, the *savoir faire*, it comes later.' And in 'The Adventure of the Christmas Pudding' he says: 'It is the time for follies, when one is young.'

However, Poirot's youthful follies only seem to extend to playing a game called 'If not you, who would you like to be?' He confessed to writing the answer in young ladies' albums. And he had once been a man of action. In *Curtain*, he says as a young man in the Belgian police force he shot a criminal who sat on a roof shooting at people in the street below.

He was certainly highly thought of in his own country. In 'The Affair of the Kidnapped Prime Minister', Poirot is called in by the British government to save the day during the First World War, though he was unknown in London, 'on the express recommendation and wish of a great man of your own country'. Poirot thinks that this is his old friend the Préfet, but it becomes clear that it is the king of Belgium himself. It seems that he saw service in the First World War before becoming a refugee. In *Murder on the Orient Express*, he reminds a French general that he once saved Poirot's life and, when he turns up at Styles St Mary, Poirot limps badly.

His famous moustache is described as 'very stiff and military'. Hastings, who knew Poirot before he arrived in England, describes Poirot a 'quaint, dandified little man' – his height was ' hardly five feet, four inches' – and 'the neatness of his attire was almost incredible'. Hastings says: 'I believe that a speck of dust would have caused him more pain than a bullet wound.'

His eyes are green, and grow steadily greener when he is puzzled, then shine like a cat's when he has a clever idea. Even when lost in thought his eyebrows make expressive motions. However, in *Murder on the Orient Express*, Mary Debenham calls him 'a ridiculous-looking little man. The sort of man one could never take seriously.'

In England, he was initially put up by Emily Inglethorp, the mistress of Styles Court, who had seven Belgian refugees staying at Leastways Cottage, not far from the park gates. There he occupied an upstairs room where he would sit looking out on the street below while smoking the occasional tiny Russian cigarette. However, the residents of Styles know nothing of Poirot's reputation. Hastings tells them: 'You've been entertaining a celebrity unawares.'

Indeed Hastings had already been singing the praises of the 'very famous detective' he had come across in Belgium once. He was 'a funny little man, a great dandy, but wonderfully clever'.

So when Mrs Inglethorp is murdered, one of the sons from her first marriage, John Cavendish, asks Hastings to call in Poirot to investigate – thus beginning Poirot's career as a private detective. He jumps at the chance, plainly bored by his enforced exile in the Essex countryside.

It is then he discovers that he 'was not finished'. Indeed, his powers were greater than ever. The method he employs, while meticulously observing the evidence, requires pure reason and a knowledge of human psychology.

His investigation, faithfully recorded by Hastings, set the template for future stories where premeditated murder takes place in genteel surroundings. Due to the diligence of Poirot, the Styles case was solved and the murderer ends up in the Old Bailey, ensuring Poirot's fame.

Poirot moves to London, with the other inmates of Styles, for the trial. There he is given a small assignment by the War Office, where Hastings is then working, and, in 'The Lemesurier Inheritance', they dine together in the Carlton.

Having triumphed at Styles, Poirot decides to begin a second career as a 'private inquiry agent'. He took rooms where he was waited on by a slapdash landlady. Poirot was always straightening the cups and saucers she threw on the table and polishing the metal teapot with his silk handkerchief. Poirot himself refers to tea as 'your English poison', preferring to boil up a thick, sweet chocolate drink in a small enamel saucepan. The landlady's other function is to announce visitors. However, she does not attend to the cleaning. In 'The Kidnapped Prime Minister', when Hastings drops in on Poirot, he finds him removing a grease spot from his grey suit with benzine and a minute sponge.

At the time, Poirot is assisting a charlady to find her missing husband, though the Belgian is sympathetic with the man who has made himself scarce. It is then that they are visited by Lord Estair – who Christie confusingly says is 'Leader of the House of Commons' – and Mr Bernard Dodge, who was a member of the war cabinet and a close personal friend of the Prime Minister. Hasting tells the story of how Poirot discovered the whereabouts of the missing Prime Minister on the eve of an important conference during the war. Some five years after the Great War is over, Hastings tells the tale because he feels that it is right and proper that England should know 'the debt it owes to my quaint little friend'. Later Poirot works for the Home Office and we learn in *Sad Cypress* that Poirot has been entertained at Sandringham.

Having performed services for his adopted country, Poirot helps the family of Captain Vincent Lemesurier who Hastings had known in France. They believed that the family was afflicted by a medieval curse and that their first-born sons would die before they inherited the estate. Going to work like 'an intelligent terrier', Poirot proved that there was no such curse.

In the spring of 1919, Japp invites Poirot to join him in the investigation of a murder at a Victory Ball, where Lord Cronshaw was found dead with a table knife in his heart. Meanwhile, Coco Courtenay, an actress rumoured to be engaged to Lord Cronshaw, had left the ball early and was found dead in her bed due to an overdose of cocaine. Poirot calls this *'une belle affaire'*. Poirot celebrates cracking the case with a *'recherché* little supper'.

By *Murder on the Links*, Hastings was sharing rooms with Poirot. Meanwhile, Poirot become fashionable.

'Oui, my friend, it is true,' he tells Hastings in 'The Adventure of the Western Star'. 'I am become the mode, the *dernier cri!'*

Even popular movie actress Mary Marvell seeks him

out when she is being blackmailed over a diamond named the Western Star. Nevertheless, Poirot continues to live in a street he calls 'not aristocratic'. In *The Big Four*, Poirot is living at 14 Farraway Street. His landlady there is Mrs Pearson, though she is dubbed 'Mrs Funnyface' by Dr Ridgeway. Her eyes are 'as round as saucers' when a uniformed guard from the mental asylum turns up. She occasionally drops her aitches.

Poirots moves rather a lot. In *The Murder of Roger Ackroyd* he is living in The Larches in King's Abbot, and in *The Hollow* he has bought a country cottage called Resthaven near the town of Market Depleach in the fictional county of Wealdshire. Being a thorough-going urbanite, he only liked it because it was quite square like a box. The surrounding landscape, though it was supposed to be a beauty spot, was 'too wildly asymmetrical to appeal to him'. And trees had the untidy habit of shedding their leaves. For Poirot, the countryside was best observed from a car on a fine afternoon before driving back to a good hotel. Poirot had been brought up to believe that all outside air was best left outside. Besides, he is hardly attired for the outdoor life. In 'The Apples of Hesperides', he ends up limping after being forced to walk some miles in the country in his patent-leather shoes. When it is suggested that a pair of brogues might be more suitable, he does not care for the idea. He liked his feet to look neat and well-shod.

In 'The Third-Floor Flat', he is living in a fifth-floor flat with a view over London. However, he appears to be on some secret assignment as he is using the alias O'Connor – pointing out, unnecessarily, that he is not Irish.

Poirot's most settled address is a service flat in Whitehaven Mansions, London W1. In *Cat Among the Pigeons* it is number 228 (28 in some editions), while in *The Clocks* it is 203. It is a thoroughly modern apartment block for the 1930s – strictly geometric. This suits Poirot as it is perfectly symmetrical. He lives on the third floor with chromium fittings, square armchairs and rectangular ornaments. One of these is a sculpture with one cube placed on top of another and about it 'a geometrical arrangement of copper wire'. There was, Christie says in *Mrs McGinty's Dead*, not a curve in the place. However, in *Third Girl*, an antique table with clawed feet appears.

There are etchings on the wall of his sitting room which are admired by his guest Anne Meredith. While his tastes in art are 'always somewhat bourgeois', he knows all about jewellery, being able to tell real stones from paste at a glance. Otherwise the sitting room gleams with chrome. The square fireplace is seldom used because Poirot considers: 'A coal fire was always shapeless and haphazard.' He prefers instead the radiators set and modern devices for excluding drafts.

He had a big, square desk – not an antique. Its drawers were locked, while the papers on the top were neatly arranged so that he could immediately put his hand on anything he wanted. And, in 'The Adventure of the Western Star', there are books. He explains to Hastings his shelving system: the tallest books go on the top shelf, the next tallest on the row beneath. Titles include *'Peerage'* – presumably Burke's – *Who's Who*, *First Steps in Russian* (though it is found on the floor in 'The Double Clue') and *The Magic of the Egyptians and Chaldeans* (though he keeps a tattered volume in his pocket in 'The Adventure of the Egyptian Tomb'). We also learn that Poirot is a fan of Shakespeare and reads Dickens and Tennyson. He must surely have an *ABC* rail guide, if only as a memento of the case, the erotic novel *Under the Fig Tree* given to him by author Salome Otterbourne in *Death on the Nile* and, simply out of loyalty, he must have something by his old friend crime novelist Ariadne Oliver, perhaps a book featuring her Finnish detective Sven Hjerson. And, presumably, he would have at least one copy of his own *magnum opus*, an analysis of great writers of detective fiction. He also keeps the dagger used to kill Samuel Ratchett in *Murder on the Orient Express*

– a souvenir given to him by the Compagnie Internationale des Wagons-Lits, he explains.

There is other reading material to hand. Hastings reads Poirot the headlines from the *Daily Blare*, a morning newspaper. In *The Murder of Roger Ackroyd*, Poirot takes the *Daily Budget*. By *Third Girl*, he is taking the *Morning News* and the *Daily Comet*. He also reads *The Times*. And in 'The Augean Stables', he admits to glancing at a scandal-sheet called *X-ray News*.

Elsewhere we learn that there is a modern writing-table set squarely in front of the window, angular upright chairs and armchairs that are 'squarely built'. Poirot's head is practically the only thing in the room that is not square.

When not at home, Poirot roughs it in the top hotels. *Three Act Tragedy* finds him in a slightly florid suite at the Ritz. He avoids, if possible, country houses in winter, unless they have been fitted with central heating. And, of course, he likes to travel on the most luxurious of trains. On the Blue Train, Poirot 'dexterously polished one of the forks' in anticipation, while on the Orient Express he 'found himself in the favoured position of being at the table which was served first and with the choicest morsels'. He is equally at home on the Riviera, where he could be found 'jauntily placing the minimum stakes on the even numbers' at the casino at Monte Carlo. In London, he goes to the theatre and, sometimes, the cinema but is often enraged by the looseness of the plot.

For Poirot, 'order and method' mean everything. As well as being almost ludicrously conscious about his appearance, he is always straightening things and tidying – to the point that, in 'The Lost Mine', he keeps £444, four shillings and four pence in his bank account. He keeps a tiny mirror in his pocket with a small comb to maintain his moustache, which is also lavished with scented pomade. He also had a pair of curling tongs heated over a small spirit stove to maintain his moustache in proper order and dyes his hair with 'Revivit' – which claims not to be a hair dye but 'brings back the natural tone of the hair'. In *Hallowe'en*, though, he admits that he is, in fact, covering up grey hair. From being a penniless refugee, sharing a house, Poirot rises rapidly in the world. It is not clear how he makes his money as he seems to do most of his work *pro bono* because a case interests him. Famously, in *Murder on the Orient Express*, he turns down a fee of $20,000 – worth some $360,000 today – to protect Samuel Ratchett because Poirot does not like his face. He only has a limited clientele, he says, and has made enough money to 'satisfy both my needs and my caprices'. And in *Taken at the Flood*, he boasts that his fees are 'enormously expensive'. However, in 'The Adventure of the Clapham Cook', he charges Mrs Todd just one guinea – twenty-one shillings (£1.05) – as a consultation fee. That would be the equivalent of £60 ($75) at today's prices. In *The Big Four* he admits, for the first time in his life, he was tempted by 'mere money'. He was offered a 'stupendous' sum to travel to Rio at the behest of the richest man in the world, American soap king Abe Ryland. But then it was near the beginning of his career as a private detective and his excuse is that he is a lonely man since his best friend, Captain Hastings, has been away in Argentina for a year and a half.

As time goes on, he gets a valet – known variously as George or Georges in deference to Poirot's native tongue – a secretary, Miss Lemon, and a chauffeur – 'a young man who enjoyed a handsome salary'. In *The Clocks*, he has a Daimler limousine, while in 'The Arcadian Deer' he's ferried in an expensive Messarro Gratz, which did not behave 'with the mechanical perfection he expected of a car'. He also has a cleaning woman, though when he took on a new one she brought in one of her children which was 'strictly against orders'. At Resthaven he also employed a Belgian gardener named Victor who laid out a vegetable garden in neat rows, while Victor's wife Françoise devoted herself to the tender care of her employer's stomach. Poirot's oft-stated ambition to retire and grow vegetable marrows ends in disaster when we find him so enraged that he flings the biggest of them over the garden wall in *The Murder of Roger Ackroyd*. In *Mrs McGinty's Dead*, he admits that he did not have the temperament for it.

While George can make an acceptable *omelette fines herbes*, the dining room in Whitehaven Mansions is 'tiny' and Poirot generally dines out. However, he has coffee delivered to his bedside by George in the morning. Despite his long sojourn in England, Poirot 'clung firmly to the Continental breakfast'. It upset and distressed him to see Hastings tucking into eggs, bacon and marmalade. He complains that eggs ruin the symmetry of the breakfast table because every hen lays eggs of a different size. However, in *Murder on the Links*, he is discovered tapping on the shell of his second boiled egg.

Poirot can even get enraged by toast. On one occasion he complains that a piece is not square, round or triangular. It has no symmetry – 'no shape remotely pleasing to the eye'. When Hastings explains that it has been cut from a cottage loaf, Poirot gives him a withering look.

He breakfasts on coffee and rolls in *Peril at End House*. If he has to have toast, he would eat it with jam, otherwise only butter. In *Third Girl* he has found a Danish patisserie that sells brioche which he consumes at the breakfast table with a steaming cup of chocolate. He will not touch tea unless forced. Otherwise he drinks tisanes, herbal teas which, like his chocolate, he sometimes prepares himself over a spirit lamp. However, by *Hickory Dickory Death* in 1955, Poirot had given up his campaign against tea and served afternoon tea to guests – strong Indian tea along with hot buttered crumpets, bread and jam, and rich plum cake – at five o'clock. For Poirot this would spoil the enjoyment of the supreme meal of the day, dinner.

In *Death in the Clouds* he invites Inspector Japp and

Monsieur Fournier of the Sûreté to dine, proving that it was possible to eat well in England. Poirot even seems to enjoy that steak-and-kidney pudding in the Cheshire Cheese pub off Fleet Street. However, his delicate sensibilities draw the line at the Chinese food he is forced to sample in Limehouse in 'The Lost Mine', crying 'Ah, *Dieu, mon estomac*', while tenderly clasping that portion of his anatomy. He again exclaims '*mon estomac*' when flying from Le Gourget to Croydon in *Death in the Clouds*. Poirot also suffers from seasickness, especially on the Channel crossing, though he seems to be able to manage on the calmer waters of the Mediterranean. He is, though, little better on a camel in 'The Adventure of the Egyptian Tomb' where his 'groans and lamentations . . . shrieks, gesticulations and invocations to the Virgin Mary and every saint in the calendar' end with him finishing the journey on a small donkey.

Poirot is a man who has always taken his stomach seriously, 'reaping his reward in old age'. In *Mrs McGinty's Dead* we learn that, for Poirot, eating was not only a physical pleasure, it was also an intellectual research. He spent the time between meals, when he was not solving crimes, tracking down new sources of delicious food. In this novel, he had just given *La Vielle Grand'mère* in Soho his seal of approval. He is only sorry that he can eat just three times a day. Sometimes Poirot manages to overcome this hurdle. In *Lord Edgware Dies*, he suggests to Hastings that they have '*une petite omelette*' before making a call. The meal actually consists of 'a delicious omelette, a sole, a chicken and a *Baba au Rhum* of which Poirot was inordinately fond'. Poirot's reasoning is that 'the brain should be the servant of the stomach'.

Outside the gastronomic milieu of London though, Poirot suffers. In the Black Swan in Hartly Dene, he had a steak that was both tough and full of gristle, Brussels sprouts that were large, pale and watery, and potatoes that had a heart of stone.

'Nor was there much to be said for the portion of stewed apple and custard which had followed. The cheese had been hard, and the biscuits soft.'

Things get worse when he visits the west of Ireland in 'The Apples of Hesperides'. The meal he consumed produced a 'curious and painful sensation in his insides' and the hot water he had been brought was tepid. His bed was broken – as were two panes of glass in his room. The hotel did not live up to his ideas of what a hotel should be. In *Mrs McGinty's Dead*, the conditions in the Summerhayes' guesthouse in Broadhinny are so bad that Poirot begins missing meals.

'Only in England is the coffee so atrocious,' he laments in *The Big Four*. 'On the Continent they understand how important it is for the digestion that it should be properly made.'

When forced to drink tea in *Sad Cypress*, he stirs the inky beverage cautiously before taking one heroic sip. To make tea palatable, he puts as many as five lumps of sugar in it. Even then, in *Dead Man's Folly*, he forgoes tomato and pâté sandwiches in favour of a cream cake – 'a particularly sweet and squelchy one'.

In the Black Swan, he is served 'a cup of liquid mud euphemistically called coffee'. In the Stag Inn in *Taken at the Flood*, Poirot is served for breakfast 'somewhat grudgingly' a concoction whose principal component is watery hot milk and you have to move from the coffee room into the lounge to be served 'small cups of a treacly and muddy liquid called black coffee'.

But there are good things to be had. After the murder in *The Hollow*, he has cold duck for supper, followed by caramel custard. And in *One, Two, Buckle My Shoe*, he has perfect clear soup, a grilled sole, saddle of lamb with tiny young garden peas, and strawberries and cream. Although this was English, not Continental, cooking, the wines served with dinner 'stirred Poirot to a passion of appreciation'.

In *The Adventure of the Christmas Pudding*, he praises Mrs Ross, the cook at Kings Lacey, saying: 'The oyster soup . . . and the stuffing. The chestnut stuffing in the turkey, that was quite unique in my experience.'

Mrs Ross is flattered, assuming that as he was a 'foreign gentleman' he would prefer Continental dishes. But Poirot is adamant that good English cooking – not the cooking in second-class hotels or restaurants – is appreciated by Continental gourmets. Then there are the puddings.

'We have nothing like that in France . . . It is worth making a journey to London just to taste the varieties and excellencies of the English puddings.'

Naturally he consumes good wines. His cellar runs to a Château Mouton Rothschild in *The Labours of Hercules*. In *Lord Edgware Dies* he drinks 'possibly a glass too much' champagne, but insists that not even the 'best and driest of champagne, the most golden-haired and seductive of women . . . influences the judgment of Hercule Poirot'.

He occasionally accepts a dry martini, but says he prefers sherry. What he cannot abide is whisky, which he claims ruins the palate, leaving you unable to appreciate the delicate wines of France. He has to hand for guests grenadine, crème de menthe, Benedictine, crème de cacao, whisky and soda . . . even beer. More often than not Poirot himself is happy with a *sirop de cassis*, which Colin Lamb in *The Clocks* says is 'blackcurrant to you and me'.

He is always neatly attired. In the foreword to *The Labours of Hercules* we find him wearing striped trousers, a correct black jacket, a natty bow tie and, of course, patent-leather shoes. Later he is found wearing a dark grey gent's suit. Visiting the offices of *X-Ray News* in *The Labours of Hercules* he is asked whether he is going to the Royal Enclosure at Ascot, but then his immaculate attire is topped off with a white camellia in his buttonhole. He even wears a white camellia in his button hole when wearing a white duck suit on the Riviera. Going to Sunday lunch in Wealdshire, he refuses to dress like a country gentleman, even donning his pale grey Homburg for the occasion. 'You stick out in a country place,' Inspector Morton tells him in *After the Funeral*.

In *Five Little Pigs* (*Murder in Retrospect* in the US), English country gentleman Meredith Blake takes exception to Poirot wearing the wrong clothes and button boots. He did not look as though he had ever hunted or shot – or even played a decent game. He was, in short, 'a foreigner'. The best Hastings can say in defence of his friends is: 'There is nothing of the Socialist about Poirot.'

In 'The Third-Floor Flat', Poirot is glimpsed in 'a resplendent dressing gown and embroidered slippers'. It is important, he says in 'The Augean Stables', to present a good appearance 'when one has few natural advantages'.

In *The Big Four*, Poirot admits that he does not play chess. However, he plays bridge. This even results in 'heavy financial gain' to Poirot and Sir Montagu Corner in *Lord Edgware Dies*. He has a horror of golf. Asked by Lucien Bex in *The Murder on the Links* if he plays, Poirot says: 'I? Never! What a game! Figure to yourself, each hole is of a different length. The obstacles, they are not arranged mathematically. Even the greens are frequently up one side! There is only one thing – how do you call them? – tee boxes! They, at least, are symmetrical.'

However, totally out of character in *Evil Under the Sun*, Poirot organizes a picnic – on Dartmoor. But on his seaside holidays he avoids the beach. He cannot abide sand.

Poirot is every bit as fastidious in his taste for women. Although he admires America, he finds American women less charming than those from his own country. A French or Belgian girl is 'coquettish, charming – I think there is no one to touch her'. He has little to do with them though. Nevertheless, he tells Hastings: 'You admire *les femmes* . . . you prostrate yourself before all of them who are good-looking and have the good taste to smile upon you; but psychologically you know nothing about them.'

There are few significant women in Poirot's life. One is Countess Vera Rossakoff, the jewel thief he meets in 'The Double Clue' – one of *Poirot's Early Cases*. Poirot is told she is a charming Russian woman, 'a member of the old regime'. At first Poirot is sceptical, saying: 'Any woman can call herself a Russian countess.' Then, without warning, she flies into the room like a whirlwind, 'bringing with her a swirl of sables . . . and a hat rampant with slaughtered ospreys'. Hastings describes her as a woman with a 'somewhat disturbing personality'.

At the Carlton, Poirot and Hastings find her 'arrayed in a marvellous négligée of barbaric design'. She calls him 'a clever little man'. Poirot is bowled over in admiration.

'What a woman,' he says. *'Mon Dieu, quelle femme . . .'*

By *The Big Four* she has become Inez Veroneau, puzzlingly 'a Spaniard, married to a Frenchman'. She accuses Poirot of hunting her from London.

However, Madame Veroneau is a widow in mourning. She is also secretary to one of the villains, Madame Olivier. Even so, Hastings notes that Poirot still had a sneaking fondness for the countess.

'Something in her very flamboyance attracted the little man . . . That she was arrayed against us, on the side of our bitterest enemies, never seemed to weigh on his judgement,' he says.

However, Poirot is vindicated when he returns the child that she thought was dead. In the end, Poirot says: 'I might even marry and range myself . . . Who knows?' But it was not to be.

Even twenty years later, she remains a woman of 'full and flamboyant form'. For him, other women were devoid of charm, lacking her rich, alluring femininity. He longs for a *'femme du monde*, chic, sympathetic, *spirituelle* – a woman with ample curves, a woman ridiculously and extravagantly dressed! Once there had been such a woman . . .'

When he glimpses her on the escalators in Piccadilly Circus Underground station, she has changed little. 'Her luxuriant henna-red hair [was] crowned with a small plastron of straw to which was attached a positive platoon of brilliantly feathered little birds. Exotic-looking furs dripped from her shoulders. Her crimson mouth open wide, her rich, foreign voice echoed resoundingly. She had good lungs . . .' She says she will meet him in Hell.

The narrator of *The Labours of Hercules* also points out that it is the 'misfortune of small precise men to hanker after large and flamboyant women'. Time had passed but he had 'never been able to rid himself of the fatal fascination the countess held for him'. She remained for him 'sumptuous and alluring'. Even the memory of her thievery 'roused the old admiration' in him. She was a 'woman in a thousand – a million'. He is, the narrators says, 'the little bourgeois . . . still thrilled by the aristocrat'.

Although he thinks he has lost her again, Miss Lemon puts him on the right track. They meet again in a chic nightclub she is running. Resplendent in a scarlet evening dress, she addresses him as 'my very dear friend' and flatters him. Again he contrives to extricate her. At the end of 'The Capture of Cerberus', she embraces Poirot with 'Slavonic fervour'. Poirot recoils when he sees in the mirror he has lipstick and mascara on this face. Nevertheless, he sends her a dozen red roses. In *One, Two, Buckle My Shoe*, he is still holding a candle for her. However, in the meantime, in *Peril at End House*, he is very soft on Nick Buckley, who exhibits many of the same ruthless traits. And in *Evil Under the Sun* he admitted he admired the dressmaker Rosamund Darnley, proprietor of Rose Mond Ltd, as much as any woman he had ever met. 'He liked her distinction, the graceful lines of her figures, the alert carriage of her head. He liked the neat sleek waves of her dark hair and the ironic quality of her smile.' And he makes no attempt to disguise his pleasure when she sits down next to him.

Plainly Ariadne Oliver is not going to inspire such passion. In *Cards on the Table*, she is described as 'an agreeable woman of middle age, handsome in a rather untidy fashion with fine eyes, substantial shoulders and a large quantity of rebellious grey hair with which she was continually experimenting'. She also has an agreeable bass voice.

They have met before at a literary dinner. But while Poirot depended on order and method, Mrs Oliver is an earnest believer in woman's intuition. In the countryside, she wears tweeds and a hat at an unfashionable angle. However, she also favours patent-leather shoes – though hers have high heels and she absent-mindedly retains them when away from London. At dinner, she wears 'iron-grey satin' and looks 'like an obsolete battleship'. She is a woman of ample proportions with a 'jutting shelf' of a bust. On one occasion, after she had almost run him down, Poirot has to help her out of her small car, whereupon she 'shook herself rather like a Newfoundland dog'.

When she first appears in 'The Case of the Discontented Soldier', she is already a 'sensational novelist', though she is also on the staff of Mr Parker Pyne. She works at the top of his house on a table with 'a typewriter, several notebooks, a general confusion of loose manuscripts and a large bag of apples'. By then she had already written forty novels that were bestsellers in England and America, and translated into French, German, Italian, Hungarian, Finnish, Japanese and, of all things, Abyssinian.

We know little of her younger life. She had a great-aunt Alice. She was sent to finishing school in Paris and daydreamed about her beloved Monsieur Adolphe, but had few boyfriends. At one time, she wanted to be a nun, then thought she'd become a nurse. But she plainly married

– though her husband is never mentioned – and began a literary career.

She is business-like and spurs herself on with the thought of how much money she is going to get for her serial rights, although she remains overdrawn. Nevertheless, she refuses to make speeches or give interviews. Politics were an anathema to her, though she thinks that a woman should be head of Scotland Yard.

Christie admitted that Mrs Oliver had a 'strong dash of myself'. This is best illustrated, perhaps, in the attitude to her vegetarian Finnish detective Sven Hjerson. She says she did not know why she had thought up the revolting man. She knew nothing about Finland. His mannerisms were idiotic. But she was tied to him for life because he was box office.

'If I met that bony, gangling, vegetable-eating Finn in real life,' she says, 'I'd do a better murder than any I've ever invented.'

Ill-suited as lovers, they remain firm friends. They investigate cases together and, in *The Pale Horse*, Ariadne goes sleuthing on her own.

The only other significant woman in Poirot's life is Miss Felicity Lemon. But there is no love interest here. In *Hickory Dickory Death*, her sister says that Felicity 'has never cared for people'. It is only then that Poirot realizes that Felicity is the severe Miss Lemon's first name. She looks 'intensely British'. When in 'The Mystery of the Spanish Chest' it is suggested that a man and a woman were 'very close friends', Miss Lemon treats the idea with faint distaste and even rushes from the room when things get too much for her.

Even in *Poirot's Early Cases*, she is 'forty-eight and of unprepossessing appearance' – elsewhere 'unbelievably ugly and incredibly efficient'. She 'seemed to be composed entirely of angles – thus satisfying Poirot's demand for symmetry. However, she is also the perfect secretary

– in Poirot's eyes at least – as she was a human machine, an instrument of precision. Completely uninterested in human affairs, her real passion in life was developing the perfect filing system.

Her job is to answer the phone, usher visitors in discreetly and handle Poirot's correspondence. She is regularly seen with her pencil hovering over her shorthand pad and typed with the 'speed and precision of a quick-firing tank'. Sometimes he seeks her advice – especially on how to handle tradesmen – and is perfectly capable of giving an opening on purely human matters. In 'How Does Your Garden Grow?' she says she has torn a piece out of the paper for Poirot – in fact, she has cut it out neatly with scissors. Later, he takes her on the investigation with him.

However, in *Hickory Dickory Death* 'that hideous and efficient woman' makes three mistakes in a letter. Poirot is bewildered, then discovers that she is worried about her sister. Before, he had never conceived of her having a sister, or for that matter parents or even grandparents. Nevertheless, he offers to grant Miss Lemon's sister his professional services.

Miss Lemon is seldom, if ever, unpunctual. Fog, storms, illness and the failure for public transportation have no affect. Once she is five minutes late – due to a suicide – and apologizes profusely. But what really lets Miss Lemon down in Poirot's eyes is that she had no imagination, which makes discussing a case with her uphill work. However, she has an instinct for what might interest him, putting important correspondence on the top of the pile.

Poirot sometimes uses her for research and she looks things up, consulting the *Encyclopedia Britannica* and a medical work over a possible instance of kleptomania. She thinks that men are silly for playing with model railways and reading Sherlock Holmes. When she gets time to read, she prefers an improving book, regarding such frivolities as crime fiction with contempt. However, she is loyal. In

Dead Man's Folly, she bristles in her employer's defence. She also has a special look to indicate that she wants to get rid of Poirot so she could get on 'with proper fervour' with her work.

Poirot's closest friend is Arthur Hastings. We know little of his background. When he first appears in *The Mysterious Affair at Styles*, he says that he has 'no near relations or friends'. However, in *Dumb Witness*, he admits to having a great-aunt Mary whose handwriting looked like a spider had got into an inkpot and walked over a sheet of notepaper.

He went to Eton, but was not wealthy and had a job with Lloyd's of London before the First World War that took him to Brussels where he first met Poirot, whose various exploits and triumphs he is happy to recite. Fighting in France, he rose to the rank of captain and was awarded the OBE. Wounded on the Somme (First Battle 1 July–13 November 1916) he was invalided home from the Front and, after some months in a rather depressing convalescent home, was given sick leave – which was when he ended up at Styles.

There, on 17 July 1916, he has a reunion with Poirot. He admits to a 'secret hankering to be a detective'. But instead of being Sherlock Holmes, he finds himself playing Watson – twenty-six of the Poirot stories and eight novels are narrated by Hastings.

Poirot praises him for his good memory, though the order he presents them in 'truly . . . deplorable' and he often omits one of paramount importance. Worse, 'you dressed in haste, and your tie is on one side'.

Throughout the books Poirot belittles Hastings' intellectual ability – and straightens his tie. 'I know the truth of the whole affair. And so could you know it if you would only use the brains the good God has given you,' he says. 'Sometimes I really am tempted to believe that by inadvertence He passed you by.'

Hastings is sometimes offended by this high-handed attitude.

However, when Hastings is not around Poirot misses him. In 'How Does My Garden Grow?' Poirot says: 'He had such an imagination. Such a romantic mind. It is true that he always imagined wrong – but that in itself was a guide.'

Nevertheless, in the beginning at least, Hastings vies with Poirot.

'My system is based on his,' he tells Mary Cavendish in *The Mysterious Affair at Styles*, 'though of course I have progressed further.'

However, by the end of the book, Hastings has a job in the War Office, while Poirot, on the strength of 'The Styles Case', was on the way to becoming a sought-after private detective – though it is Hastings that the family and Poirot himself have asked to write an account.

Invalided out of the army, he takes up residence with Poirot in London and continues his work as his chronicler. Early on, they are inseparable, though Hastings still has a 'recruiting job' in 'The Kidnapped Prime Minister'. Indeed, Poirot is handling some matter for the War Office in 'The Lemesurier Inheritance'. By *The Murder on the Links*, Hastings is private secretary to an MP who had been entrusted with transacting some business in Paris.

Hastings is about thirty years old when their association begins. He gets his own back by making remarks abut Poirot's age and assuming he has lost the plot. Hastings is much taller that Poirot with a straight back and broad shoulders. Poirot chides him for parting his hair at the side, rather than in the middle. 'What a difference it would make to the symmetry of your appearance.' And, if Hastings must have a moustache, it should be a real moustache – 'a thing of beauty' – like his own. However, in *The ABC Murders*, Hastings admits to being touchy about the thinness of his hair.

An old-fashioned English gentleman, Hastings favours eggs and bacon, and whisky and soda – though he can force down a dry Martini in *Peril at End House*. He is appalled at Poirot's willingness to eavesdrop, pry, read private letters and dissemble. In *Peril at End House*, he says primly: 'The English character is averse to lying on a wholesale scale and that, no less, was what Poirot's plan required.'

Nevertheless his loyalty is absolute. In *Lord Edgware Dies*, Inspector Japp says: 'Where the master goes, the dog follows.' Hastings does not think this is in the best of taste.

The feisty Miss Peabody in *Dumb Witness* (*Poirot Loses a Client*) even doubts Hastings' ability as an amanuensis.

'Can you write decent English?' she asks.

'I hope so,' says Hastings.

'H'm – where did you go to school?'

'Eton.'

'Then you can't.'

However, for the readers of Agatha Christie's Poirot novels, he does a pretty good job of it.

Hastings is wary of being embraced by Poirot, who kisses him a couple of times in *The Mysterious Affair at Styles*. However, Hastings is a ladies' man. He is taken by the fresh-looking young Cynthia Murdoch. When she kisses him, he finds it 'very nice . . . but the publicity of the salute rather impaired the pleasure'.

Half-a-lifetime later, in *Curtain*, Hastings still remembers Cynthia Murdoch, a young girl with auburn hair, running across the lawn. Poirot perpetually teases Hastings about the 'auburn hair that so excites you'.

In *The Murder on the Links*, Hastings meets a young woman on the Calais express who swears. Being old-fashioned, he considers that a woman should be womanly and has no patience with 'the modern neurotic girl who jazzes from morning till night, smokes like a chimney and uses language which would make a Billingsgate fishwoman blush'. What's more she is wearing make-up and is little more than seventeen. Nevertheless, Hastings engages her in conversion.

She is an actress, a former child acrobat and an American. Although Hastings does not believe in 'marrying out of one's class', by the end of the book, he has kissed her – though she is 'only a little scullion'. She has black hair. Nevertheless, Hastings marries her and they move to a ranch in Argentina. In *The Big Four*, Hastings receives a cable telling him that she has been kidnapped. In fact, Poirot has her in a place of safety. By then Poirot knows not to embrace Hastings or to show any emotion. He says, he will be 'very British. I will say nothing – but nothing at all.'

While Mrs Hastings stays in South America, bringing up their two sons and two daughters, Hastings himself travels back and forth, staying in England for long periods to assist his friend and record his exploits.

By *Curtain*, Hastings is a widower, though his daughter Judith appears in the tale. In a postscript, Poirot urges Hastings to seek out Elizabeth Litchfield, an attractive young woman who believes herself tainted by murder in the family, as he is 'still not unattractive to women' himself. We do not know whether Hastings took his advice.

The other recurring figure in the Poirot stories is Detective Inspector James Japp. When they first meet in *The Mysterious Affair at Styles*, Poirot already knows Japp well enough to call him Jimmy, an unusual informality for Poirot. Over the years, their association flourishes, with Japp calling Poirot in on particularly puzzling cases. With the help of Poirot, Japp has become a chief inspector by *Death on the Nile*.

Japp is described as 'little, sharp, dark and ferret-faced', while remaining 'jaunty and dapper'. Poirot has a high opinion of Japp's abilities, though deplores his lack of method, while Hastings saw his highest talent lay in 'seeking favours under the guise of conferring them'. He often gets to do Poirot's legwork. In 'The Disappearance of Mr Davenheim', Japp pays up after betting Poirot £5 that he cannot solve the case without leaving his chair. And Poirot boasts that in 'The Plymouth Express' mystery, Japp had gone to make a survey of the railway line and, when he returned, without moving from his apartment, Poirot told him everything he had found. Nevertheless he remains 'good-humoured' and he, too, gets his tie adjusted by Poirot.

Having already retired from the Belgian police force before we even meet him, Poirot makes several attempts to retire as a private detective. After retiring to King's Abbot to grow marrows in *The Murder of Roger Ackroyd*, he tries again in *The Labours of Hercules*, which are supposed to be his last ten cases before he returns to the cultivation of his beloved green-skinned gourds.

In *Peril at End House*, Poirot claims: 'I am not a stage favourite who gives the world a dozen farewells.' However, in *The ABC Murders*, he admits that he is like 'the prima donna who always makes one more appearance' – until, of course, he finally dies in *Curtain*. By then, he is so famous worldwide that he appeared on a Nicaraguan postage stamp commemorating the fiftieth anniversary of the foundation of Interpol. Agatha Christie complained that he appeared to have 'large quantities of intestines coming out of his head'. She supposed that this was someone's idea of little grey cells.

4

HERCULE POIROT INVESTIGATES

By the time Agatha Christie killed him off, Poirot had appeared in thirty-three novels, one play and more than fifty short stories.

The Mysterious Affair at Styles
New York: Dodd, Mead & Co., 1920; London: The Bodley Head, 1921

The story is told by Captain Arthur Hastings, who is on a month's sick leave after being invalided home from the Front in the First World War. He is invited by his friend John Cavendish to stay at the Cavendish estate, Styles Court, near Styles St Mary in Essex. John's stepmother Emily Inglethorp, who is now in control of the family fortune, has married a much younger man, Alfred Inglethorp, who John describes as a 'rotten little bounder'. Both John and his younger brother Lawrence, a would-be poet, are dependent on their stepmother. Also on hand are John's beautiful wife Mary, Mrs Inglethorp's secretary and companion Evelyn Howard and Cynthia Murdoch, an orphan taken in by Mrs Inglethorp who works in the dispensary in the nearby hospital and consequently has access to poisons. In the village is a strange foreigner named Dr Bauerstein to whom Mary Cavendish is mysteriously attracted. Out on a stroll Hastings meets Hercule Poirot, a celebrated detective and now a refugee who Hastings knew in Belgium before the war.

Late that night the Styles' household is awoken by Mrs Inglethorp who is having some kind of a fit. The door to her bedroom is locked from the inside. After they break it down, they find her having convulsions. She cries out the name of her husband and dies. The cause: strychnine. Detective Inspector James Japp arrests her husband. But Poirot is not so sure. Christie provides a plan of the first floor to help the reader follow the well-constructed plot.

The story appeared as a special in the long-running *Poirot* series in 1990 to celebrate the centenary of Agatha Christie's birth. BBC Radio 4 turned it into a five-part serial in 2005 and the Great Lakes Theater toured a stage adaptation in 2012.

The Murder on the Links
London: The Bodley Head, 1923; New York: Dodd, Mead & Co., 1923

Hastings is travelling back from Paris. On the train to Calais he meets a young flapper, who wears scarlet lipstick and swears. Although he disapproves of 'new' women, he is immediately charmed. She and her twin sister are actresses-cum-acrobats.

Arriving in London, Hastings finds that Poirot has received a letter from a wealthy businessman named Paul Renauld who lives at Merlinville-sur-Mer between Boulogne and Calais. He wants to hire a detective, but by the time Poirot and Hastings reach Merlinville, Renauld has been murdered. He had been stabbed and his body was found beside an open grave, dug on a new golf course adjoining his estate. In his villa, his wife had been found bound and gagged.

Because of Poirot's reputation, he is allowed to join the investigation. However, Inspector Giraud of the Sûreté arrives and he treats Poirot with contempt for his old-fashioned and unscientific methods. After a series of bruising encounters, Poirot bets Giraud 500 francs that he can find the murderer first.

A second body is found while Poirot is away in Paris. Nevertheless he is able to describe the circumstances in detail when he returns. Poirot has spotted similarities with a murder that happened twenty years before. This proves to be the key to the case. Poirot wins his bet and Hastings gets to kiss his flapper.

BBC Radio 4 produced a radio adaptation in 1990 and it appeared in the long-running *Poirot* TV series in 1996. It has also appeared as a graphic novel published by Harper-Collins in 2007.

Poirot Investigates
London: The Bodley Head, 1924; New York: Dodd, Mead & Co., 1925

These short stories were originally serialized in the *Sketch* magazine, beginning on 7 March 1923. Eleven were collected in the UK edition, while all fourteen appeared in the US.

'The Adventure of the Western Star'
First published in issue 1576 of the Sketch, *11 April 1923; in the US, Volume 38, Number 4 of* Blue Book *magazine, February 1924 as 'The Western Star'*

The movie star Mary Marvell visits Poirot and tells him that she has received threatening letters saying that she must return her famous diamond, the Western Star, which is said to have come from the left eye of an idol. It was given to her by her husband, actor Gregory Rolf. The couple are going to stay at the home of Lord and Lady Yardley, Yardley Chase, where they plan to make a film. Hastings recalls that, some years before, there was gossip linking Lady Yardley and Gregory Rolf. Poirot advised Miss Marvell not to take her diamond to Yardley Chase, but she is determined to do so as Lady Yardley has its twin, the Eastern Star.

After Miss Marvell has gone, Lady Yardley turns up – Poirot had been recommended by Mary Cavendish from *The Mysterious Affair at Styles*. She has received similar letters. However, Lord Yardley is short of money and aims to sell the Eastern Star. As Mary Marvell would not take Poirot's advice, she accepts Lady Yardley's commission instead.

Poirot arranges to visit Yardley Chase where Lady Yardley's diamond is stolen. Mary Marvell's diamond also goes missing, but Poirot solves the mystery and gets Lady Yardley's stone returned.

The Adventure of the Western Star appeared in the *Poirot* TV series in 1990.

'The Tragedy at Marsdon Manor'
First published in issue 1577 of the Sketch, *18 April 1923; in the US, Volume 38, Number 5 of* Blue Book *magazine, March 1924, as 'The Marsdon Manor Tragedy'*
The North Union Insurance Company asks Poirot to investigate the death of Mr Maltravers, apparently of a brain haemorrhage, soon after taking out a large life insurance in favour of his young wife. Visiting Maltravers' home, Marsdon Manor, he discovers that a small rook rifle was found next to the body.

After he has interviewed Mrs Maltravers, a young man named Captain Black arrives. Poirot interviews Captain

Black and discovers that he knew a man who had committed suicide with a rook rifle when he was out in East Africa. He had told the story at dinner at Marsdon Manor the night before Mr Maltravers died. From this, Poirot deduces that Mr Maltravers was murdered and use trickery to unmask the killer.

This appeared in the *Poirot* TV series in 1991.

'The Adventure of the Cheap Flat'
First published in issue 1580 of the Sketch, *9 May 1923; in the US, Volume 39, Number 1 of* Blue Book *magazine, May 1924*
Hastings was visiting friends when he was told by the newly-weds, Mr and Mrs Robinson, that they had just rented a flat in Knightsbridge at an unbelievable low price. Poirot is immediately interested. Visiting the apartment block, he discovers that, while the Robinsons said they had only just moved in, the porter says that they have lived there for six months. Poirot rents another flat in the block.

He then reveals that Inspector Japp had told him of the theft of the plans for harbour defences in the US. The suspect had been killed. His girlfriend, who had disappeared at the time of his death, bears a striking resemblance to Mrs Robinson. Poirot and Hastings break into the Robinsons' apartment and apprehend a would-be assassin. Poirot's little grey cells not only linked the theft of the plans with the cheap rent on the apartment, he goes on to track down the rest of the spy ring and recover the plans.

This appeared in the *Poirot* TV series in 1990.

'The Mystery of the Hunter's Lodge'
First published in issue 1581 of the Sketch, *16 May 1923; in the US, Volume 39, Number 6 of* Blue Book *magazine, June 1924, as 'The Hunter's Lodge Mystery'*
Poirot is ill, so Hastings takes on a case for him. Roger Havering, who had been staying in his club in London, says that his wife has phoned saying that his wealthy uncle,

Harrington Pace, had been murdered the previous evening at their home, Hunter's Lodge, and he should bring a detective. Poirot sends Hastings, telling him to follow any instructions he wires.

When Hastings arrives at Hunter's Lodge, Inspector Japp is there. The housekeeper, Mrs Middleton, says that, after dinner, a man with a black beard came to see Mr Pace. The two men were talking in the gun-room. Then there was a shot. The man with the black beard then disappeared along with one of a pair of pistols. Mrs Havering confirms this story and Inspector Japp confirms Mr Havering's alibi. Poirot sends word that they are to arrest Mrs Middleton, but she has vanished. Further investigation casts doubt on whether she ever existed at all. Poirot fingers the crooks, but Japp does not have enough evidence to arrest them. However, in the moral world of Agatha Christie, they get their comeuppance anyway.

This appeared in the *Poirot* TV series in 1991.

'The Million-Dollar Bond Robbery'
First published in issue 1579 of the Sketch, *2 May 1923; in the US, Volume 38, Number 6 of* Blue Book *magazine, February 1924, as 'The Great Bond Robbery'*

The charming Esmée Farquhar asks Poirot to prove the innocence of her fiancé Philip Ridgeway. He was taking a million dollars-worth of Liberty Bonds to New York when they went missing. After being counted by two of the bank's general managers, one of which was Mr Ridgeway's uncle, they were sealed in a package and locked in his portmanteau which had been fitted with a special lock. Ridgeway had the only key and sailed with the trunk from Liverpool on the *Olympia*. Just a few hours before the liner arrived in New York, the bonds went missing. A search of the ship was made, but they seemed to have disappeared into thin air. However, within half an hour of the ship docking, they were on sale.

Interviewing Ridgeway, Poirot discovers that an attempt had been made to force the lock, but had apparently failed. Everyone leaving the ship was searched. No one could have carried the bulky package off. Ridgeway also says that one broker swore that he had bought some of the bonds before the *Olympia* had docked. Even though Ridgeway himself was searched as he left the ship, people were beginning to say that he had stolen the bonds.

At the bank, the general managers confirm his story, but Poirot comes away saying that he knows who stole the bonds. Hastings and Poirot then travel to Liverpool, where the *Olympia* has just docked, to interview the stewards. Poirot gives an accurate description of the passenger who occupied the cabin next to Mr Ridgeway. However, the man concerned was one of the last to leave the ship in New York. Hastings believes that fact has sunk Poirot's theory. Instead it has confirmed it.

On the train back to London, Poirot writes a note to Inspector McNeil at Scotland Yard. Over dinner with Miss Farquhar, Poirot explains how the bonds had been stolen and who had done it.

This appeared in the *Poirot* TV series in 1991.

'The Adventure of the Egyptian Tomb'
First published in issue 1600 of the Sketch, *26 September 1923; in the US, Volume 39, Number 4 of* Blue Book *magazine, August 1924 as 'The Egyptian Adventure'*
The archaeologist Sir John Willard dies suddenly of heart failure shortly after opening the Tomb of King Men-her-Ra in Egypt. Two weeks later, his sponsor, the wealthy American Mr Bleibner, dies of blood poisoning. Then his nephew Rupert shoots himself in New York. The newspapers claim that the deaths are due to the 'curse of Men-her-Ra'.

Poirot is summoned by Lady Willard, Sir John's widow. Their son has headed out to Egypt to continue his father's work. Lady Willard is afraid that he, too, may succumb to the curse. To Hastings' surprise, Poirot admits that he believes in the force of superstition and takes the case.

He asks about other members of the expedition and a cable to New York reveals that Rupert Bleibner had been at a low ebb for several years, after being a beachcomber in the South Seas. Recently he had raised enough money to get to Egypt where he said he had a good friend he could borrow money from. However, this uncle was not forthcoming. Rupert returned to New York where he killed himself, leaving a note saying that he was a leper and an outcast.

Hastings and Poirot travel to Egypt. There they discover that there has been another death among the party. This time the cause was tetanus. Poirot pretends to believe in the curse. That night, he is served a cup of camomile tea and has a fit. The expedition's doctor comes running. But Poirot has only feigned the fit. He sends the tea for chemical analysis. The doctor then kills himself, leaving Poirot to explain how and why the victims had died.

This appeared in the *Poirot* TV series in 1993.

'The Jewel Robbery at the Grand Metropolitan'
First published in issue 1572 of the Sketch, *14 March 1923 as 'The Curious Disappearance of the Opalsen Pearls'; in the US, Volume 37, Number 6 of* Blue Book *magazine, October 1923 as 'Mrs Opalsen's Pearls'*

Hastings takes Poirot to Brighton for the weekend. They stay at the Grand Metropolitan where they meet the wealthy Mr Opalsen and his wife. Mrs Opalsen wants to show Poirot her pearls, only to discover that they have been stolen. The only two suspects are her maid Célestine, who was in the room, and the chambermaid who came in to turn down the beds. The two women accuse one another. The pair were apart for only a few seconds when Célestine went to get cotton and scissors from the adjoining room. This was too short a time to take out the jewel case, open it and steal the pearls. Poirot notices that there is another connecting door leading to the next suite. However, it is bolted on the inside.

Célestine's room is searched and the pearls are found under her mattress. She is arrested and that appears to be the end of the case. But Poirot examines the next suite which is unoccupied. It has not been dusted and there is a rectangular mark on a table near the window.

Poirot then reveals that the pearls found under the mattress were not real. He interviews the chambermaid and asks her whether she has seen a white card like the one he hands her to examine. He asks a valet attending Mr Opalsen the same thing. He also notices French chalk on the runners of the drawer where the jewel-case is kept.

The next day Poirot is triumphant. The pearls have been returned and a pair of well-known jewel thieves arrested.

This appeared in the *Poirot* TV series in 1993.

'The Kidnapped Prime Minister'
First published in issue 1578 of the Sketch, *25 April 1923; in the US, Volume 39, Number 3 of* Blue Book *magazine, July 1924, as 'The Kidnapped Premier'*
Towards the end of the First World War, Hastings and Poirot are discussing an assassination attempt on the Prime Minister – he escaped with a bullet grazing his cheek. Then they are visited by Lord Estair – who Christie confusingly says is 'Leader of the House of Commons' – and Mr Bernard Dodge, who was a member of the war cabinet and a close personal friend of the Prime Minister who has now been kidnapped in France on his way to an important conference. A car sent to pick him up was found in a side road with the driver and the commander-in-chief's ADC bound and gagged inside. A second car was found with the Prime Minister's secretary Captain Daniels inside, similarly bound and gagged, but there is no sign of the PM. Poirot's interest is immediately piqued by Captain Daniels,

who had been in the car with the Prime Minister during the earlier assassination attempt, which reportedly took place near Windsor. The driver's name was Murphy, which sounded suspiciously Irish. Nevertheless, he seems to have behaved heroically. However, he has since gone missing and the car he had been driving was found abandoned outside a Soho restaurant thought to be a meeting place for German spies.

Poirot travels to France, but goes no further than Boulogne where he sits thinking in his hotel room. Then he returns to England and tours the hospitals to the west of London. Armed with the vital clue he has gathered, Poirot then organizes a raid on a house in Hampstead, rescues the Prime Minister and has him flown to France in time for the conference.

This appeared in the *Poirot* TV series in 1990.

'The Disappearance of Mr Davenheim'
First published in issue 1574 of the Sketch, *28 March 1923; in the US, Volume 38, Number 2 of* Blue Book *magazine, December 1923, as 'Mr Davenby Disappears' (the name was changed throughout in the original US magazine publication)*
Inspector Japp is visiting Poirot and Hastings for tea and they discuss the disappearance of the banker Mr Davenheim. He walked out of his house one afternoon to post some letters and has not been seen since. Poirot has a bet with Japp that he can solve the case within a week without moving from his chair.

When he disappeared Davenheim was expecting a Mr Lowen. He had left instructions that Lowen should be shown into the study. Though jewels and other valuables were missing from the safe, Lowen had not been arrested. It also transpires that Davenheim had spent the previous autumn in Buenos Aires and a picture in the newspaper shows him with long hair, a full moustache and a beard.

Japp returns, announcing that, while they have not found Davenheim's body, they have found his clothes. A gold ring that Davenheim always wore has been pawned in London by a man name Billy Kellett, who has already served three months for stealing a watch. He says he saw a man answering Lowen's description throw it over a hedge. With the proceeds, he got drunk, assaulted a policeman and was arrested.

Poirot has only one question: Did Mr and Mrs Davenheim share a bedroom? It transpires they did not. Poirot then advises Hastings and Japp to withdraw any money they might have in Davenheim's bank. The following day it collapses. Poirot then reveals where Davenheim is hiding – in prison – and Japp sends him £5.

This appeared as a thirty-minute play in the series *Grand Electric Theater* on CBS in 1962 and in the *Poirot* TV series in 1990.

'The Adventure of the Italian Nobleman'
First published in issue 1604 of the Sketch, *24 October 1923; in the US, Volume 40, Number 2 of* Blue Book *magazine, February 1924, as 'The Italian Nobleman'*
A neighbour named Dr Hawker visits Poirot and Hastings one evening. His housekeeper then turns up saying that a patient named Count Foscatini has phoned saying that he was being killed. They rush around to his flat where they find Foscatini has been bludgeoned to death with a marble statuette. He was at the dining table that had been set for three people. Poirot examines the remains of the meal. Although the main courses had been consumed, very little of the rice had been eaten and the desserts were untouched. Poirot also remarks that Foscatini, while being bludgeoned, had managed to call the doctor, then carefully hung up the receiver.

Foscatini's valet, Graves, said that the previous morning two Italians, one of whom was named Signor Ascanio had visited. Money was discussed and there was a threat. The valet said that Foscatini then invited the two men for dinner, so they could continue their discussion.

After he had brought the port and coffee, Graves said he had been given the rest of the night off. That was about 8.30 p.m. and a broken clock set the time of the murder at 8.47 p.m. But Poirot noticed that the curtains were not drawn.

Signor Ascanio is arrested. He denies even knowing Count Foscatini and is vouched for by the Italian ambassador. However, in confidence to Poirot, he does admit that he knew Foscatini, who was a blackmailer. During his visit in the morning, he had handed over a huge sum of money in return for incriminating documents. Poirot had noticed that while the coffee was served black, Foscatini's teeth were dazzlingly white, unstained though all three coffee cups had been used. This tells him who the real murderer is.

This appeared in the *Poirot* TV series in 1993.

'The Case of the Missing Will'
First published in issue 1605 of the Sketch, *31 October 1923; in the US, Volume 40, Number 3 of* Blue Book *magazine, January 1925 as 'The Missing Will'*
Girton-graduate Violet Marsh approaches Poirot to ask him to help her find the will of her late uncle. He did not approve of educated women and had threatened to pit his wits against hers. When he died, he left his estate to her for a year. After that, his house and large fortune would pass to various charities. His will was witnessed by her uncle's servants, Mr and Mrs Butcher. Miss Marsh believes that there is a second will hidden around the house. Finding it is her uncle's challenge.

Poirot and Hastings visit the estate. The house is neat and tidy. Everything is in order except for the key to a roll-top desk that is attached to a dirty envelope. Mr and Mrs

Butcher say that they signed two wills for their master. He said he had made a mistake in the first one and had to tear it up before going to pay the tradesmen.

Poirot follows various clues and discovers what he takes to be a destroyed will. They are on the train back to London when Poirot realizes the key fact he has overlooked. They travel back to the house and find the will.

This appeared in the *Poirot* TV series in 1993.

'The Veiled Lady'

First published in the US in Volume 40, Number 5 of Blue Book magazine, March 1925

Poirot is bored. There do not seem to be enough challenging cases for him in England. He dismisses a recent smash-and-grab raid at a jewellery shop in Bond Street and the mysterious death of an Englishman in Holland. Then a heavily veiled lady turns up, introducing herself at Lady Millicent Castle-Vaughan. She had written a compromising letter to a soldier killed in the war and was now being blackmailed by a man called Lavington who keeps the letter in a Chinese puzzle box.

Knowing that Lavington is away, Poirot and Hastings break into his house and take the puzzle box. Lady Millicent is delighted at the return of her letter and asks to keep the box as a souvenir. Poirot refuses; something is wrong with her shoes. As a result, he manages to clear up the jewel theft and the murder in Holland.

This appeared in the *Poirot* TV series in 1990.

'The Lost Mine'

First published in the US in Volume 40, Number 6 of Blue Book magazine, April 1925

Poirot has 14,000 shares in a Burma mine that he earned by the exercise of his little grey cells. It had been worked out as a silver mine and abandoned, though there were still quantities of lead ore still to be extracted. However, only one Chinese family knew where it was. The head of the family, Wu-Ling, sailed to England with the papers. He was to be met at Southampton by Mr Pearson, one of the directors of the company who wanted to buy the mine.

However, Pearson returned saying that he had missed Wu-Ling who had taken a special train to London. A call came from the Russell Square Hotel, but Wu-Ling did not turn up to a board meeting the next day. When the company called the hotel they were told that a Chinaman had gone out with another man earlier that morning. When he did not reappear, Pearson called the police. A body was found in the Thames, but there was no sign of the papers. So Pearson called in Poirot.

On board the ship, Wu-Ling had befriended a young man named Charles Lester and invited him to visit him at the Russell Hotel. When he did, a man purporting to be Wu-Ling's servant appeared who took him by taxi in the direction of Limehouse. But Lester grew suspicious and fled.

However, Wu-Ling had no servant and the taxi driver said that he had taken the two men to an opium den in Limehouse, but only Lester had emerged.

At Pearson's insistence, he and Poirot visited the opium den where they overheard a conversation indicating that Lester had the papers, then slipped away. After this, Poirot had no problem identifying the culprit; it was a harder job convincing Inspector Miller of Scotland Yard who, in the end, took all the credit. But Poirot got the shares in the mine.

This appeared in the *Poirot* TV series in 1990.

'The Chocolate Box'
First published in the US in Volume 40, Number 4 of Blue Book *magazine, February 1925*

One night Poirot tells Hastings of one of the failures he had when he was with the Belgian police force. It concerned a rising French deputy, Paul Déroulard, who was bitterly anti-Catholic and a well-known womanizer. He married a wealthy aristocrat from Brussels who died after falling down stairs two years later. He subsequently died one night after dinner in the house his wife had bequeathed him. His death was of little interest to Poirot as he was a *'bon Catholique'*. However, Virginie Mesnard, cousin of Déroulard's dead wife, asked him to investigate.

She had been at dinner the night Déroulard had died, along with M. de Saint Alard, a neighbour of Déroulard's from France, and John Wilson, an English friend. Poirot visited the house, pretending to be a journalist, a ruse to fool Déroulard's ageing mother who was in failing health. After dinner Déroulard had retired to his study with de Saint Alard and Wilson. Suddenly he went red in the face, fell down and died. In the study, Poirot spotted a full box of chocolates, but strangely, while the box was pink, the lid was blue. Déroulard, it seems, always ate a few chocolates after dinner. He had finished a box on the day he died.

De Saint Alard was an ardent Catholic, so had a motive to kill Déroulard. Then Poirot discovered that Wilson had a prescription made up for trinitrine, which lowers the blood pressure and was made up into tiny tablets of chocolate.

Poirot then visited the house of de Saint Alard, disguised as a plumber. There he discovered an empty bottle of Wilson's trinitrine tablets. When he returned to Brussels, he was writing up his report when he was summoned by someone he had not suspected, though they had left the most obvious clue. However, Poirot was satisfied as both Déroulard and his murderer got their comeuppance.

This appeared in the *Poirot* TV series in 1993.

'The Murder of Roger Ackroyd'
London: Collins, 1926; New York: Dodd, Mead & Co., 1926
The book is set in the fictional village of King's Abbot, a place 'rich in unmarried ladies and retired military officers'. It begins with the death of a wealthy widow, Mrs

Ferrars. Dr Sheppard, who is also the narrator, concludes she had died from an overdose of veronal, which she was taking for insomnia.

The following day, Sheppard is invited to dine at Fernly Park, the home of Roger Ackroyd, who was thought to have been romantically involved with Mrs Ferrars. After dinner, Sheppard and Ackroyd talk privately in his study. Ackroyd had asked Mrs Ferrars to marry him, but they decided to delay the announcement until her year of mourning for her first husband was up. Then she told him that she had poisoned her husband; he was a brute. Since then, she had been blackmailed for huge sums. However, Mrs Ferrars would not say who the blackmailer was – though he is convinced that she would have left a letter or word of some kind before she killed herself.

The evening post arrives. There is a letter from Mrs Ferrars, but Ackroyd puts off reading it until he is alone later. Sheppard leaves, but is summoned back to Fernly Park by a mysterious telephone call, purportedly coming from Ackroyd's butler, Parker, saying that Ackroyd has been murdered. Parker denies making the call. When they go to check on Ackroyd, they find the study door locked from the inside and break in to find him dead with an ornate dagger sticking out of his neck.

Ackroyd had been heard talking in the study half-an-hour after Sheppard had left. There were a number of suspects on hand with possible motives. Major Hector Blunt, a big-game hunter, was a house guest at Fernly Park at the time of the murder. Mrs Cecil Ackroyd, widow of Ackroyd's ne'er-do-well younger brother, and her daughter Flora live at Fernly Park and are entirely dependent on Ackroyd for their support. Flora is in love with Ackroyd's estranged stepson, Captain Ralph Paton, who is secretly visiting King's Abbot. The butler Parker had been eavesdropping on his master on the evening of the murder. Miss Russell, the housekeeper at Fernly Park, was once thought to have had romantic intentions towards Mr Ackroyd. That was before Mrs Cecil Ackroyd came along and, finally, Mrs Ferrars became available. Then there was the parlour maid Ursula Bourne who had questionable references. Even Ackroyd's secretary Geoffrey Raymond is set to receive a much-needed £500 legacy.

The mystery begins to unravel when Dr Sheppard's next-door-neighbour turns out to be Hercule Poirot, who has retired to King's Abbot to grow marrows. Sheppard is employed as his assistant, taking over from Hastings. His spinster sister Caroline, thought to be a prototype of Miss Marple, also lends a hand. Poirot rules out the suspects one by one, until only the most unexpected is left. While the twist at the end divided readers and critics, Dorothy L. Sayers rode to Christie's defence, saying that 'it is the reader's business to suspect everyone'.

The Murder of Roger Ackroyd was adapted for the stage as *Alibi* in London in 1928, and as *The Fatal Alibi* in New York in 1932. A British movie of *Alibi* was made in 1931. Orson Welles adapted the novel for radio in the Campbell Playhouse on CBS in 1939. BBC Radio 4 produced another radio version in 1987. It appeared in the *Poirot* TV series in 2000, with Japp instead of Sheppard assisting Poirot. The Russians made a movie version called *Neudacha Puaro* (*Poirot's Failure*) in 2002 and a graphic novel was published by HarperCollins in 2007.

The Big Four
London: Collins, 1927; New York: Dodd, Mead & Co., 1927
In *The Big Four*, Agatha Christie used a series of short stories she had originally published in issues 1614 to 1925 of the *Sketch* magazine between 2 January and 19 March 1924, which she then rewrote as a single narrative. The stories included 'The Unexpected Guest', 'The Adventure of the Dartmoor Bungalow', 'The Lady on the Stairs', 'The Radium Thieves', 'In the House of the Enemy', 'The Yellow

Jasmine Mystery', 'The Chess Problem', 'The Baited Trap', 'The Adventure of the Peroxide Blonde', 'The Terrible Catastrophe', 'The Dying Chinaman' and 'The Crag in the Dolomites'. Most of these stories also appeared in the US in *Blue Book Magazine* between March and December 1927. *The Big Four* also introduces mysterious jewel thief Countess Vera Rossakoff, who later wins Poirot's heart. Here she is introduced as 'our old antagonist' who 'engineered a particular smart jewel robbery in London'. Later this is related in *Poirot's Early Cases*.

The book begins with Hastings returning from Argentina. He pays a surprise visit on Poirot at their old lodgings, but Poirot is packed and ready to travel to Rio where he is to work for the richest man in the world, American soap king Abe Ryland. Hastings asks Poirot what is meant by the 'Big Four', outside the major powers at the Versailles Conference and the movie industry. Poirot says that it refers to 'a gang of international criminals or something of that kind'.

Hastings asks Poirot to delay his trip and travel back to South America with him. Poirot demurs unless an 'unexpected guest' arrives. Then they hear a noise from the bedroom, though there is no access to it except through the room they are in or a high window. Inside, they find a man who is thin and emaciated, covered from head to foot in dust and mud. They revive him with some brandy.

In a mechanical voice, the man repeats the words 'Monsieur Hercule Poirot of 14 Farraway Street'. They call a doctor who says that the man is suffering from some kind of shock. Suddenly the man begins to scribble the figure 4 on a piece of paper.

Poirot's boat-train is due and they leave the exhausted man in the care of the landlady. But before they can go, the man tells them, as if quoting from a report, that Li Chang Yen is the brains of the Big Four and is designated Number One. Number Two is an American whose name is represented by a dollar sign. Number Three is a French woman. And Number Four is known only as 'the destroyer'.

On the train Poirot is lost in thought, but when the train is stopped by a signal outside Woking Poirot declares he has been an imbecile and they jump off. He has realized that the summons to Rio was a way to get him out of the way. They rush back to Poirot's apartment where the unexpected guest is dead. The doctor diagnoses asphyxiation though the windows are open and there is no gas in the flat. To Hastings' surprise, Poirot calls Inspector Japp.

A warder from Hanwell Asylum turns up, who claims that the dead man is an escapee. He was insane, the warder says. Poirot questions this. After the warder has gone, Japp arrives and recognizes the dead man as Mayerling, a Secret Service agent who went missing in Bolshevik Russia five years earlier.

Poirot then realizes that he did not open the windows before he left. It seems that the dead man was not asphyxiated, but poisoned. At that point he notices that the clock had been stopped at four o'clock. Mayerling has been murdered, he deduces, by Number Four – 'the destroyer'.

Poirot and Hastings go in pursuit of Number Four and – through a web of international intrigue, underground laboratories, kidnapped physicists and secret weapons – unmask the Big Four.

It was published as a graphic novel by HarperCollins in 2007 and will air in the *Poirot* TV series in season 13, 2013–14.

The Mystery of the Blue Train
London: Collins, 1928; New York: Dodds, Mead & Co., 1928
The luxurious Blue Train carried rich Brits from Calais to the Riviera. The year is 1927 and on board is twenty-eight-year-old heiress Ruth Kettering with her maid Ada Mason. After an affair with the Comte de la Roche, Ruth had

married Derek Kettering, soon to become Lord Leconbury. However, he is involved with the French dancer Mirelle. They too are on board.

Ruth is on her way to an assignation with the Comte de la Roche. She is carrying with her a fabled ruby known as the Heart of Fire, bought for her by her father, millionaire Rufus Van Aldin. A famous jewel thief known as the Marquis is after it. On board, Ruth strikes up a conversation with thirty-three-year-old Katherine Grey who had been companion to the late Mrs Emma Hatfield and, on her death, had inherited the old lady's savings. They lived in the village of St Mary Mead, later home of Miss Marple.

There is a murder on board and the Heart of Fire is stolen. Fortunately, also on the train is Hercule Poirot, who begins to investigate at the behest of Mr Van Aldin's secretary Major Knighton. He steers the police from the obvious suspects, eventually fingering someone no one suspected.

This appeared as a special in the *Poirot* TV series in 2005.

Black Coffee
London: Embassy Theatre, 1930; St Martin's Theatre, 1931

Poirot and Hastings are summoned to the home of physicist Sir Claud Amory, who fears that someone is trying to steal the formula for his new explosive. But they arrive too late. The formula was already missing from the safe. Sir Claud had the lights switched off, so that the culprit could return it. Indeed, the formula had been returned, but by the time Poirot enters, Sir Claude is dead from poison in his black coffee.

A film of the play was made in 1931. A French version appeared the following year as *Le Coffret de Laque* and was released internationally as *The Lackered Box*. The play was novelized by Charles Osborne in 1998 and published in the UK by HarperCollins, in the US by St Martin's Press.

Peril at End House

London: Collins, The Crime Club, 1932; New York: Dodd, Mead & Co., 1932

Hastings and Poirot are staying at the Majestic Hotel in St Loo on the south coast of Cornwall. In the garden, Poirot trips and falls at the feet of a pretty girl. Her name is Magdala 'Nick' Buckley and she is the last of a long line of Buckleys to live at End House on the point visible from the hotel. She claims to have a charmed life, having escaped death three times in as many days.

While they are talking, a wasp – or bee – flies past her face. Later Poirot notices that a hole in the brim of her hat was made by a bullet he has retrieved. Though her closest friend thinks Nick is a liar, Poirot investigates the other supposed accidents that had threatened her life. The bullet that pierced her hat came from a Mauser. She had one that her father brought back from the war, but it is missing. Poirot and Hastings offer her their protection.

The house is heavily mortgaged and run down. The lodge is rented out to an Australian couple, named the Crofts. There is little to inherit. The house will go to her cousin Charles Vyse, a lawyer; the rest to Nick's closest friend Freddie Rice, who has left an abusive husband. He has disappeared so she cannot divorce him and marry her boyfriend Jim Lazarus, a Bond Street art dealer. Also on hand is Commander George Challenger, who wants to marry Nick.

Poirot suggests that Nick has a friend to stay with her. She invites her cousin Maggie. Over dinner they discuss the daredevil pilot Michael Seton who is missing presumed dead. Watching fireworks outside, Maggie, who is wearing Nick's shawl, is shot dead. Hastings reassures Nick that Poirot will find out who did it.

Hastings lists the suspects, but no one seems to have sufficient motive. Then Nick says that she was engaged to Michael Seton who, it has now been confirmed, is dead.

The engagement had been kept secret, she says, from Seton's millionaire uncle who has now died. Consequently, it is Nick who stands to gain.

The story was adapted for the stage and appeared at the Vaudeville Theatre, London, in 1940. A Russian film version called *Zagadka Endkhauza* was made in 1989. The story appeared as part of the *Poirot* TV series in 1990. A PC game version appeared in 2007 and a graphic novel was published by HarperCollins in 2008.

Lord Edgware Dies
London: Collins, The Crime Club, 1933; New York: published as Thirteen at Dinner, *Dodd, Mead & Co., 1933*

Hastings relates the case of the fourth Baron Edgware as one of Poirot's triumphs. It took place when Carlotta Adams, an American actress known for her imitations, was quite the rage in London. One of her impressions was of Jane Wilkinson, another American actress well known on the London stage.

Wilkinson had quit acting to marry Lord Edgware, but left him to return to stage and screen. At that night's performance, she had been in the audience. Afterwards Hastings and Poirot have supper at the Savoy.

Lady Edgware approaches Poirot. She must talk to him privately, upstairs in her suite. There she tells him she has to get rid of her husband. She had tried lawyers. An American divorce is no good to her as she wants to marry the Duke of Merton, who is incidentally a Catholic. Poirot points out that he does not take divorce cases. But Miss Wilkinson is adamant. Either Lord Edgware 'agrees to a divorce – or dies', she says. Carlotta Adams joins the party in Lady Edgware's suite and Poirot, after a glass too much champagne, agrees to go to see her husband. Not only does he agree to a divorce but says that he wrote to his wife six months before telling her so.

The next day Inspector Japp comes around to tell Poirot

that Lord Edgware has been found murdered – 'stabbed in the neck by his wife'. Beforehand, the butler had ushered her into the library. Ten minutes later she was heard leaving. However, that night, Jane Wilkinson had been at a dinner party in Chiswick with twelve other people who gave her a cast-iron alibi.

Suddenly Poirot is concerned for the safety of Carlotta Adams. At her flat, they find she is dead from an overdose of veronal. After a luncheon party at Claridge's where Jane Wilkinson shows her ignorance of the mythological Paris, a young actor named Donald Ross, who had been one of the thirteen at dinner in Chiswick, phones Poirot. But before he can say what he is calling about he is killed – stabbed in the back of the neck, just like Lord Edgware.

A torn letter gives Poirot his final clue. Hastings calls Inspector Japp and Poirot reveals all. During the action, Poirot takes time off to investigate the disappearance of an ambassador's boots in a case curiously similar to 'The Ambassador's Boots' tackled by Tommy and Tuppence Beresford in *Partners in Crime*. The book ends with a letter from the culprit confessing the crime.

A film of *Lord Edgware Dies* was made in 1934 and a TV movie was made in 1985 using the US title *Thirteen at Dinner*. The story appears in the *Poirot* TV series in 2000.

Murder on the Orient Express
London: Collins, The Crime Club, 1934; New York: published as Murder on the Calais Coach, *Dodd, Mead & Co., 1934*
Returning from 'a little affair in Syria', Poirot meets Monsieur Bouc, the director of the Compagnie Internationale des Wagons-Lits that runs the Orient Express, in Istanbul. The coach travelling through to Calais is unusually full for the time of year. However, a Mr Harris has not arrived and Poirot takes his berth. His fellow passengers are a colourful bunch. They include shady American businessman Samuel

Edward Ratchett, his secretary Hector MacQueen and valet Masterman, stiff-upper-lipped British officer Colonel Arbuthnot, American widow Mrs Hubbard, Hungarian diplomat Count Andrenyi and his wife, imperious Russian Princess Natalia Dragomiroff and her German maid Hildegarde Schmidt, English governess Mary Debenham, loquacious Italian-American automobile salesman Antonio Foscarelli, Swedish missionary Greta Ohlsson, and private eye and bodyguard Cyrus Hardman.

Poirot is approached by Mr Ratchett who says that his life has been threatened and offers Poirot big money if he will take the case. He refuses. When asked why, Poirot says simply: 'I do not like your face.'

Poirot's compartment is next to Ratchett's. During the night there is a cry and various comings and goings which Poirot overhears or glimpses. Then the train comes to a halt in a snowdrift, somewhere in Yugoslavia. After breakfast, Poirot is summoned by Bouc. Ratchett is dead. During the night he had been stabbed some twelve times. Bouc asks Poirot to solve the murder before the Yugoslav police arrive. As they are caught in a snowdrift, the killer must be on board the train.

After examining all the evidence, interviewing the suspects and exercising the little grey cells, Poirot calls all the passengers into the restaurant car where he outlines two solutions. In one an enemy of Mr Ratchett's boarded the train along its route, murdered Ratchett, then escaped. Monsieur Bouc declares that this is absurd. The doctor who examined the body also refuses to accept this explanation.

Poirot then outlines a complex and tightly argued scenario taking in all the evidence. It is totally convincing. However, Monsieur Bouc then says that the first theory Poirot put forward was correct. The doctor agrees and Poirot says: 'Having placed my solution before you, I have the honour to retire from the case.'

Murder on the Orient Express was filmed in 1974 and

2001. It appeared in the *Poirot* TV series in 2010. A PC game was made in 2006 and a graphic novel was published by HarperCollins in 2007.

Three Act Tragedy

New York: published as Murder in Three Acts, *Dodd, Mead & Co., 1934; London: Collins, The Crime Club, 1935*

Mr Satterthwaite is staying with retired actor Sir Charles Cartwright at his house, the Crow's Nest, overlooking the harbour at Loomouth. Another guest is Harley Street doctor Sir Bartholomew Strange, a specialist in nervous disorders. Other dinner guests, largely theatrical types from London, are arriving by train, while Lady Mary Lytton Gore and the Reverend Stephen Babbington and his wife will be fetched by car. Then there is her daughter Hermione, usually known as 'Egg', who is often seen in Sir Charles' company, though he is twice her age. They are to be joined by Sir Charles' secretary Miss Milray; otherwise there would be thirteen at dinner. Among them is someone Sir Charles calls 'the most conceited little devil I have ever met' – Poirot.

'I hope we shan't have a crime this weekend,' says Strange.

However, while they are having cocktails, the Reverend Babbington keels over and dies.

During a discussion of the incident, Poirot is called upon to venture an opinion. He says that it is unlikely that anyone would want to hurt such a harmless old gentleman. He also dismisses suicide and agrees that if they had the contents of the Reverend Babbington's glass analyzed they would only find 'the remains of a very excellent dry Martini'.

Soon after, the death of Sir Bartholomew Strange was announced. He was drinking a glass of port when he collapsed and died. Present were several of the guests from the dinner party at the Crow's Nest. At the inquest it is found that he died from nicotine poisoning. Mr Satterthwaite returns from the South of France to investigate. Poirot, who he meets in Monte Carlo, follows.

Babbington's body is exhumed and he too died of nicotine poisoning. While the others try their best to discover the identity of the murderer, Poirot remains aloof at the Ritz Hotel exercising the little grey cells. He solves the mystery, but not before the murderer can kill again.

The story was made into a TV movie called *Murder in Three Acts* with Satterthwaite replaced by Hastings and it appeared in the *Poirot* TV series in 2010.

Death in the Clouds

New York: published as Death in the Air, *Dodd, Mead & Co., 1935; London: Collins, The Crime Club, 1935*

Poirot, minus Hastings, boards a passenger place at Le Bourget, bound for Croydon, along with twenty other passengers, two stewards . . . and a wasp. During the flight, one of the passengers dies. Her name is Madame Giselle. There is a mark on her neck and it is initially thought that the wasp stung her, precipitating her death. However, Poirot finds a knot of orange and black silk tied to a peculiar-looking thorn on the floor at her feet. Another passenger, detective novelist Daniel Clancy, says it is a dart from a blow-pipe.

When the passengers disembark, they are corralled by Inspector Japp, who takes Poirot aside. The woman had died at least half an hour before they landed and Poirot had slept through the whole thing. He asks Japp for a list of everyone's possessions.

Japp questions the passengers. Among them are Countess Cicely Horbury, the Honourable Venetia Kerr and London dentist Norman Gale. Clancy immediately comes under suspicion after admitting to owning a blow-pipe, obtained while researching a murder in one of this novels. Then a blow-pipe is found on the plane – behind Poirot's seat.

It transpires that Madame Giselle is a money-lender. Her clientele were of the upper and professional classes. She also indulged in blackmail. Her money is left to her daughter Anne Morisot, who she abandoned as a baby in the *Institut de Marie* in Quebec. Anne is on board the plane posing as Lady Horbury's maid. Poirot recognizes that she is in imminent danger. But when he arrives at her hotel she has left and is found dead on the boat-train to Boulogne.

Poirot's suspicions rest on an empty matchbox and the fact that Madame Giselle had two coffee spoons on her saucer, then names as the killer someone who had never been seen near the victim. Clancy, who is present at the dénouement, is thrilled to see a real detective at work.

This appeared in the *Poirot* TV series in 1992.

The ABC Murders
London: Collins, The Crime Club, 1936; New York: published as The Alphabet Murders, *Dodd, Mead & Co., 1936*

In June 1935, Hastings comes home from his ranch in South America and looks up Poirot. He has received a letter telling him to look out for Andover on the twenty-first of the month. It is signed 'ABC'. That day, a shopkeeper named Alice Asher is killed in Andover. An *ABC Railway Guide* was found on the counter.

A second letter draws Poirot's attention to Bexhill-on-Sea. There Betty Barnard is found dead on the beach with an *ABC* guide under her. A third taunting letter mentions Churston in Devon, but it is wrongly addressed so Poirot and Hastings cannot get there on time. However, the police warn all people with a name beginning with C. Nevertheless, the wealthy surgeon Sir Carmichael Clarke is found with his head bashed in. An *ABC* was found face down on his dead body. He was married with no children and his wife is ill. While the newspapers blame a 'homicidal maniac', Sir Carmichael's brother Franklin brings a delegation of the victims' loved ones to see Poirot.

A fourth letter from ABC says that the next incident will take place in Doncaster on the day that the St Leger is being run on the racecourse there.

Alongside Hastings' account runs the seemingly unrelated narrative of Alexander Bonaparte Cust – initials ABC. He goes to Doncaster where he goes to the cinema. A man is found slumped in a seat with an *ABC* guide. Cust finds blood on his sleeve.

The dead man's name is George Earlsfield, but the man next to him was named Downes. The police think that ABC made a mistake and killed the wrong man.

A. B. Cust comes under suspicion. Eight *ABC* guides are found in his room, along with a blood-stained knife. Cust gives himself up, saying that he had committed the murders though had no memory of actually doing them. He also knew nothing of the letters to Poirot. The police are convinced that Cust committed the Doncaster murder at least, but Poirot is not so sure.

The novel was filmed as *The Alphabet Murders* in 1966. BBC Radio 4 dramatized it in 2008. It appeared in the *Poirot* TV series in 1992 and was made into a video game in 2009.

Murder in Mesopotamia
London: Collins, The Crime Club, 1936; New York: Dodd, Mead & Co., 1936

A foreword to the book is ostensibly written by Giles Reilly, MD. In it, he says he asked Miss Amy Leatheran to write this account of the events that occurred four years earlier and have since been surrounded by wild and ridiculous rumours.

Amy was a nurse and had been invited to be a companion to the wife of the archaeologist Dr Eric Leidner who is on a dig in Iraq. Apparently Louise Leidner has 'fancies' and is in a nervous state. Amy takes the job.

Mrs Leidner opens up to Amy. In 1918, she married a

young man in the State Department who turned out to be a German spy. Louise turned him in. He was sentenced to be shot, but managed to escape when the train he was travelling on crashed. She then received a letter from him, telling her that if she ever married another man he would kill her. Indeed, every time she got on intimate terms with a man she received another threatening letter.

After she married Eric Leidner, she received letters saying that she was going to die. They woke one morning to find the gas had been turned on in their apartment. For her own safety, she accompanied her husband out to Iraq. But then she received another threatening letter, this time with an Iraqi stamp on it. It strikes Amy that the writing on the letters in similar to Mrs Leidner's own handwriting.

Dr Leidner was working on the roof. When he comes down, he goes to see his wife who is resting in her room. Leidner emerges to summon Nurse Leatheran who finds Louise quite dead. She had been hit on the head, and had been dead at least an hour before Dr Leidner found her. There was no sign of the weapon with which she had been struck.

The suspicion is that she has been murdered by her first husband. But the windows to her room were locked and heavily barred. The only way in was through a door that opened onto a central courtyard, so the murderer must be a member of the expedition.

Fortunately, after dealing with some scandal in Syria, Hercule Poriot is passing by. He begins to investigate and speculates that whoever wrote the threatening letters was deliberately imitating Mrs Leidner's handwriting – and that, possibly, her first husband was a member of the expedition.

Miss Johnson, one of the veterans of the expedition, says that she thought she heard Mrs Leidner cry out, but decides she must have been mistaken as all the windows to her room were shut. Then she figures out 'how someone could come in from outside – and no one would ever guess'. But before she explains she is poisoned with hydrochloric acid, used for cleaning pottery, which had been substituted for the water she kept on a bedside table. Before she dies, she says: 'The window . . .' And under her bed, they find the murder weapon.

Poirot considers the possibilities and not only works out who the killer is but also solves another crime – the theft of antiquities.

This appeared in the *Poirot* TV series in 2001 and was published as a graphic novel by HarperCollins in 2008.

Cards on the Table
London: Collins, The Crime Club, 1936; New York: Dodd, Mead & Co., 1937
In a foreword, Agatha Christie warns the reader that this is a different kind of detective story. Normally, you can just pick the least likely suspect and the job is over. Here there are four suspects who have already committed murder, so the deduction must be entirely psychological.

Poirot is invited to a party by Mr Shaitana, an acquaintance of Mephistophelian appearance, to meet his 'exhibits' – four murderers who have got away with it – Dr Roberts, Mrs Lorrimer, Major Despard and Miss Anne Meredith. Also present are Mrs Ariadne Oliver, author of detective stories, Superintendent Battle, and Colonel Race of the Secret Service. Over dinner, they discuss murder, leading Shaitana to remark: 'Poison is a woman's weapon.' Poirot spends a good deal of time studying Shaitana's upper lip which bears a fine moustache – perhaps the only one in London that could compete with his own.

After dinner, they play bridge – the four sleuths in one room, the four murderers in another. When they have finished, they find Shaitana is dead. He has been stabbed. No one else was present. It is up to the sleuths to figure out who has done it.

The story was adapted for the stage, opening at the Vaudeville Theatre, London, in 1981 and appeared in the *Poirot* TV series in 2005.

Dumb Witness

London: Collins, The Crime Club, 1937; New York: published as Poirot Loses a Client, *Dodd, Mead & Co., 1937*

Emily Arundell dies at the age of seventy. Ten days before her death her family gathered at Littlegreen House, her home in Market Basing. They expect to inherit. Instead, the bulk of her fortune goes to her companion Miss Wilhelmina Lawson.

Sometime later, Poirot receives a letter from Miss Arundell. She is fearful 'ever since the incident of the dog's ball' and asks Poirot what his fees are. The letter was written on 17 April, but delivered on 28 June, over two months later.

Poirot and Hastings head to Market Basing, where they discover Littlegreen House is up for sale. Posing as a buyer, Poirot discovers that his client, Miss Arundell, is already dead. In the house they meet a terrier named Bob.

The doctor says that Miss Arundell died from rich food and a chill. She had been ill for some time. However, a week or two before she died, she had fallen downstairs. Bob was blamed for leaving his ball on the stairs. Poirot reveals that he has received a letter from Miss Arundell giving him a commission and learns that the family comprises nephew and niece Charles and Theresa Arundell, and niece Bella who has married Dr Tanois. They were all visiting shortly before she died.

Poirot notices that there is a nail driven into the skirting board at the head of the stairs, disguised with varnish. He believes that Miss Arundell had fallen over tripwire at the top of the stairs, not Bob's ball.

The plot is further complicated when he discovers that the doctor has no sense of smell. Meanwhile, the Tripp sisters, who held a séance with Miss Arundell, say they saw a luminous haze around her head. Miss Lawson also saw luminous ectoplasm. Putting these facts together Poirot realizes how Miss Arundell was murdered.

Theresa Arundell comes under suspicion when Miss Lawson says she saw a figure in a female dressing gown wearing a brooch with the letters 'T A' on it in a mirror. Then Bella Tanios dies of an overdose of sleeping-draught . . .

An adaptation appeared in the *Poirot* TV series in 1996 and was published as a graphic novel by HarperCollins in 2009.

Death on the Nile
London: Collins, The Crime Club, 1937; New York: Dodd, Mead & Co., 1937

Heiress Linnet Ridgeway has just refurbished her country house in Malton-under-Wode. Her oldest friend, Jacqueline de Bellefort, who has been left penniless by the Wall Street crash, calls. She begs Linnet to take her penniless fiancé Simon Doyle on as her estate manager. However, Linnet and Simon marry and they head to Egypt for their honeymoon. Poirot is planning to holiday there, too.

On a terrace overlooking the Nile, Linnet and Simon are confronted by Jacqueline. Linnet appeals to Poirot for help. Jacqueline is following them wherever they go. Linnet says that Jacqueline has even threatened to kill them and Poirot agrees to have a word with Jacqueline. But Jacqueline tells Poirot that if she wanted to kill Linnet, he could not stop her.

Poirot is taking a Nile cruise on the SS *Karnak*. In an attempt to give Jacqueline the slip Linnet and Simon are also on board; along with erotic novelist Salome Otterbourne and her daughter Rosalie; Linnet's American trustee Andrew Pennington who had brought documents for her to sign; American socialite Miss Marie Van Schuyler and her companion and nurse Miss Bowers; an outspoken socialist named Ferguson; Italian archaeologist Signor Richetti and Austrian physician Dr Bessner. Jacqueline is on board too.

Things get serious when Linnet and Simon are sunning themselves ashore and a boulder comes crashing down a cliff, narrowly missing them.

Colonel Race joins the steamer. He tells Poirot he is on the track of a killer who is on the boat. After dinner, Poirot is sleepy and goes to bed. Jacqueline gets drunk, takes out a gun and pulls the trigger. Simon falls, a red stain soaking through his trouser leg as Jacqueline drops the pistol.

Jacqueline is sent to her cabin with Nurse Bowers to look after her and Dr Bessner is summoned to attend Simon, who is insistent that Linnet should not be told. In the morning Linnet is found dead. She has been shot in the head. On the wall of her cabin is the letter 'J' scrawled in blood. A string of pearls are also missing.

But Jacqueline can't have done it as she was pumped full of morphine and Miss Bowers stayed with her. Simon stayed in Dr Bessner's cabin and was also incapacitated with drugs and a gunshot wound.

Poirot figures out who killed Linnet Ridgeway, but not before her maid Louise, who discovered the body, is also murdered.

Christie adapted the story for the stage, appearing as *Murder on the Nile* at the Ambassadors Theatre, London, and *Hidden Horizon* at the Plymouth Theater, New York, in 1946. It was filmed as *Death on the Nile* in 1978. *Murder on the Nile* appeared on TV as part of the *Kraft Television Theater* series in 1950. BBC Radio 4 broadcast a dramatization in 1997 and it appeared in the *Poirot* TV series in 2004. A PC game, *Death on the Nile*, appeared in 2007 and HarperCollins published a graphic novel that year.

Murder in the Mews

London: Collins, 1937; New York: published as Dead Man's Mirror *and Other Stories, Dodd, Mead & Co., 1937*

This collection of Poirot stories was published without 'The Incredible Theft' in the US in 1937. However, it was restored in the Berkeley Books edition in 1987.

'Murder in the Mews'

First published in Woman's Journal, *December 1936; in the US, in Volume 37, Numbers 5 and 6 of* Redbook *magazine, September and October 1937*

It is Guy Fawkes' Night and Poirot and Japp agree that, with all the fireworks going off, it is a good night for a murder. The next morning, Japp summons Poirot to Bardsley Gardens Mews where young widow Mrs Barbara Allen has been found dead, an apparent suicide. She had lived with a friend, Jane Plenderleith, who had been away in the country. The doctor points out that, while the pistol is in Mrs Allen's right hand, the bullet hole is on her left side, just above her ear. It would be impossible to fire a shot that way. The door was locked and the key is missing. It appears to be a murder made to look like a suicide.

Miss Plenderleith tells Poirot and Japp that Mrs Allen was engaged to Charles Laverton-West MP. She has no enemies and only a small income so no one would benefit from her death. On the other hand, she was not in financial difficulties and was about to be married, so there was no reason for her to commit suicide.

However, examining her chequebook, they discover that she was overdrawn. Large sums have been withdrawn – £200 on the day she died – though little money had been found in the house.

A man was seen calling on Mrs Allen on the evening of her death. He had been seen at the house before, but he did not answer the description of Charles Laverton-West.

Miss Plenderleith says that the description of Mrs Allen's

visitor sounds like Major Eustace, someone Mrs Allen had known in India who had turned up now and again. Poirot suggests that Major Eustace was blackmailing Mrs Allen. However, he says, the crime is the wrong way round – the victim usually kills the blackmailer, not the blackmailer the victim.

Searching the house, they find a locked cupboard. When Miss Plenderleith opens it, there are golf clubs and an attaché case inside. Miss Plenderleith claims that she brought the attaché case back with her that morning, but the two magazines in it are four months old.

The butts of Turkish cigarettes and a piece of a cufflink prove that Major Eustace visited Mrs Allen. He admits it, but says she gave no indication that she was going to commit suicide. He also admits taking £200 from her and when blackmail is mentioned asks for a solicitor and Japp arrests him.

Eustace has a long record, but when Poirot and Japp visit the mews to tell Miss Plenderleith, Poirot notices that the golf clubs and the attaché case are missing. The attaché case was found in the lake at Wentworth where Miss Plenderleith had been playing golf. This convinces Poirot that Mrs Allen had not been murdered, though someone else was about to be.

This appeared in the *Poirot* TV series in 1989.

'The Incredible Theft'
First published in the Daily Express, *6–12 April 1937 (as an expanded version of 'The Submarine Plans' published in issue 1606 of the* Sketch, *7 November 1923; in the US, Volume 41, Number 3 of* Blue Book *magazine, July 1925)*
Lord Mayfield, minister for armaments, is hosting a house party. At dinner are the head of the air force Air Marshal Sir George Carrington, his wife Lady Julia and son Reggie, Mrs Macatta MP, Lord Mayfield's private secretary Mr Carlile and Mrs Vanderlyn, who is thought to be a spy.

Alone after dinner, Lord Mayfield and Sir George

discuss a new bomber that will give Britain air supremacy. Meanwhile, Mayfield says he aims to entrap Mrs Vanderlyn. On the terrace, Mayfield claims to have seen a fleeting figure, though Sir George did not see it.

In the study, Carlile is arranging papers by the safe. He is just about to leave the room when Mayfield says that he has forgotten the most important ones – the papers about the new bomber. Carlile says they are on top. But when he checks they are not.

Nobody else has been in the room and Carlile had only left for a moment when he heard a woman scream. Mrs Vanderlyn's French maid said she had seen a ghost. Sir George suggests they call in Hercule Poirot.

Carlile is quickly ruled out because he could have copied the plans at any time. Poirot then asks Lord Mayfield why he did not have the man he saw crossing the terrace pursued. Sir George says they have to avoid publicity. Poirot finds that there were no footprints on the grass. It has to be an inside job.

While interviewing Lord Mayfield, Poirot suddenly announces that he knows where the plans are. Nevertheless, he goes on interviewing all the guests one after the other, examining their motives.

Poirot then tells Mayfield to get rid of his guests. Before she leaves, Lady Julia promises to have the plans returned, if no questions were asked, thinking her son had stolen them. In fact, they have not been stolen at all.

This appeared in the *Poirot* TV series in 1989.

'Dead Man's Mirror'

An expanded version of 'The Second Gong' published in issue 499 of Strand Magazine, *July 1932; in the US, Volume 58, Number 6 of the* Ladies Home Journal, *June 1932*

Poirot is summoned to Hamborough St Mary by Gervase Chevenix-Gore who, according to Satterthwaite, is 'the last of the baronets'. When Poirot arrives at Hamborough, the guests are already dressed for dinner. The gong sounds and they go in to dinner. But Sir Gervase is not among them. He is found dead in his study with the door locked. A small pistol is on the floor under his hand. The immediate assumption is that he shot himself. Under a shattered mirror there is a bullet. The key to the study door is in his pocket and a champagne cork popping or a car backfiring heard just after the first gong may in fact have been the shot.

There seemed to have been no motive for suicide. However, Sir Gervase did not get on with his family and any one of them might have had a motive for killing him. Poirot is concerned that Sir Gervase must have got himself into a very awkward position if the bullet was going to pass through his head into the mirror. But only his fingerprints are on the pistol. The one detail inconsistent with suicide was his summons to Poirot.

Chief Constable Major Riddle and Poirot interview those present. Some maintain that Sir Gervase was mad; others are plainly mad themselves. They also question Sir Gervase's solicitors about his will.

Poirot realizes that it is possible to leave the study via the French windows and have them lock themselves behind you and that the mirror had been broken because, in it, you could see the murder being committed from the windows. With everyone assembled in the study, Poirot says that the mirror was not shattered by the bullet that killed Sir Gervase. That bullet hit the gong. Poirot then makes a wild accusation – and the guilty party steps forward.

This appeared in the *Poirot* TV series in 1993.

'Triangle at Rhodes'
First published in issue 545 of the Strand Magazine, *May 1936, as 'Poirot and the Triangle at Rhodes'*
Poirot is taking a holiday on Rhodes. On the beach he sees former Chanel model Valentine Dacres, now married to

Tony Chantry. She also attracts the attention of the handsome Douglas Gold who arrives with his mousy wife Marjorie. While she goes swimming, Douglas falls into conversation with Valentine. The attention he shows her makes Chantry angry. Observers see an eternal triangle developing.

As tension between Gold and Chantry mounts, a distraught Mrs Gold consults Poirot, who recommends that she leave the island if she values her life. Someone is planning a murder.

While they are having a drink one evening, Valentine drains a pink gin and feels ill. Her husband says it was his drink and accuses Gold of putting something in it. Five minutes later Valentine Chantry is dead.

The poison is identified as strophanthin. A packet is found in Douglas Gold's dinner jacket. Poirot is blamed for warning Mrs Gold rather than Tony or Valentine Chantry. But he maintains that Douglas Gold is not the killer. Everyone is looking at the wrong triangle.

This appeared in the *Poirot* TV series in 1989.

Appointment with Death
London: Collins, The Crime Club, 1938; New York, Dodd, Mead & Co., 1938

On his first night in Jerusalem, Hercule Poirot hears the words 'You do see, don't you, that she's got to be killed?' drift in though his bedroom window. He goes to bed, believing that the words are a recitation from a play or a book.

However, the words were said by Raymond Boynton to his sister Carol. They are talking of their brutish stepmother and they are determined to kill her to protect their other siblings.

The grotesque Mrs Boynton is a tyrannical matriarch who has the children cowed. She even dominates her thirty-year-old stepson Lennox and his wife Nadine. The family are of interest to Dr Gerard, a famous French psychologist, and medical student Sarah Walker, who are also staying at the Solomon Hotel. They travel to Petra. There, Mrs Boynton is left sitting in the mouth of a cave where she is later found dead. Poirot investigates. Miss Walker has to examine the body because Dr Gerard has come down with a bad bout of malaria. A hypodermic syringe goes missing. When it is returned, Gerard's stock of digitoxin, the active constituent of digitalis, disappears.

Mrs Boynton suffered from a heart condition and took digitalis anyway. While there is no proof that a murder has been committed, Poirot promises to clear the matter up in twenty-four hours.

Christie adapted the story for the stage and it opened at the Piccadilly Theatre, London, in 1945. It was filmed in 1988 and appeared in the *Poirot* TV series in 2008.

Hercule Poirot's Christmas

London: Collins, The Crime Club, 1939; New York: published as Murder for Christmas, *Dodd, Mead & Co., 1939*

The tyrannical Simeon Lee, who made his fortune from diamond mining in South Africa, calls his family together at his home, Gorston Hall, for Christmas. His son Alfred, who panders to his father's every whim, and his wife Lydia already live at the Hall. Then there is David Lee, an artist who hates his father for his flagrant unfaithfulness to his mother, which drove her to an early grave. His wife Hilda thinks that her husband should forgive and forget. George Lee, a portly politician, and his young wife Magdalene are also attending, along with Harry, the black sheep of the family, and Pilar Estravados, Simeon's granddaughter from Spain who is coming to live at Gorston Hall. An unexpected guest is Stephen Farr, the son of Simeon's partner in Kimberley, who meets Pilar on the train. All the family members live off allowances provided by the old man, and on Chrismas Eve Simeon Lee assembles them to overhear him on the telephone, telling his solicitors that he wants to change his will on Boxing Day. He then upbraids his sons, saying they inherited 'the brains of a louse' from their mother and that Pilar is worth any two of them put together.

That evening the doorbell rings. It is a Superintendent Sugden who says he is collecting for the Police Orphanage. After dinner, the noise of china smashing and furniture being knocked over is heard. Then there is a scream. But the door to Simeon Lee's room is locked. They break the door down to find him dead in a pool of blood.

Superintendent Sugden returns just in time. He notices Pilar pick something up. It is a wisp of rubber and a small piece of wood, which he takes. However, unfortunately for the murderer, Hercule Poirot is spending Christmas with the local chief constable.

This appeared in the *Poirot* TV series in 1994.

Sad Cypress
London: Collins, The Crime Club, 1940; New York: Dodd, Mead & Co., 1940

Elinor Carlisle receives an anonymous letter warning her that someone is 'sucking up to' her aunt, seeking to do her and her fiancé Roddy Welman out of their inheritance. The person in question is Mary Gerrard, daughter of the lodge keeper on the estate of Laura Welman, aunt to both Elinor and Roddy. Laura has had a stroke and Mary reads to her.

Laura Welman wants to see her lawyer to make a will, but dies in the night. Then Roddy falls in love with Mary, and Elinor breaks off their engagement. As Mrs Welman died intestate, everything passes to Elinor as her closest blood relative. However, she is generous and intends to give £2,000 to Mary, who then makes a will leaving everything to her aunt in New Zealand who she has not seen for years.

After having tea and sandwiches, Mary dies. She had been poisoned. Elinor is accused of murdering her, and the local doctor, who believes that she is innocent, calls in Hercule Poirot. Later Agatha Christie said that this was a mistake; the book, whose title comes from *Twelfth Night*, was ruined by the presence of Poirot.

BBC Radio 4 adapted the story as a five-part serial in 1992 and it appeared as a special in the *Poirot* TV series in 2003.

One, Two, Buckle My Shoe
London: Collins, The Crime Club, 1940; New York: published as The Patriotic Murders, *Dodd, Mead & Co., 1940 (later published by Dell as* An Overdose of Death)

Again Christie bases a novel on a nursery rhyme; this time lines are used as the titles of the chapters. The book begins with London dentist Henry Morley complaining to his sister about the government and the busy day he has ahead of him, and also that his assistant has been called away to attend a sick aunt. One of his patients that day is Poirot. The next patient is powerful financier Alistair Blunt. As Poirot leaves, he notices a woman arriving. The buckle from her shoe falls off. Poirot picks it up.

That afternoon, Poirot takes a phone call from Chief Inspector Japp. Morley has shot himself, or so Japp thinks. However, he is not quite satisfied. Morley was in good health and had no trouble with money or women. Besides, he did not own a gun.

The aunt of Morley's assistant was not ill after all, and Japp has been put on the case because of the involvement of the bigwig Blunt. The last patient to see Morley, a Greek named Amberiotis who was staying at the Savoy, died of the anaesthetic administered at the dentist's. According to his file at Scotland Yard, he was a spy and a blackmailer. Then the woman Poirot saw arriving at Morley's disappears . . .

This appeared in the *Poirot* TV series in 1992 and was adapted for radio by BBC Radio 4 in 2004.

Evil Under the Sun

London: Collins, The Crime Club, 1941; New York: Dodd, Mead & Co., 1941

One, Two, Buckle My Shoe mentions Hitler and Mussolini, Communists and Blackshirts, but *Evil Under the Sun* returns to untroubled times, with Poirot holidaying at the Jolly Roger Hotel on Smugglers' Island off the Devon coast. However, while the mood is tranquil and the sea is blue, Poirot remarks 'there is evil everywhere under the sun'.

Also staying there is the impossibly handsome Patrick Redfern and his pale-skinned wife Christine, a schoolteacher, along with the beautifully bronzed actress Arlena Stuart, her husband Captain Kenneth Marshall and his teenage daughter Linda, who hates her stepmother and wants her dead. The Reverend Stephen Lane says that Arlena is 'evil through and through'. Dressmaker Rosamund Darnley, who carries a torch for Captain Marshall, condemns her as a gold-digger and man-eater, and begs Kenneth to get a divorce.

It transpires that Arlena has met Patrick before and Kenneth suspects that she has contrived to meet him there in Devon. Christine also thinks that Patrick picked that spot because he knew Arlena was going to be there. Poirot warns those concerned; he is convinced that there is going to be a murder. Then Arlena is found dead on the beach. She has been strangled.

Evil Under the Sun was filmed in 1982 and was adapted for radio by BBC Radio 4 in 1999. It appeared in the *Poirot* TV series in 2001 and was turned into a PC game in 2007.

Five Little Pigs

London: Collins, The Crime Club, 1942; New York: published as Murder in Retrospect, *Dodd, Mead & Co., 1942*

Again Christie uses a nursery rhyme to structure a novel; here, 'This Little Piggy'. Lines from the nursery rhyme:

'This Little Pig Went to Market'; 'This Little Pig Stayed at Home'; 'This Little Pig Had Roast Beef'; 'This Little Pig Had None'; and 'This Little Pig Cried "Wee Wee Wee"' are used as the titles for five chapters. They introduce the five suspects.

A woman named Carla Lemarchant comes to visit Poirot and reveals that her real name is Caroline Crale. This was the same name as her mother who, sixteen years earlier, had been tried and convicted for the murder of her husband, the painter Amyas Crale and the visitor's father. She was sentenced to penal servitude for life and died after serving one year, leaving a letter for her daughter which would tell her the truth when she was twenty-one. As Carla Lemarchant is soon to be married and plans to start a family of her own, she wants Poirot to investigate the case and prove that her mother was innocent, as the condemned woman insists in the letter. Intrigued, Poirot takes the case, knowing how difficult it will be to investigate a case that is sixteen years old – in retrospect.

He interviews the lawyers involved, the police and the five suspects – the five little pigs – and gets each to write narrative of what happened. He then reconstructs the events and reveals the killer. Christie adapted the story for the stage. It opened at the Duchess Theatre, London, as *Go Back for Murder* in 1960 and it appeared in the *Poirot* TV series in 2003.

The Hollow

London: Collins, The Crime Club, 1946; New York: Dodd, Mead & Co., 1946 (reprinted by Dell as Murder After Hours)

Lady Lucy Angkatell is planning a house party at her country estate, The Hollow. Along with her husband Sir Henry and her cousin Midge Hardcastle, those present include Harley Street physician Dr John Christow and his downtrodden wife Greda, Christow's mistress, the sculptress Henrietta Savernake, heir to the estate Edward

Angkatell and the rebellious student David Angkatell. Added to this brew is Christow's former lover, the actress Veronica Cray, who is staying at a neighbouring cottage and has come over to borrow some matches. Then she insists that John walk her home; they have so much to talk about. He does not return until three in the morning and knows that he is in trouble with both Greda and Henrietta. The next morning Christow receives a letter from Veronica, telling him to come to her. He dutifully does so. She says she wants them to get back together again; he tells her that he does not love her. While he is walking back to The Hollow, he is shot, falling dead at the edge of the swimming pool.

Coincidentally, another neighbour, one Hercule Poirot, has been invited to lunch that day. When he arrives he is directed to the swimming pool where he finds a tableau he thinks is staged for his benefit. A woman is standing over a body, revolver in hand. Others converge on the scene. Then Poirot realizes what he is witnessing is real. The victim opens his mouth to deliver his dying word: 'Henrietta.'

The woman standing over the body is the wronged wife Greda. It seems like an open-and-shut case until Poirot exercises his little grey cells.

Christie dropped Poirot completely for the stage version, which opened at the Fortune Theatre, London, in 1951. He reappeared in the adaptation made for the *Poirot* TV series in 2004.

The Labours of Hercules
London: Collins, The Crime Club, 1947; New York: Dodd, Mead & Co., 1947

Over a bottle of Poirot's Château Mouton Rothschild, Dr Burton, a Fellow of All Souls, says that Hercule does not resemble his mythical namesake. Nor do his labours resemble the labours of Hercules. Poirot rises to this challenge. Before retiring to cultivate vegetable marrows, he decides to accept twelve cases that reflect the Hercules classical labours. The entire book is being shot as a feature-length episode of the *Poirot* TV series.

'The Nemean Lion'

First published in issue 587 of Strand Magazine, *November 1939*

A letter comes asking Poirot to investigate the kidnapping of a Pekinese dog. He treats this suggestion with disgust. Nevertheless, he is curious. The letter is from Sir Joseph Hoggin who tells Poirot that his wife had paid £200 to get her dog back. He would have left the matter there, but the same thing had happened to a friend at his club. There was a racket going.

Poirot visits Hoggin's wife and discovers that her Pekinese is 'a veritable lion'. It went missing when walked by her downtrodden companion Amy Carnaby. Investigating Miss Carnaby, Poirot solves the mystery of the dognappings and puts a stop to it. Along the way he captures another 'Nemean Lion' and prevents a murder.

'The Lernean Hydra'

First published in issue 588 of Strand Magazine, *December 1939; in the US, in* This Week *magazine, 3 September 1939 as 'The Invisible Enemy'*

Dr Charles Oldfield consults Poirot. His invalid wife has died and gossip is circulating that he poisoned her. The tittle-tattle is like the nine-headed Hydra of Lernea because as fast as one head is lopped off two grow in its place. Poirot agrees to slay the many-headed monster.

Oldfield's wife had died from a gastric ulcer whose symptoms are similar to that of arsenic poisoning. She was older than Oldfield and left him a considerable sum of money. Much of the gossip concerns his young dispenser, Jean Moncrieffe. She wants to marry Oldfield but is afraid that people will say he killed his wife to marry her.

Mrs Oldfield's body is exhumed and arsenic is found. Jean is implicated. But Poirot kills the Hydra by catching out the real killer.

'The Arcadian Deer'

First published in issue 589 of Strand Magazine, *January 1940; in the US, in* This Week *magazine, 19 May 1940 as 'Vanishing Lady'*

Poirot's car – a Messarro Gratz – breaks down. The mechanic who fixes it has the perfect physique of a Greek god – 'a young shepherd in Arcady'. He asks Poirot to find the lady's maid to a Russian dancer who had visited a country house nearby. She was a blonde named Nita. They had spent the afternoon together, walking along the river bank. She said that she would return two weeks later. But when the Russian dancer returned, she had a new maid.

Poirot discovers that the Russian dancer Katrina Samoushenka's previous maid was an Italian. He tracks her to Pisa, where she has died. Then he goes Switzerland to see Samoushenka. There he discovers his golden hind and persuades her to return to her mechanic.

'The Erymanthian Boar'

First published in issue 590 of Strand Magazine, *February 1940; in the US, in* This Week *magazine, 5 May 1940 as 'Murder Mountain'*

Still in Switzerland, Poirot is on the funicular when he is handed a note concerning the killer Marrascaud who is described by the Swiss police as a 'wild boar'.

Marrascaud is meeting secretly with his cohorts at a hotel at Rochers Neiges; the hotel can only be reached by funicular as it's above the snow line. Poirot continues his ascent to the hotel which, although it is early in the season, is full. Poirot pretends to be Monsieur Poirier, a silk merchant from Lyons. The funicular breaks down so they are cut off there, while Poirot tracks down his wild boar.

'The Augean Stables'
First published in issue 591 of Strand Magazine, *March 1940*
Poirot is approached by the Home Secretary Sir George
Conway and the Prime Minister Edward Ferrier. A newspaper called *X-Ray News* is going to publish accusations
of chicanery and misuse of party funds against Ferrier's
father-in-law, the former Prime Minister John Hammett,
now Lord Cornworthy. He cannot sue for libel as the
accusations are true, while Ferrier is trying to clean up the
mess. Poirot can barely stifle a yawn until Sir George mentions the Augean Stables. He then agrees to help in this
Herculean task.

Poirot co-opts Mrs Ferrier and uses the public tastes for
scandals involving sex and drugs as the river to wash out
the Augean Stables, putting *X-Ray News* out of business in
the process.

'The Stymphalean Birds'
First published in issue 592 of Strand Magazine, *April 1940; in the
US, in* This Week *magazine, 17 September 1939 as 'The Vulture
Woman'*
Rising politician Harold Waring is holidaying in Herzos-
lovakia where he meets Mrs Rice and her daughter Elsie
Clayton. He sees two strange women with hook noses,
wearing cloaks that flap like the wings of birds in the wind.
They are, apparently, Polish.

Mrs Rice tells Waring that Elsie is in an abusive marriage. One evening Elsie bursts into his room saying that
her husband has arrived. The door is flung open and the
figure in the doorway, armed with a heavy spanner, says
that the Polish women are right: she is having an affair and
he is going kill her.

Elsie is chased back to her room where she brains her
attacker with a paperweight while Harold looks on. Things
look bad for both of them. No one must find Harold there,
so he flees. Half an hour later, Mrs Rice tells him that

Elsie's husband is dead. Harold was now implicated in a murder case. The only thing he can do is bribe the manager of the hotel, the local police and a few others.

Harold wires for money but, as Mrs Rice speaks the local language, she handles the arrangements. The next afternoon, she says everything is okay. She has paid out a considerable sum. But then the Polish women approach. Mrs Rice translates, saying they intend to blackmail him.

Harold bumps into Poirot and tells him his troubles. He seizes on the connection with the Stymphalean Birds. Poirot then has the blackmailers arrested, but they are not the Polish women.

'The Cretan Bull'
First published in issue 593 of Strand Magazine, *May 1940; in the US, in* This Week *magazine, 24 September 1939 as 'Midnight Madness'*
Diana Maberly comes to see Poirot. Her fiancé Hugh Chandler has broken off their engagement because he fears he is going mad. She thinks he is the sanest person she knows, but there is madness in the family.

Hugh lives with his father, Admiral Chandler, at Lyde Manor. There have been strange occurrences in the district. Sheep have had their throats cut. Poirot goes to Lyde Manor to see for himself and is impressed by Hugh's magnificent physique – he is a 'young bull'.

Poirot interviews Colonel Frobisher, Admiral Chandler's oldest friend, who tells him of the insanity in the Chandler family. Hugh's mother had died in a boating accident when the boy was ten. She had been a childhood friend of Frobisher's before he went out to India as a subaltern. Despite his concern about his son, Admiral Chandler will not let Hugh see a doctor, preferring to shut him up like a wild beast. Hugh suffers hallucinations and there are more bloodthirsty incidents before Poirot realizes that there is insanity in the family – but not Hugh's.

'The Horses of Diomedes'

First published in issue 594 of Strand Magazine, *June 1940*

Dr Michael Stoddart summons Poirot to the scene of a cocaine-fuelled party given by Patience Grace. She has had a row with her boyfriend, Tony Hawker, and taken a pot-shot at him out of the window. But Stoddart does not want the police involved because of another girl, Sheila Grant, who he met at a hunt ball in Mertonshire. Her father is a general whose four daughters have got in with a bad set. After meeting Sheila, who is suffering the after-effects of a night on cocaine, Poirot heads out to Mertonshire. There he talks to Lady Carmichael about the Grant girls who, she says, are man-eaters. She assumes that he is investigating a crime. He says that he is there to tame wild horses – symbolically, at least.

He finds General Grant a real *pukka sahib* who drinks heavily and complains of gout. Getting up to leave, Poirot stumbles against the general. Then he goes to a party and meets another of the Grant sisters, Pamela. Sheila arrives with Hawker, for whom nobody has a good word. Pamela asks Poirot: 'What's the stuff Tony's been giving Sheila?' Then he finds Hawker's hip flask is full of white powder.

Poirot says that those who profit from the degradation of others are vampires preying on flesh and blood. He then accuses Sheila Grant of feeding on human flesh, like the mares of Diomedes.

'The Girdle of Hyppolita'

First published in issue 595 of Strand Magazine, *July 1940; in the US, in* This Week *magazine, 10 September 1939 as 'The Disappearance of Winnie King'*

Poirot's friend Alexander Simpson asks him to help recover a recently discovered Rubens masterpiece stolen from his gallery by a gang of art thieves and thought to have been taken to France. But Poirot is more interested in the case of an English schoolgirl named Winnie King who has gone missing on her way to her first term at Miss Pope's finishing school in Paris. She disappeared from the train after it left Amiens and her hat was found at the side of the line. Later she turned up on the roadside fifteen miles from Amiens; she had been doped and remembered nothing after leaving home in Cranchester.

Among the other passengers were a crook and his flashy wife. A pair of shoes are then found beside the line, although Winnie was wearing shoes when she was found.

In Paris, Poirot visits Miss Pope's exclusive school. She complains that two sets of policemen searched Winnie's possessions. But pupils' bags were routinely unpacked when they arrived. Poirot notices a painting of Cranchester on Miss Pope's wall. It was a present addressed to her from Winnie. With this clue, Poirot solves the mystery of the disappearing schoolgirl and recovers the missing Rubens which is called 'The Girdle of Hyppolita'.

'The Flock of Geryon'
First published in issue 596 of Strand Magazine, August 1940; in the US, in This Week magazine, 26 May 1940 as 'Weird Monster'

Miss Carnaby, last seen in 'The Nemean Lion', has been inspired by Poirot to take up fighting crime. She wants to consult him on a case she wishes to pursue. After a friend of hers was widowed, she joined a religious sect called the Flock of the Shepherd, which has a retreat in Devon and is run by the handsome Dr Andersen. When Mrs Carnaby's friend died, she left all her property to the movement. Three other wealthy women have done the same recently.

Poirot suggests that Miss Carnaby infiltrates the sect while Poirot contacts Inspector Japp. Japp discovers that Andersen was a German chemist whose career was curtailed by the Nazis. The women in question died from diseases some had suffered for years before joining the sect. Three died in their own homes; the fourth in a hotel in the south of France. Nevertheless, Poirot says that Dr Andersen is the Monster Geryon who it is his mission to destroy.

'The Apples of the Hesperides'
First published in issue 597 of Strand Magazine, *September 1940; in the US, in* This Week *magazine, 12 May 1940 as 'The Poison Cup'*
Renowned art collector Emery Power hires Poirot to find a Renaissance goblet used by Pope Alexander VI, the Borgia pope, to poison his guests. Made by Benvenuto Cellini, the gold goblet was decorated by a jewelled serpent coiled around an apple tree, with priceless emeralds representing the fruit. Power bought it in 1929, but it was stolen from the vendor before he took possession of it.

The thieves were a well-known gang. Two of them were captured, but the goblet was not among their swag. The third, an Irish cat burglar named Patrick Casey, died falling from a building. There has been no sign of the goblet since and Power's former rival for its possession is now a business partner.

Poirot discovers that Casey's daughter became a nun. With the help of a man called Atlas, Poirot undertakes a little burglary and recovers the goblet – only to convince Power to return it.

'The Capture of Cerberus'
First published in This Week *magazine, 16 May 1947, as 'Meet Me in Hell'*
Poirot is going up the escalator at Piccadilly Circus tube station when Countess Vera Rossakoff calls out to him from the down escalator. He asks where he can find her. She replies: 'In Hell.' Miss Lemon later explains that Hell is a nightclub and books Poirot a table. At the door is a guard dog named Cerberus.

There Poirot meets the Countess. With her are Professor Liskeard, who advised on the Hadean decorations, and the psychologist Dr Alice Cunningham who is engaged to the countess's son. She is writing a book on criminal psychology and expresses an interest in Vera's penchant for stealing jewels. In response, Poirot comments on Alice's attire – a heavy coat and skirt with a big pocket more suitable for a round of golf. After parrying Poirot, she goes to dance with a man called Paul Varesco who, she says, lives on women and has strange cravings.

Inspector Japp tells Poirot that the club is a front for selling dope bought by the idle rich, not with money, but with jewels. Poirot tries to warn Vera Rossakoff that there is going to be a raid. But Vera needs no help from Poirot to escape from being set up. Poirot employs a dog trainer to capture Cerberus who reveals the hiding place of the drugs. He also fingers the drug dealers and has to wipe a grateful Vera's lipstick and mascara from his face before reporting to Japp.

Taken at the Flood
London: Collins, The Crime Club, 1948; New York: published as There is a Tide, *Dodd, Mead & Co., 1948*
The book contains an epigraph from Julius Caesar:

> There is a tide in the affairs of men,
> Which, taken at the flood, leads on to fortune,
> Omitted, all the voyage of their life
> Is bound in shallows and in miseries.
> On such a full sea are we now afloat,
> And we must take the current when it serves,
> Or lose our ventures.

In the Coronation Club during an air raid, Major Porter, late of the Indian Army, is holding forth about the death of a neighbour named Gordon Cloade, who has just returned from the US after marrying a young widow named Mrs Underhay. A bomb hit Cloade's house in Camden Hill, killing everyone except Cloade's brother-in-law and his wife, who was found naked after her clothes had been blasted off her. Major Porter had known Mrs Underhay's first husband in Nigeria. After their marriage failed, he had intended to fake his own death, perhaps adopting the pseudonym Enoch Arden. Overhearing this were Gordon Cloade's brother Jeremy, a lawyer, and Hercule Poirot.

Eighteen months later, after the war is over, Poirot is visited by the wife of Dr Lionel Cloade, another of Gordon Cloade's brothers. She wants him to prove that Underhay is still alive, but she can hardly afford his fees. Five days later, Poirot reads of the death of a man named Enoch Arden in Warmsley Vale, home of the Cloades.

Life in Warmsley Vale is getting back to normal after the war, but the Cloades are having a tough time. They were all dependent on Gordon's money, which has now gone to his second wife Rosaleen, formerly Mrs Underhay. She was accompanied by her over-protective brother David Hunter, who warns Rosaleen to watch out for strychnine in her soup. Enoch Arden turns up at the local inn having written to Hunter, saying he had news of Captain Underhay and asking for £10,000.

After Enoch Arden is found dead Superintendent Spence is called in to investigate. He suspects David Hunter of murdering Arden. Poirot seeks out Major Porter who identifies the dead man as Robert Underhay, but Porter later commits suicide; then Rosaleen Cloade is found dead, further confusing the police.

This appeared in the *Poirot* TV series in 2006.

The Under Dog and Other Stories
New York: Dodd, Mead & Co., 1951

Not published as a volume in the UK, this is a collection of Hercule Poirot short stories published in magazines between 1923 and 1926. The title story appeared in book form in the UK for the first time in *The Adventure of the*

Christmas Pudding (1960). The rest appear in *Poirot's Early Cases* (1974).

'The Under Dog'
First published in Volume 8, Number 6 of Mystery Magazine, *1 April 1926; in the UK,* The London Magazine, *October 1926*
Lily Margrave, a companion of Lady Astwell, visits Poirot. Sir Reuben Astwell has been murdered and his nephew, Charles Leverson, has been arrested. Late at night, the butler, Parsons, heard them rowing, then heard a thud. Sir Reuben had been found dead the following morning, bludgeoned with a heavy instrument.

Although Leverson, who is financially embarrassed and had blood on his sleeve, will inherit, Lady Astwell does not think he is the killer. Rather, her intuition tells her that Sir Reuben's secretary Owen Trefusis is the culprit. Poirot is also intrigued by Lily's involvement.

Arriving at the Astwell abode, *Mon Repos*, Lady Astwell reveals that Lily tried to put her off calling in Poirot. Again she asserts that Trefusis killed her husband, though he has been with him for nine years and has nothing to gain. Leverson also worked for Sir Reuben; they were always having rows, but then Reuben was not an easy man to get on with. Parson confirms that Leverson was drunk when he came home and, after shouting at his uncle, there was a heavy thud, then silence. Poirot finds Trefusis excessively meek and easy to bully. He says that Leverson had a row with his uncle earlier in the evening, leaving Sir Reuben in a very bad temper. He had later had a row with Lady Astwell about Lily – Sir Reuben found her interfering his papers and wanted to send her away. Smearing blood on a piece of fabric from the frock Lily was wearing on the night of the murder, Poirot forces a confession out of her. Lady Astwell then agrees to undergo hypnosis allowing Poirot to set up an elaborate trap for the killer.

This appeared in the *Poirot* TV series in 1993.

'The Plymouth Express'
First published in issue 1575 of the Sketch, *4 April 1923 as 'The Mystery of the Plymouth Express'*

The body of Mrs Rupert Carrington, née Flossie Halliday, is found under a seat on the Plymouth Express. After her father, Ebenezer Halliday, the steel king of America, put an end to her affair with the adventurer, the Count de la Rochefour, she had married the Honourable Rupert Carrington, a gambling addict, who would now inherit. Halliday hires Poirot to find her killer.

Flossie was on her way to a house party at Avonmead Court and travelled to Bristol with £100,000-worth of jewellery, which was missing. She had informed her maid Jane Mason that she was going on beyond Bristol alone and would return on the uptown train that afternoon. But Mrs Carrington did not return. According to Jane Mason, when Flossie left Bristol, there was a man with her in her carriage.

Her husband was out of town at the time and Mason, though she did not see the man's face, said her mistress's companion was of the same build. Halliday has found a letter that shows his daughter and Armand de la Rochefour were in contact again. He is of a similar build to Flossie's husband and had checked out of the Ritz on the day of the murder.

A newspaper boy has seen the distinctively dressed Mrs Carrington at Weston and the murder weapon is found at the side of the tracks between Weston and Taunton. One of the missing jewels is passed by a jewel thief named 'Red Narky' who works with a female accomplice called Gracie Kidd. Poirot heads for the Halliday mansion in Park Lane where he finds an outfit similar to the one worn by Mrs Carrington when she was murdered.

An extended and modified version of this story became *The Mystery of the Blue Train*. *The Plymouth Express* appeared in the *Poirot* TV series in 1991.

'The Affair at the Victory Ball'
First published in issue 1571 of the Sketch, 7 March 1923
Christie's first published short story. It is narrated by Captain Hastings who assumes the role of Watson to chronicle the adventures of his own great detective. In the rooms they share, they are reading an account of the murder of Lord Cronshaw at the Victory Ball. That same night showgirl Coco Courtenay was found dead from an overdose of cocaine. Inspector Japp arrives and invites them to join the investigation.

There were rumours that Cronshaw was engaged to Coco. They were together at the ball with a party of six all dressed as figures from the *Commedia dell'arte*. Cronshaw was Harlequin; Miss Courtenay Columbine. But they were not on speaking terms and she was escorted home by actor Chris Davidson, outfitted as Pierrot.

After supper in a private room Cronshaw was notably unsociable. Later, he was found dead on the floor of the supper room with a table knife through his heart and a small pompon of emerald green silk in his hand. The body was unnaturally stiff. Poirot's knowledge of the costumes of the characters of the *Commedia dell'Arte* leads him to the culprit.

This appeared in the *Poirot* TV series in 1991.

'The Market Basing Mystery'
First published in issue 1603 of the Sketch, 17 October 1923
Poirot, Hastings and Inspector Japp take a weekend's break in the country town of Market Basing. A local constable approaches them. Walter Protheroe at Leigh Hall has been found dead, a supposed suicide. But he can't have shot himself. That morning, Protheroe's housekeeper Mrs Clegg had found his bedroom door locked. She became alarmed and called the doctor and the police. After breaking down the door, they found Protheroe shot through the head with a pistol in his right hand, but the bullet hole was

just behind his left ear – an impossible shot. Poirot quickly picks up some fresh clues by sniffing the air and examining an apparently spotless handkerchief tucked up Protheroe's sleeve.

The window was locked and bolted and the key to the door could not be found. Protheroe was a heavy smoker and there were cigarette butts in the ashtray. Houseguests Mr and Mrs Parker are adjudged to be a 'bad lot'; the evidence stacks up and Mr Parker is committed for trial. Poirot, however, demurs.

Christie uses the same plot device later in 'Murder in the Mews'.

'The Lemesurier Inheritance'
First published in issue 1609 of the Sketch, *18 December 1923*
Shorting after renewing their acquaintanceship in *The Mysterious Affair at Styles*, Poirot and Hastings are dining at the Carlton when Hastings spots Captain Vincent Lemesurier who he had known in France. Lemesurier was with his Uncle Hugo.

A cousin named Roger arrives, bringing the news that Vincent's father has had a bad fall from a horse. Vincent turns white. He and Hugo rush off, leaving Roger Lemesurier to explain the family curse – that no first-born son would live to inherit.

Vincent Lemesurier dies falling from a train on the way to see his stricken father. There follows a series of deaths of first-born sons in the family and Uncle Hugo eventually inherits. His wife subsequently visits Poirot, telling him that her eldest son has had three near scrapes with death recently.

Realizing the boy is in danger, Poirot visits their Northumberland estate where he unmasks a human agency behind the curse.

In the *Poirot* TV series, this story was woven into *The Labours of Hercules* feature-length episode, first aired in November 2013.

'The Cornish Mystery'

First published in issue 1612 of the Sketch, *28 November 1923*

Mrs Pengelley comes to consult Poirot. She believes that her husband is trying to poison her. They live in Polgarwith in Cornwall. Their niece, Freda Stanton, who had been living with them for eight years, has just moved out following a row. Her friend Jacob Radnor suggests that they should leave her to come to her senses. As for the poisoning, Mrs Pengelley thinks that her husband's blonde secretary is behind it.

The next day, Poirot and Hastings head down to Cornwall. By the time they reach Polgarwith, Mrs Pengelley is dead. Poirot berates himself. They visit Miss Stanton and find her with Mr Radnor. They were engaged. This was the cause of the row as Mrs Pengelley had been infatuated with Radnor herself.

Mrs Pengelley's doctor thinks that she died of gastritis. While Radnor says that he thinks she was poisoned by her husband, he asks Poirot to hush it up as she would be the last person who would want a scandal.

Some time later Hastings reads in the paper that Mr Pengelley and his secretary are engaged. Then Mrs Pengelley's body is exhumed and found to be full of arsenic. Mr Pengelley is arrested and charged with murder.

At this point, Poirot intervenes. He summons the real killer and gets them to sign a confession.

This appeared in the *Poirot* TV series in 1990.

'The King of Clubs'

First published in issue 1573 of the Sketch, *21 March 1923*

Hastings reads in the newspaper of the murder of theatrical impresario Henry Reedburn. Nearby, the four members of the Oglander family – father, mother, son and daughter – were playing bridge when a woman covered with blood burst through the French windows and collapsed with the word 'murder' on her lips. She is the famous dancer Valerie Saintclair. However, Poirot is already involved in the case having previously been contacted by Prince Paul of Maurania who hopes to marry Valerie Saintclair. Reedburn had a hold over her, though, and professed to be in love with her, although she did not reciprocate. Valerie had consulted a clairvoyant for a card reading. The last card she turned up was the king of clubs. This warned Valerie to be wary of the man who has power over her. Plainly this was Reedburn and Prince Paul fears that she has killed him.

Poirot goes to Reedburn's house in Streatham. His body has been found outside the library window in the back garden. A lady's voice had been heard coming from the library. Outside the library door is marble seat decorated with a lion's head. The doctor who had attended the body said that, if Reedburn had fallen back on it, it could have caused the fatal head wound, only the angle of the body would have made that impossible. Besides, there were no blood stains on it. And the wound, he says, could not have been inflicted by a woman.

They then cross the garden to the Oglander's house. Miss Saintclair is still there, recovering. She admits Reedburn was blackmailing her, but denies killing him and claims to have been molested by a blood-stained tramp.

In the drawing room where the Oglanders were supposed to have been playing bridge Poirot finds the king of clubs missing from the pack – and solves the mystery.

This appeared in the *Poirot* TV series in 1989.

'The Submarine Plans'
See 'The Incredible Theft' in Murder in the Mews
Here, Lord Alloway, head of the Ministry of Defence, replaces Lord Mayfield; and Sir Harry Weardale, First Sea Lord, replaces Air Marshal Sir George Carrington. There are other name changes, but the plot remains the same.

'The Adventure of the Clapham Cook'
First published in issue 1607 of the Sketch, *14 November 1923*
While they are living together, Hastings often searches the newspapers for interesting cases for Poirot. One day, he reads of a missing typist, a suicide and a bank clerk who has gone missing with £50,000 of securities. But Poirot is more interested in his toilette. He says that he will only touch a case of national importance.

Then a red-faced lady named Mrs Todd arrives who wants him to find her missing cook; she left without giving notice. After being berated for being 'too proud' to take the case, Poirot deigns to investigate as a 'novelty'.

He suggests that the cook had an accident while she was out. However, she had sent for her trunk which was already packed. Hastings and Poirot visit the client's Clapham home where Poirot discovers that there is a lodger named Simpson who works in the City. Hastings notes that he works in the same bank as Mr Davis, the missing bank clerk he had read about in the paper.

An ad in the newspaper elicits a visit from the missing cook. She tells Poirot that she was stopped in the street by a man with a beard and a big hat; he purported to come from a wealthy well-wisher in Australia who offered her a position in Cumberland, provided she leave immediately. However, when she sent for her things, they arrived in paper parcels, not in her trunk.

Not only has Poirot solved the mysteries of the missing cook and the missing bank clerk, he has uncovered a murder.

This appeared in the *Poirot* TV series in 1989.

Mrs McGinty's Dead
London: Collins, The Crime Club, 1952; New York: Dodd, Mead & Co., 1952 (also appeared in a Detective Book Club edition as Blood Will Tell)
Poirot is returning from dinner in Soho. He is bored. Even the hoarding announcing the verdict in the McGinty trial

does not interest him. When Poirot gets home, Superintendent Spence of the Colchester Police awaits him; he has been working on the McGinty case.

Poirot asks: 'How did she die?'

The question reminds Spence of the old children's game 'Mrs *McGinty's* Dead'.

Her lodger James Bentley has just been convicted of her murder. The jury found that he bludgeoned her with a heavy implement to steal £30. Her hair and blood group matched the hair and blood found on his sleeve. However, Spence does not think he did it and he wants Poirot to investigate. Having too much time on his hands, Poirot welcomes the challenge to his little grey cells.

Poirot travels to Broadhinny, the village of just four cottages, a post office and a shop, were Mrs McGinty lived. He suffers in a terrible guesthouse where the cooking is foul. It was one of the places Mrs McGinty came to clean and she is sorely missed. Poirot overhears his host, Major Summerhayes, say that he looks like a hairdresser. Poirot insists to Mrs Summerhayes that he is perhaps the most famous detective in the world and that he is investigating the murder of Mrs McGinty.

Poirot interviews the locals. They are convinced that Bentley was the murderer. He was a little mad or 'queer'. They were fed up with the police investigation and disliked foreigners. So Poirot says that he is looking into the case for rich relatives of Bentley. When Maude Williams expresses doubt about Bentley's guilt, Poirot claims his investigation has already made considerable progress. Maude, he thought, would talk, making someone, somewhere uneasy.

Soon the investigation is making progress. A bottle of ink, a Sunday paper and some old murder cases put Poirot on the right trail. Soon someone is so rattled that they try to push him under a train. But he is not to be dissuaded and, after another murder, Poirot names someone that not even Ariadne Oliver, who makes an appearance, suspects.

The story was adapted for the screen as *Murder Most Foul* in 1964 where Poirot is replaced by Miss Marple. Poirot was restored for the *Poirot* TV series in 2007.

After the Funeral
London: Collins, The Crime Club, 1953; New York: published as Funerals are Fatal, *Dodd, Mead & Co., 1953*

Nobody is surprised when Richard Abernethie dies. He has outlived the rest of his siblings except for his invalid brother Timothy and his younger sister Cora who was thought to be 'simple'. She ran off with an artist and has not been seen by the family for twenty-five years. After the funeral, the solicitor Mr Entwhistle reads the will. In it, Abernethie divides his estate equally among the surviving family members.

Then in typical fashion, Cora blurts out: '. . . it's been hushed up very nicely . . . he was murdered, wasn't he?'

There was no reason to think that Richard Abernethie had been killed, but Cora's outburst sets family members thinking. The following afternoon Cora is murdered. A window in her cottage has been smashed and she has been bludgeoned with a hatchet. The housekeeper, Cora's companion, Miss Gilchrist was out at the time and a few trinkets were missing, perhaps to make it look like a robbery.

While Cora's legacy returns to the family, her paintings – including those bought at local sales – are left to Miss Gilchrist. Mr Entwhistle then employs Poirot to investigate the two deaths. In turn, Poirot employs the now retired Mr Goby, who had gathered evidence on Derek Kettering in *The Mystery of the Blue Train*, to do some of the legwork for him. But it is, of course, Poirot's little grey cells that put the clues together.

The story was filmed as *Murder at the Gallop* in 1963, with Poirot replaced by Miss Marple, played by Margaret Rutherford. Poirot returned when *After the Funeral* was produced in the *Poirot* series in 2006.

Hickory Dickory Dock

London: Collins, The Crime Club, 1955; New York: published as Hickory Dickory Death, *Dodd, Mead & Co., 1955*

The normally faultless Miss Felicity Lemon, Poirot's secretary, has made three mistakes in a simple letter. This is because, she explains, of her widowed sister. Having returned from Singapore, the sister has become the matron of a hostel for students in Hickory Road belonging to a Greek lady named Mrs Nicoletis, where there had been a spate of petty thieving. This is not Poirot's usual line, but he invites Miss Lemon's sister to tea.

When she lists the disparate items that have been stolen, Poirot congratulates her for bringing a 'unique and beautiful problem' to him.

While Poirot goes about trying to solve the problem of the missing items one by one, Miss Lemon's sister, Mrs Hubbard, returns to Hickory Road, where she discovers that one of the West Indian law students has had her notes ruined. Green ink has been spilt over them. When Poirot hears of this, he arranges to give a lecture at Hickory Road.

Over dinner at the hostel (which fortunately has a good Italian chef), Poirot sizes up the suspects. After his lecture, the conversation turns to the thefts. Poirot is asked what he advises. He says that Mrs Hubbard or Mrs Nicoletis should call the police as soon as possible. Mrs Hubbard agrees, but does not think she will get the consent of Mrs Nicoletis.

The students say they consider Poirot's methods old-fashioned, but then one of the students, Celia Austin, begs Mrs Hubbard not to call the police, admitting the thefts. However, she insists that she did not steal a missing stethoscope. Nor did she spill the ink or cut up a rucksack. There were other missing items she knew nothing about – light bulbs, boracic powder or bath salts. She was only trying to attract the attention of a man.

Mrs Nicoletis is angry when she hears that Poirot has

been snooping around, but Mrs Hubbard is relieved that the matter is closed. Then Celia Austin is found dead. It is said that she committed suicide. Mrs Hubbard does not think she did and Poirot is back on the case.

This appeared in the *Poirot* TV series in 1995.

Dead Man's Folly
London: Collins, The Crime Club, 1956; New York: Dodd, Mead & Co., 1956

Ariadne Oliver invites Poirot to Nasse House in Nasse-combe, Devon. On the way from the station they give two lady hitchhikers – one Dutch, the other Italian – a lift, dropping them at a nearby youth hostel.

Mrs Oliver tells Poirot that she had been hired to organize a 'murder hunt' for the fête the following day. However, she feels that she is being manipulated and suspects that the next day there is going to be a real murder, not a fake one.

She has a list of suspects. Among them are the owner of the house, the rich though plebian Sir George Stubbs who complains of the encroachment of the youth hostellers, his half-witted foreign wife Hattie, who is twenty years his junior; the architect Michael Weyman, who is repairing a folly in the grounds; and Mrs Folliat, whose family had owned the house since Tudor times but, after the men-folk were thought to have perished in the war, had to sell it, although she was allowed to stay on as a lodger. In the fête's murder hunt, the body is going to be in the boathouse. It is to be played, at the last minute, by girl guide Marlene Tucker. But when Poirot and Mrs Oliver go to check up on Marlene, she really is dead. Prior to that discovery, Lady Stubbs' cousin Etienne de Sousa arrived. But Hattie has herself disappeared; she is thought to be afraid of him. Suspicion falls on Amanda Brewis, Sir George's secretary, who Lady Stubbs asked to take a tray of refreshments to Marlene. There was a certain antagonism between Miss Brewis and Lady Stubbs. More confusion is caused by

Alec Legge and his wife Sally. He is an atomic physicist who thinks that all unintelligent people should be prevented from breeding. Then the boatman Merdell drowns; he was Marlene's grandfather. Marlene's mother says: 'There's been Merdells at Nasse for years.' This reminds Poirot that Merdell himself had said: 'There'll always be Folliats at Nasse House.'

This is the vital clue that allows Poirot to solve the crime.

The story was filmed in 1986 and BBC Radio 4 broadcast a dramatization in 2007. It appeared in the *Poirot* TV series in 2013.

Cat Among the Pigeons

London: Collins, The Crime Club, 1959; New York: Dodd, Mead & Co., 1960

A prologue covers the opening of the summer term at Meadowbank School for Girls and its formidable staff who discuss the exotic trips they have taken during the holidays.

The main text starts with a revolution in the Middle Eastern sheikhdom of Ramat. Preparing to flee, the young Sheikh, Prince Ali Yusuf, gives the family jewels to his pilot Bob Rawlinson, his fag at school, to smuggle out of the country.

Bob's sister Joan Sutcliffe and her daughter Jennifer were in Ramat. He goes to their hotel while they are out and conceals the gems among their luggage. The woman on the next balcony has seen what he has done.

The British Consulate warns Joan and Jennifer to leave the country because of the revolution. They go by sea. Bob and Prince Ali Yusuf choose to fly and are killed.

When Joan and Jennifer return to England both British Intelligence and others take an interest in their luggage. Jennifer is then sent to Meadowbank School where British Intelligence already have an agent in place, posing as a gardener, to keep an eye on Princess Shaista, first cousin of Ali Yusuf, who is starting there that term.

Jennifer has trouble with her tennis racket, believing it to be warped from the heat of the Persian Gulf. So her friend Julia Upjohn swaps hers for it. After the games mistress is murdered in the sports pavilion Miss Rich says she suspects that there is someone among them who does not belong – a 'cat among the pigeons'. A woman then turns up, bringing Jennifer a new racket, saying it is from her Aunt Gina, and taking the other one, thinking it to be Jennifer's, to be restrung.

During the murder investigation, Princess Shaista insists that, as she was going to marry Prince Ali Yusuf, the missing jewels now belong to her. She expresses a fear of being kidnapped or assassinated, then goes missing and another teacher is found dead in the sports pavilion.

Julia Upjohn finds the missing gems. Fearing that she may now be in danger, she goes to consult Hercule Poirot who she knows of through a friend of her mother. This appeared in the *Poirot* TV series in 2008.

The Adventure of the Christmas Pudding and a Selection of Entrées
London: Collins: The Crime Club, 1960

By 1960, the 'Christie for Christmas' had become an institution, but with no novel to offer that year, the publishers put together five Poirot stories, plus one from Miss Marple.

'The Adventure of the Christmas Pudding'
First published in a shorter form in issue 1611 of the Sketch, *18 December 1923*

A Christmas in the countryside has been arranged for a reluctant Poirot by the emissary of the son of an eastern potentate, who is about to marry. However, a famous ruby that he has brought to England to be reset by Cartier has been taken by an accommodating young lady. As there must be no scandal, he cannot go to the police. Instead, he hires Poirot, who is persuaded when he hears that the historic jewel has been responsible for many deaths. To recover it, he must spend Christmas in Kings Lacey, as a guest of Colonel and Mrs Lacey.

His quarry, it appears, is Desmond Lee-Wortley. He is beau of the hosts' orphaned granddaughter and heir-ess Sarah, though he is not thought to be suitable due to his unsavoury reputation. Mrs Lacey thinks that, if they spend Christmas together in the family home, Sarah will tire of him. Her grandmother is then charmed by him, par-ticularly as he has asked to bring his sister with him. Con-valescing after an operation, she is confined to her room. However, the Laceys ask Poirot for his help to thwart any marriage between Sarah and Lee-Wortley.

The young people in the party find Poirot faintly ridicu-lous and plan to stage a fake murder for him to investigate. On Christmas Eve, Poirot finds a note pinned to his pillow warning him not to eat the Christmas pudding. But when it arrives after Christmas lunch, Poirot tucks in anyway. However, the Colonel nearly chokes on what he takes to be a piece of red glass in his portion. Poirot retrieves it and drops it into his pocket.

On Boxing Day, the youngsters stage their fake murder. Bridget, a great-niece of Mrs Lacey, is found sprawled in snow-covered Kensington Gore. Poirot says they must call the police. They insist that it is a joke, but Poirot gets Lee-Wortley to check her pulse. There is none. The footprints in the snow match Lee-Wortley's. He then notices what appears to be large ruby in the palm of Bridget's hand, grabs it and makes off.

But there has been no murder. Poirot has recovered the ruby and foiled any marriage between Sarah and Lee-Wortley.

This story appeared in the *Poirot* TV series as *The Theft of the Royal Ruby* in 1991.

'The Mystery of the Spanish Chest'
First published as 'The Mystery of the Baghdad Chest' in issue 493 of
Strand Magazine, January 1932; in the US in Volume 58, Number 1
of the Ladies Home Journal, January 1932
Poirot takes an interest in a murder that has been in the newspaper. Major Rich invited Mr and Mrs Clayton to a party. Mr Clayton is called away to Scotland and drops in to tell Major Rich that he cannot attend. The morning after the party his body is found in a chest in the room where the party was held. Major Rich is arrested and Poirot is hired by Mrs Clayton – Major Rich's lover – to prove that he did not do it.

In the original shorter version, 'The Mystery of the Baghdad Chest', Hastings, rather that Miss Lemon, is Poirot's foil.

This appeared in the *Poirot* TV series as *The Mystery of the Spanish Chest* in 1991.

'The Under Dog'
See The Under Dog and Other Stories

'Four and Twenty Blackbirds'
First published in Volume 106, Number 19 of Collier's magazine,
9 November 1940
Poirot is dining out with his friend Henry Bonnington, who points out an old man with a beard. He has come to the same restaurant every Tuesday and Thursday for ten years, but last week he came on Monday and ordered things he had previously abhorred. Bonnington maintains that a doctor had told him to change his diet. Poirot is sceptical.

Three weeks later, Bonnington tells Poirot that the old man concerned has died. Poirot discovers who the old man is and, after consultation with his doctor, tracks down his murderer.

This appeared in the *Poirot* TV series in 1989.

'The Dream'

First published in Volume 210, Number 17 of the Saturday Evening Post, *23 October 1937*

Poirot is summoned to the ancient mansion of eccentric millionaire Benedict Farley who says that, every night, he dreams of committing suicide in exactly the same way. A week later, Poirot gets a call from his old friend Dr Stillingfleet who tells him that Farley is dead. He appears to have shot himself in exactly the same way he described in his dream. As the note inviting Poirot to consult with Farley is found, he is called in on the investigation. It also leads the police to suspect that Farley has been murdered. Poirot proves that he had – and identifies the culprits.

It appeared in the *Poirot* TV series in 1989.

'Greenshaw's Folly'

First published in Woman's Journal, *August 1960*

Miss Marple's nephew, novelist Raymond West, and literary critic Horace Bindler visit an oddball mid-Victorian mansion known as Greenshaw's Folly. While trespassing on the grounds they meet the only remaining family member, Miss Greenshaw. She asks them to witness her will, which leaves the house to her housekeeper, Mrs Cresswell.

Miss Greenshaw also wants her father's diaries prepared for publication. West recommends his wife's niece, Louise, for the job. On her second day, Miss Greenshaw asks Louise to phone her own nephew, an actor playing in a stock company. The next day, Louise looks out of the window to see Miss Greenshaw stagger away from the rockery where she had been weeding with an arrow in her chest.

'. . . he shot me,' she gasps.

Louise tries to go for help, but finds the door to the library where she is working locked. The housekeeper is locked in too. Soon after they are released, Miss Greenshaw's nephew turns up to learn that his aunt has been murdered.

Subsequently it is discovered that Miss Greenshaw did not leave the house to Mrs Cresswell, but to Alfred Pollock the gardener – he is a member of an archery club, but has an alibi.

Miss Marple realizes that Louise has witnessed a charade put on to conceal the real murderer. The clue was in the rockery.

This is being filmed as part of the *Marple* TV series.

The Clocks
London: Collins, The Crime Club, 1963; New York: Dodd, Mead & Co., 1964

In the prologue, the Cavendish Secretarial and Type-writing Bureau send shorthand-typist Sheila Webb to 19 Wilbraham Crescent at three o'clock. She is told that, if Miss Pebmarsh is not there when she arrives, she is to go in and wait. Doing as instructed, she finds a room with a number of clocks in it. They all show a little after ten past four, though a cuckoo clock on the wall sounds three. Suddenly she notices the body of a man on the floor. A woman enters and almost steps on the corpse, and Sheila screams.

In a first-person narrative, Colin Lamb, who appears to be an officer with Special Branch, says that he was looking for number 61 Wilbraham Crescent although the numbers only go up to 35 when a girl comes running out of number 19, straight into him. Sheila takes him back into the house where they meet the woman who has come in – Millicent Pebmarsh, who is blind.

Lamb calls Detective Inspector Hardcastle at Crowdean Police Station. When interviewed by the inspector, Miss Pebmarsh denies ordering a stenographer from the Caven-dish Secretarial and Typewriting Bureau. She also insists that there are only two clocks in the sitting room – just the cuckoo clock on the wall and a grandfather clock in the corner. When taken to examine the others, she denies that they are hers. There are no fingerprints on the other clocks. They have not been wound up and all point to 4.13.

The dead man is carrying the card of a Mr R. H. Curry of the Metropolis and Provincial Insurance Co. Ltd, 7 Denvers Street, London W2. This means nothing to Miss Pebmarsh. She feels the dead man's face and says that he is no one she knows.

It seems that Lamb works for counter-intelligence, and is on the track of someone he thinks lives at number 61, Wilbraham Crescent. Hardcastle explains to Lamb that there is a number 61, around the back of the Crescent, with the corner touching number 19. It belongs to a builder named Bland who was going bankrupt until his Canadian wife inherited.

The police can find no trace of Mr Curry. The Metropolis and Provincial Insurance Co. Ltd does not exist. Nor does Denvers Street. All they know is that he has been killed with a kitchen knife.

Hardcastle and Lamb visit the neighbours in number 18 and 20 and go around the back to 61, 62 and 63. They draw a blank. Frustrated by the lack of progress – though he had found a Czech coin in the back garden of number 19 – Lamb goes to see his old friend Hercule Poirot who attempts to solve the mystery without leaving his apartment, until driven out by the smell of paint. The building is being redecorated, so Poirot heads for Crowdean.

This story appeared in the *Poirot* TV series in 2011.

Third Girl
London: Collins, The Crime Club, 1966; New York: Dodd, Mead & Co., 1967

Poirot has just finished his *magnum opus* – an analysis of the great writers of detective fiction – when his valet George announces a young lady who wants to consult him about 'a murder she might have committed'. However, when she sees him, she changes her mind, saying he is too old.

Ariadne Oliver phones and invites Poirot over for a cup of chocolate. She had met the girl at a party and had mentioned Poirot to her. Her name is Norma Restarick. She is a 'third girl' in a flat at 67 Borodene Mansions. The first girl is the owner Claudia Reece-Holland, the daughter of an MP; the second is her friend, Frances Cary. However, Norma has now gone missing.

Poirot goes to the village of Long Basing to find Norma's parents and is talking to her stepmother when Norma's boyfriend David Baker turns up looking for her. No one has any idea where she is. Again Poirot employs Mr Goby to do the footwork. One of the porters at Borodene Mansions tells him that Norma fired a revolver in the block. He found drops of blood, but was given £5 by Miss Holland to hush things up. Frances also found a flick-knife in Norma's drawer after a boy got stabbed in a knife fight. Another porter tells Mrs Oliver that a woman fell from the window of number 76, probably a suicide. She also discovers that Miss Holland is the secretary of Norma's father and he was the one who asked her to take his daughter in.

Mrs Oliver tracks down David and Norma to a café. She phones Poirot, who arrives to find Norma alone as if 'lost in a kind of oblivion'. Mrs Oliver has left a note saying that she is following David.

Norma tells Poirot of her tangled relationship with her family and that she suspects her stepmother is being poisoned. But she suddenly takes offence and leaves. Meanwhile, Mrs Oliver follows David to his studio where Frances is posing as a model. After she leaves, she is hit on the head.

Norma too is injured. She steps in front of a car and is now in the care of Dr Stillingfleet, though actually he has kidnapped her. She is full of hallucinogenic drugs. With his 'client' now in safekeeping, Poirot has a free hand in solving the mystery.

This appeared in the *Poirot* TV series in 2008.

Hallowe'en Party

London: Collins, The Crime Club, 1969; New York: Dodd, Mead & Co., 1969

Agatha Christie dedicated this book to P. G. Wodehouse 'whose books and stories have brightened my life for many years. Also to show my pleasure in his having been kind enough to tell me that he enjoys my books.'

Ariadne Oliver is helping to organize a Hallowe'en party for children at the home of the widowed Mrs Rowena Drake at Woodleigh Common. Naturally, the amusement features bobbing for apples. Thirteen-year-old Joyce tells Mrs Oliver that she did not like one of her books because there 'wasn't enough blood in it'. Next, she boasts that she has seen a real murder. Nobody believes her.

When Joyce is found drowned in the bucket they had used for bobbing for apples, Mrs Oliver calls Poirot. He quickly concludes that she was murdered by someone who had 'no time to lose'. Woodleigh Common is Poirot's next destination, where he soon finds he has a roster of murders to investigate.

This appeared in the *Poirot* TV series in 2010 and a graphic novel was published by HarperCollins in 2008.

Elephants Can Remember

London: Collins: The Crime Club, 1972; New York: Dodd, Mead & Co., 1972

Ariadne Oliver is at a literary lunch where she is approached by a Mrs Burton-Cox about her god-daughter Celia Ravenscroft. What she wants to know is whether Celia's mother killed her father or was it the father who killed the mother? Their bodies had been found on top of a cliff. They had been shot, the result of a suicide pact, according to the police. Mrs Oliver thought it rather impertinent of Mrs Burton-Cox to ask and is outraged when she suggests asking Celia.

Mrs Oliver flees to Poirot's. She tells him about Mrs

Burton-Cox and her query. It seems that Celia is going to marry her son Desmond. Mrs Burton-Cox is against the match because of the murder-suicide.

Although Poirot advises her to do nothing, Mrs Oliver decides to look up some 'elephants' – people who knew the circumstances of the death and were unlikely to forget. Naturally, Poirot gets involved. He discovers that Mrs Ravenscroft had been bitten by the family dog a week or two before she died. This is the clue that leads him to unravel the mystery.

But Poirot is nothing if not thorough. He gets Mr Goby to look into the background of Mrs Burton-Cox and discovers a family secret there, too.

This is being filmed for the *Poirot* TV series.

Poirot's Early Cases
London: Collins, The Crime Club, 1974; New York: Dodd, Mead & Co., 1974

Also published as *Hercule Poirot's Early Cases*, this is a collection of Poirot short stories all published in periodicals between 1923 and 1935, and previously anthologized. 'The Affair of the Victory Ball', 'The Adventure of the Clapham Cook', 'The Cornish Mystery', 'The Lemesurier Inheritance', 'The Plymouth Express', 'The Submarine Plans' and 'The Market Basing Mystery' appeared in *The Under Dog and Other Stories* in the US in 1951. 'The Lost Mine', 'The Chocolate Box' and 'The Veiled Lady' appeared in *Poirot Investigates* in 1924. 'The Adventure of Johnnie Waverly' and 'The Third-Floor Flat' appeared in *Three Blind Mice and Other Stories* in the US in 1950. 'The Double Clue', 'Double Sin' and 'Wasps' Nest' appeared in *Double Sin* in the US in 1961. And 'Problem at Sea' and 'How Does Your Garden Grow?' appeared in *The Regatta Mystery and Other Stories* in the US in 1939.

'The Adventure of Johnnie Waverly'
First published in Volume 41, Number 2 of Blue Book *magazine, June 1925*

Mrs Waverly is the daughter of a self-made steel magnate. Her husband is the scion of one of the oldest families in England. They engage Poirot after their son Johnnie has been kidnapped.

Curiously, the kidnappers announced the fact in advance, giving the exact time and date of the abduction in a series of notes. One is even found pinned to Mr Waverly's pillow. While Mrs Waverly is indisposed by a mysterious illness, Mr Waverly fires all the staff he does not trust and calls in the police. At the forecast time of the abduction, a derelict is captured in the gardens carrying a parcel containing chloroform and another note. But the clocks have been tampered with. Then a car with a child in it is seen speeding away from the house and Johnnie is missing. But the car is stopped, the child is not Johnnie.

Poirot quickly works out who the kidnapper is and no further action is taken.

This appeared in the *Poirot* TV series in 1989.

'The Double Clue'
First published in the Sunday Dispatch, *23 September 1928*

Connoisseur Marcus Hardman calls in Poirot when medieval jewellery is stolen from his wall safe. One of the guests at a tea party he showed them to was a Countess Vera Rossakoff. After she had said goodbye he found her gazing into his cabinet of fans. She is trying to sell some of her family jewels via Bernard Parker, a young man who handles commissions for Hardman. Also present were a South African millionaire named Johnston and Lady Runcorn, a middle-aged aristocrat who has a kleptomaniac in the family.

When Poirot examines the safe he finds a man's glove stuck in the hinge. Inside there is a cigarette case with the initials B. P. on it. This is the double clue.

Hastings and Poirot visit Parker, who denies the glove and cigarette case are his. When Poirot threatens to put the matter in the hands of the police, Parker says that he will talk to Hardman. But Countess Rossakoff bursts in and leaps to the defence of Parker. However, Poirot has already recovered the other half of the pair of gloves. Returning to Hardman the following morning, Poirot gives him a piece of paper with the name of the jewel thief on. Hardman tells him not to go to the police, but simply to get the jewels back.

Then Poirot visits Countess Rossakoff, who congratulates him on clearing Parker. Later he explains to Parker how his knowledge of the Russian alphabet allowed him to solve the case.

This appeared in the *Poirot* TV series in 1991.

'The Third-Floor Flat'

First published as 'In the Third Floor Flat' in Volume 106, Number 6 of Detective Story Magazine, *5 January 1929*

Patricia Garnett and three friends get locked out of her flat, so Jimmy Faulkener and Donovan Bailey try to get in using the coal-lift. However, they get out in the wrong flat and stumble around in the dark. Returning to the lift, they alight at the right flat at which point Donovan finds he is covered in blood.

They return to the first flat where they find a dead body hidden behind the curtains and they are just about to call police when Poirot, a neighbour, introduces himself. The apartment is liberally sprinkled with clues and Poirot quickly deduces who had committed the murder, how and why.

This appeared in the *Poirot* TV series in 1989.

'Double Sin'

First published in the Sunday Dispatch, *23 September 1928*

Hastings finds Poirot overworked and persuades him to take a holiday in Ebermouth. After four days, Poirot gets a letter from his friend Joseph Aarons at Charlock Bay, who asks them to visit. Buying their tickets for the bus, Hastings notices a pretty young lady, while Poirot notices an odd young man who is trying to grow a moustache. Both have small suitcases that are stowed by the driver.

Hastings and Poirot talk to the young lady and discover her name is Mary Durrant. She works in an antiques shop with her aunt Elizabeth Penn. They are selling a collection of miniatures to American connoisseur J. Baker Wood for £500.

When the bus stops for lunch, Mary suddenly runs out of the restaurant, explaining on her return that she had seen a man taking a suitcase exactly like hers from the coach. It was the man with the feeble moustache. She claims never to have seen him before.

After checking into the Anchor Hotel in Charlock Bay, Mary claims the miniatures have been stolen. Poirot spots that, while an inner case containing the miniatures has been forced, the suitcase itself has been opened with a key. When they contact Mr Baker Wood, they find that a representative of Mrs Penn has already been there, sold him the miniatures and made off with the £500.

Baker Wood says that the person who sold him the miniatures was a middle-aged woman with a budding moustache. They find the young man with the moustache, but he has an alibi – Poirot knew he would. They return to Ebermouth and, in Elizabeth Penn's antique shop, Poirot delivers his solution to the mystery.

This appeared in the *Poirot* TV series in 1990.

'Wasps' Nest'
First published in the Daily Mail, *20 November 1928*
Poirot visits keen gardener John Harrison. He is investigating a murder – one that has not taken place yet. The topic of conversation turns to a wasps' nest. An acquaintance named Claude Langton is going to destroy it using

petrol rather than with cyanide, which is dangerous stuff to have about the place, Harrison says. However, Poirot had seen the poison book at a chemist's in nearby Barchester where Langton had signed for cyanide. Harrison says that Langton would never dream of using the stuff.

It transpires the Harrison has just got engaged to a young lady who Langton had previously affianced. Harrison insists that Langton has been 'amazingly decent' about it.

Having delivered a warning, Poirot asks what time Langton is coming to kill the wasps. Harrison says nine o'clock. Poirot returns a little before nine to find Langton leaving. Harrison is on the terrace where Poirot discovers that he has prevented not a murder but a suicide.

Christie adapted this story as a television play which was broadcast by the BBC in 1937. It appeared in the *Poirot* TV series in 1991.

'Problem at Sea'
First published in This Week, *12 January 1936*
Poirot is sailing to Egypt. On board are Colonel and Mrs Clapperton. He is a former musical-hall artiste; she the former Lady Carrington. She is overweening and nobody on board would be surprised if he took a hatchet to her. She is then murdered in a locked cabin. Poirot resorts to using a ventriloquist's dummy to expose the killer.

'How Does Your Garden Grow?'
First published in Volume 52, Number 6 of the Ladies Home Journal *in June 1935; in the UK, issue 536 of* Strand Magazine, *August 1935*
Poirot receives a letter from Amelia Barrowby requesting help in a 'delicate family matter'. However, before he can find out more Miss Barrowby dies and Poirot receives another letter, this time from a Mary Delafontaine saying that the matter was of no importance. This piques Poirot's curiosity. He visits Miss Barrowby's house to find that he

is investigating a murder and the clue to the culprit is in the garden.

This formed the basis of an episode of the *Poirot* TV series in 1991.

Curtain: Poirot's Last Case
London: Collins, The Crime Club, 1975; New York: Dodd, Mead & Co., 1975

Agatha Christie had written *Curtain* in the 1940s, but kept it locked away. At the age of eighty-five she realized that her writing career was coming to a close, so she could, at last, kill off Hercule Poirot.

Now a widower, Hastings returns to Styles, which has been converted into a hotel. Poirot has written inviting him there. As an incentive, he has invited the Franklins, the employers of Hastings' daughter Judith, who they have brought with them.

Apparently crippled with arthritis, Poirot is in a wheel-chair, but his hair and moustache are still dyed jet black, though both give the impression of being wigs. However, Poirot is still working as a detective. He wants Hastings to go 'hunting once again' with him. One of the guests at Styles is a murderer. He gives Hastings newspaper cuttings concerning five cases. The culprit – identified by Poirot solely as X – is in the house and there will shortly be a murder. Poirot will not tell Hastings who X is as his honest face would give it away. Nevertheless, Hastings is to be on the lookout for anything suspicious.

Colonel and Mrs Luttrell, the current owners of Styles guesthouse, have a row. The colonel shoots his wife, but she is only injured and it is probably an accident.

While on the prowl, Hastings begins to fear that his daughter Judith had fallen for the womanizer Major Aller-ton. Stephen Norton tells Hastings that Allerton had used his 'technique' on a girl who then committed suicide using veronal. While out bird watching, Norton appears to see something untoward through his binoculars. This provokes Hastings to plan to murder Allerton, but in the morning he thinks better of it.

The semi-invalid Mrs Franklin then dies from the poison physostigmine, which comes from the Calabar beans her research scientist husband, Judith's boss, is working with. The inquest verdict was suicide.

Then Norton is found dead in a locked room with a bullet hole in the middle of his forehead. Poirot gives Hastings one last lesson in how to evaluate evidence, then is found dead of natural causes – though Hastings refuses to believe that Poirot's death is natural. Poirot left some intriguing clues behind, on top of which four months after his death a manuscript arrives. In it, Poirot unravels the entire mystery.

This is being filmed for the *Poirot* TV series.

Life After Death
Thirty-nine years after Hercule Poirot was found dead, Agatha Christie's estate has commissioned crime novelist Sophie Hannah to write another Poirot novel, due to be published in September 2014.

5

THE SLEUTH OF ST MARY MEAD

Jane Marple is thought to have had her genesis in Caroline Sheppard, the sister/housekeeper of Dr Sheppard in *The Murder of Roger Ackroyd*. When playwright Michael Morton adapted the book for the stage, he replaced the character with a young girl. Christie responded by creating the ultimate old maid detective. She was, Christie said, 'the sort of old lady who would have been rather like some of my grandmother's Ealing cronies – old ladies whom I have met in so many villages where I have gone to stay as a girl'.

Miss Marple first appears in 'The Tuesday Night Club' in 1927, where novelist Raymond West introduces his Aunt Jane. She is knitting in a big grandfather chair at the fireside. Her eyes are 'faded blue', her hair snowy white, piled up under a black lace cap. She also wore black lace mittens and a black brocade dress, pinched at the waist, with Mechlin lace cascading down the front. Already she was between sixty-five and seventy, but she would last another fifty years.

However, by *A Pocket Full of Rye* in 1953, Miss Marple has developed into the woman the reader has always had in their mind's eye – 'a tall, elderly lady wearing an old-fashioned tweed coat and shirt, a couple of scarves and a small felt hat with a bird's wing [carrying] a capacious handbag with an aged but good quality suitcase reposed at her feet'. She does, however, continue the knitting throughout.

Along the way, she makes many deft changes of clothing. In *The Murder in the Vicarage*, she wears a very fine Shetland shawl thrown over her head and shoulders, while in *Nemesis* she wears a light tweed skirt, a string of pearls and a small velvet toque. She has a blue enamel watch pinned to the side of her dress and, when visiting the Caribbean, she replaces her stout walking shoes with sandals and plimsolls, which she finds 'not . . . elegant, but suited to the climate and comfortable and roomy for the feet'. Her nephew's wife Joan had induced her to accept a small cheque to purchase suitable clothing for the tropics, but at her age she could not bring herself to buy anything thin. And for evening wear, she adopts 'the best traditions of the provincial gentlewoman of England – grey lace'.

Miss Marple has a 'light spare figure'. Her hair is grey or snow-white, her face pink and crinkled, her teeth 'ladylike' and she rests her head to one side 'like an amiable cockatoo'. Often she carries an umbrella. In 'The Case of the Perfect Maid' her handbag is found to contain 'a handkerchief, an engagement book, an old-fashioned leather purse, two shillings, three pennies, and a striped piece of peppermint rock'. And by *Nemesis*, Miss Marple is a bit more businesslike and carries a small notebook and a Biro.

Miss Marple's health is generally good. However, she spends time at a spa in 'A Christmas Tragedy' and *A Murder is Announced*. By *The Mirror Crack'd from Side to*

Side, we find that stooping, digging and planting are now forbidden, and her gardening activities have been curtailed to a little light pruning. Although her doctor admits that she is a healthy woman for her age, she is 'pulled down a bit by bronchitis'. He also fears that, as an old lady, she might fall down the stairs, fall out of bed or slip in the bath, and needs a companion to keep an eye on her. Indeed, in *The Mirror Crack'd from Side to Side*, she does fall on loose stones while out walking.

She also suffers a bout of pneumonia – at which point Raymond West arranges for someone to look after her. When Miss Marple has recovered sufficiently he sends her to the Caribbean for convalescence. There she boasts that her doctor had told her that her blood pressure was really very good for her age.

The ageing Miss Marple has trouble with her eyesight. In 'The Thumb Mark of St Peter', the doctor has prescribed eye-drops of atropine sulphate. However, in *They Do It with Mirrors*, we hear that 'her long-distance sight was good (as many of her neighbours knew to their cost . . .)'. But ten years later in *The Mirror Crack'd from Side to Side*, Miss Marple complains that even her new spectacles did not seem to do any good. She reflects that 'there came a time when oculists, in spite of their luxurious waiting rooms, the up-to-date instruments, the bright lights they flash in your eyes, and the high fees they charged, couldn't do anything much more for you'. To solve the case, she has to resort to a magnifying glass to read the small print in movie magazines. By her stay *At Bertram's Hotel*, Raymond West suspects that she does not read the books he sends her because her eyes are failing. This, we are told, is wrong. Miss Marple 'had remarkable eyesight for her age'. She does not read them because modern novels are so difficult – 'all about such unpleasant people, doing such very odd things and not, apparently, even enjoying them'.

As to her hearing, in *4.50 from Paddington* (*What Mrs*

McGillicuddy Saw!), she complains that people did not seem to enunciate their words as clearly as they used to.

Although she does what her local GP Dr Haydock advises, she says she has too much experience of life to believe in the infallibility of doctors – 'I have no truck with doctors and their medicines myself.'

She readily admits that she knows nothing about drugs – 'nasty dangerous things I call them. I have got an old recipe of my grandmother's for tansy tea that is worth any amount of your drugs.' Other homespun cures Miss Marple recommends include putting cobwebs on a cut, a linseed poultice on the chest and rubbing in camphorated oil for a bad cough, cowslip wine and camomile tea for over-excitement, and Easton's Syrup which seems to be variously a tonic and a sedative.

It seems that she had begun her career as a detective with the case of Mrs Carruthers' missing gills of pickled shrimps. Before she arrives in the full-length novel *The Murder at the Vicarage* in 1930, she has also applied herself to the theft of Miss Hartnell's opal pin and the churchwarden's separate establishment. Nevertheless she is willing to pit her wits against the likes of Sir Henry Clithering, former commissioner of Scotland Yard, because 'living all these years in St Mary Mead does give one an insight into human nature'. She points out later: 'There is a great deal of wickedness in village life.'

Raymond West says that she is 'hopelessly Victorian'. This means having a mind like a sink. Indeed, Miss Marple, though kindly, thinks the worst of people and is usually right. She remarks how often tittle-tattle is true – nine times out of ten, she reckons.

She is, of course, nosy. The Reverend Leonard Clement, narrator of *The Murder at the Vicarage*, says: 'Miss Marple always sees everything. Gardening is as good as a smoke screen, and the habit of observing birds through powerful glasses can always be turned to account.'

However, there is more to Miss Marple than a collector of village gossip. She says that she was well educated for the standard of her day. She and her sister had a German governess. Along with German, she apparently taught them the dates of the kings and queens of England and general knowledge, though Miss Marple notes in *They Do it With Mirrors* (*Murder with Mirrors*): 'To youth it seems very odd to think that age was once young and pigtailed and struggled with decimals and English literature.' In that book, Miss Marple also mentions that she was at school in Italy. She was then, she says, a 'pink and white English girl from a Cathedral close'. In *The Mirror Crack'd From Side to Side*, she mentions that her uncle was the canon of Chichester Cathedral and she used to stay with him in the cathedral close. Another uncle was canon of Ely.

All we know about her father is that he brought some bronzes back from the Paris Exhibition. When Miss Marple was young, she went to Paris with her mother and grandmother. They were having tea in the Elysée Hotel when her grandmother noticed that she was the only woman wearing a bonnet. When she got home, he packed up all her bonnets and 'beaded mantles' and sent them to a theatrical repertory company.

Miss Marple's mother taught her that a gentlewoman should always be able to control herself in public, however much she may give way in private. Elsewhere she vouchsafes that a 'true lady can neither be shocked nor surprised'. And she inherited a certain *noblesse oblige*. Her mother used to take port-wine jelly and calf's head broth to the sick. Miss Marple, punctilious about etiquette, would not take medicine at meals or blow her nose at the dinner table. And she sits bolt upright because she had been taught to use a back-board as a girl. Miss Marple does not loll. There are standards to maintain.

'When I was a girl,' she tells Inspector Welch in 'Greenshaw's Folly', 'nobody ever mentioned the word stomach.'

As for 'sex', it was not a word much used in Miss Marple's young day though, she remarks, there was plenty of it, even if it was not talked about so much. Back then it had been labelled 'sin'. Miss Marple, Christie said, 'couldn't help feeling that was preferable to what it seemed to be nowadays – a kind of duty'.

Living in the country, Miss Marple had acquired a comprehensive knowledge of rural life – 'plenty of sex, natural and unnatural. Rape, incest and perversions of all kinds.' However, 'she had no urge to talk about, far less to write about them . . .'

Although we only see Miss Marple with her nephew Raymond and his wife Joan, she mentions that, 'in the old days' there were 'big family reunions'. She mentions her Great-Aunt Fanny who told her at the age of sixteen: 'The young people think that old people are fools; but the old people *know* the young people are fools.' There is an Aunt Helen who wore a bonnet and a black poplin mantle, and seems to have been something of an expert on grocery shopping. Another aunt was a forerunner in the detecting game. She could smell when people told a lie. Then there was one aunt who had been shipwrecked on five occasions. And Uncle Henry kept his money hidden behind volumes of sermons in the library. A bachelor, he was a man of unusual self-control whose motto was 'Never display emotion.' He was very fond of flowers. Great-Uncle Thomas was a retired admiral who lived in a large terraced house in Richmond, while her distant cousin, Lady Ethel Merridew lived in Lowndes Square in Belgravia, though her house had later been supplanted by a skyscraper.

Plainly there is money in the family. Miss Marple herself is not rich, but she has never been known to work. Unlike Poirot, she does not hire out her detective skills. She employs a series of maids and, in later years, a companion. However, she takes holidays at the Bertram Hotel and in the Caribbean at the munificence of her nephew

Raymond. And *A Caribbean Mystery* reveals: 'Long experience of nursing made Miss Marple almost automatically straighten the sheet and tuck it under the mattress on her side of the bed.' However, as a spinster, she may also have spent years nursing ailing parents.

Miss Marple also has two cousins, Antony and Gordon. In 'Tape-Measure Murder', she says: 'Whatever Antony did always went right for him, and with poor Gordon it was just the other way about; race horses went lame, and stocks went down, and property depreciated . . .'

Nephew Raymond, the Reverend Leonard Clement says, was a brilliant novelist and had made a name for himself as a poet. His poems had no capital letters in them, which was the essence of modernity, and his books were 'about unpleasant people leading lives of surpassing dullness'. However, he made a lot of money from them. His wife Joan is a modern artist who, during the course of the books, has become rather old-fashioned. (Some fans assume she is Joyce Lemprière and the romance spawned at the Tuesday Night Club.) They have two sons. The younger David works for British Railways and is consulted by Miss Marple in *4.50 from Paddington* (*What Mrs McGillicuddy Saw!*).

Miss Marple keeps pictures of nephews and nieces as babies and children which she proudly shows off in *A Caribbean Mystery*. She also rides of the rescue of her niece Mabel in 'The Thumb Mark of St Peter'.

Although Miss Marple has never been married, there had been romance in the past when she was an eager young girl – 'Such a silly girl in many ways,' she recalls. But cannot remember the name of the unsuitable young man in question. Her mother had, wisely, nipped it in the bud. At the time, she cried herself to sleep for at least a week, but when she came across him years later, she found him quite dreadful.

There was also a young man she met at a croquet party

– 'so nice – rather gay, almost Bohemian in his views'. Nevertheless, he had been warmly welcomed by her father. He was deemed 'suitable', even 'eligible', and invited to the house more than once. In the end, she found him very dull – particularly compared with the man she recalls dancing with in 'The House of Astarte' who was dressed as a brigand chief. He had five kinds of knives and daggers, which made dancing with him 'awkward and uncomfortable'. Nevertheless, in *A Murder is Announced*, she rues that there is no one left who remembers her as a young girl, which leaves her feeling rather lonely.

However, Miss Marple draws comfort from her numerous kind friends, most of whom inhabit the small village of St Mary Mead. In the handy map provided in *The Murder in the Vicarage* there are no more than a dozen houses, including the vicarage, a handful of shops, a church, a station, a pub – the Blue Boar – and the doctor's house where, presumably, he holds his surgery. Nearby there is Gossington Hall, home of Colonel Arthur Bantry and his wife Dolly. By *The Mirror Crack'd from Side to Side* in 1962 it had been bought by faded movie star Marina Gregg. By then the village had changed. There is a bingo club and a new housing estate has been built on the outskirts.

St Mary Mead is about twenty-five miles south of London in the fictional county of Downshire in *The Murder in the Vicarage* and in Radfordshire in *The Body in the Library*. It is midway between Market Basing and the unfortunately named Loomouth, both places that Poirot visits, though sadly the sleuths never meet.

6

MISS MARPLE MYSTERIES

Bored with Poirot, Christie created Miss Marple, although she said that she 'had no intention of continuing her for the rest of my life' and had no idea that she would become a rival to Hercule Poirot. Eventually, the redoubtable Miss Marple appeared in twelve novels and twenty short stories.

The Murder at the Vicarage
London: Collins, The Crime Club, 1930; New York: Dodd, Mead & Co., 1930

At luncheon at the vicarage in the village of St Mary Mead, the vicar remarks that 'anyone who murdered Colonel Protheroe would be doing the world at large a service'.

Protheroe is the village busybody. He wants to go through the church accounts, suspecting embezzlement. He makes a fuss on every conceivable occasion and the vicar's wife, Griselda, says that both his second wife Anne and daughter are fed up with him. His first wife had left him.

Protheroe has also made a 'shemozzle' when he found out that his daughter, Lettice, is sitting for the good-looking young painter Lawrence Redding in her bathing dress. The vicar then finds Redding kissing Anne Protheroe. Redding also says that he hopes the old man will die – 'and good riddance to everyone'. As a magistrate, Colonel Protheroe takes pleasure in sentencing three poachers in one day, earning him fresh enemies. With that, the vicar finds Colonel Protheroe dead in the study in the vicarage, shot through the head. The list of suspects is a long one.

Inspector Slack comes to investigate. While Christie says 'never did a man more determinedly strive to contradict his name', it is Miss Marple – who knows everything that goes on in the village – who unravels the labyrinthine plot and unmasks the murderer. At the same time she exasperates the chief constable, telling him: 'I'm afraid there's a lot of wickedness in this world. A nice honourable upright soldier like you doesn't know about these things, Colonel Melchett.'

The story was adapted for the stage, appearing first at the Playhouse, London, in 1949. The BBC filmed it in the *Miss Marple* series in 1986 and it appeared in the *Marple* TV series in 2004. A graphic novel version was published by HarperCollins in 2008.

The Thirteen Problems
London: Collins, The Crime Club, 1932; New York: published as The Tuesday Club Murders, *Dodd, Mead & Co., 1933*
The book is a collection of thirteen short stories. Miss Marple is entertaining and, naturally, the talk turns to unsolved mysteries. Her guest, the artist Joyce Lemprière, suggests they form a club meeting each Tuesday, where each member presents a mystery for the others to solve. After each of the six sessions, the Tuesday Night Club moves to neighbours Colonel and Mrs Bantry for another six tales. The thirteenth involves a crime that

occurs while club member Sir Henry Clithering is staying with the Bantrys.

'The Tuesday Night Club'

First published in issue 350 the Royal Magazine, *December 1927; in the US, Volume 101, Number 5 of* Detective Story *magazine, 2 June 1928 as 'The Solving Six'*

Once it has been decided to proceed with the Tuesday Night Club, Sir Henry Clithering, a former commissioner of Scotland Yard, is chosen to start things off.

His tale is a simple one. Mr and Mrs Jones, and her companion Miss Clark, sit down to dine on tinned lobster, trifle, bread and cheese. All three are taken ill. Mr Jones and Miss Clark recover; Mrs Jones dies. Botulism is blamed.

A commercial traveller, Mr Jones had been staying in a hotel in Birmingham, returning immediately before supper. However, a chambermaid from a hotel discovers a piece of blotting paper displaying the words: 'Entirely dependent on my wife . . . when she is dead I will . . . and hundreds and thousands . . .'

When Mrs Jones grew ill, the maid Gladys, who had prepared the meal, made a bowl of cornflour to quell her stomach, but Miss Clark, who was otherwise dieting, ate it. Noting this clue, Miss Marple quickly names the culprits. Sir Henry confirms she is correct.

'The Idol House of Astarte'

First published in issue 351 the Royal Magazine, *January 1928; in the US, Volume 101, Number 6 of* Detective Story *magazine, 9 June 1928 as 'The Solving Six and the Evil Hour'*

Next it is the turn of elderly cleric Dr Pender. As a young man, he attended a fancy dress party at the home of Sir Richard Haydon on Dartmoor. Also attending was the notorious beauty Miss Diana Ashley. There are prehistoric relics all around, including a grove that Sir Richard claims belonged to the Phoenician goddess Astarte.

When Diana Ashley appears at the grove, dressed as Astarte and issuing threats against those who defy her, Haydon moves forward, but he stumbles and falls. His cousin Elliot goes to examine him, then calls for a doctor. Sir Richard is dead. He has been stabbed in the heart. But Diana had no knife and was too far away to have touched him.

Elliot insists on going back to the grove to look for the weapon. By then Diana is knocked out by a sleeping draught. In the morning, Elliot is found in the grove, unconscious but still alive, with a bronze knife sticking out of his shoulder.

Again Miss Marple names the killer and Dr Pender confirms she is correct.

'Ingots of Gold'

First published in issue 352 of the Royal Magazine, *February 1928; in the US, Volume 102, Number 1 of* Detective Story *magazine, 16 June 1928, as 'The Solving Six and the Golden Grave'*

Raymond West tells of a mystery that he does not know the answer to. One Whitsun, he was visiting a friend called John Newman, who told him of a treasure ship of the Spanish armada that had foundered on the Serpent Rocks there.

Taking the train to Polperran in Cornwall, where Newman lived, West got talking to an Inspector Badgworth who was investigating the sinking of another ship, the *Otranto*, on those same rocks six months earlier. It had been carrying bullion.

In the local pub, West is warned off by the landlord, Mr Kelvin. The following morning, he sees Newman's gardener hard at work, but Newman himself has gone missing. He is found bound and gagged in a ditch.

He says he had been down at Smugglers' Cove where he noticed men unloading something heavy from a small boat and stashing it in a cave. Suddenly, he had been set upon, transported on a lorry and flung in a ditch.

Inspector Badgworth visits the caves and says that bullion had been stored there, but has since been removed. There are tyre tracks. These match the tyres on the lorry belonging to the publican Mr Kelvin. He is arrested, but witnesses swear that the lorry could not have left the garage.

Sir Henry then names the culprit, while Miss Marple describes how it was done.

'The Blood-Stained Pavement'

First published in issue 353 of the Royal Magazine, *March 1928; in the US, Volume 102, Number 3 of* Detective Story *magazine, 23 June 1928, as 'Drip! Drip!'*

Joyce Lemprière's story also takes place in Cornwall. She was sketching the front of the Polharwith Arms when a man called out to a woman named Carol who he has not seen for year. He then introduced her to his wife Margery.

They talked about bathing. The husband was to take a boat to see some caves. Carol wanted to come too, but was afraid of boats and said she would walk.

Painting that afternoon, Joyce notice two bathing dresses, one scarlet, one dark blue, drying on the balcony and assumed that the bathing party had returned safely. After a bloodthirsty tale by one of the locals, she discovered she had painted something that was not there – bloodstains on the pavement.

The husband came out of the pub to enquire whether Carol had returned after they had bathed together. He called up to his wife, saying she had not. The couple then drove on to Penrithar. Soon after Carol returned and drove off. Later, the papers reported that there had been a bathing accident. Margery Dacre had gone swimming but had not returned. When her body was found, there was a wound to the side of her head as if she had dived into the sea and hit her head on a rock.

Miss Marple, of course, knew what had happened. The

following year, Joyce witnessed a similar scenario and reported the matter to the police.

'Motive v. Opportunity'
First published in issue 354 of the Royal Magazine, *April 1928; in the US, Volume 102, Number 4 of* Detective Story *magazine, 30 June 1928, as 'Where's the Catch?'*
Mr Petherick, a solicitor, tells the story of a wealthy client of his named Simon Clode. After a series of deaths in the family, he took in his two nieces Mary and Grace, and his nephew George. His will would share his estate equally between the three of them.

However, he fell under the thrall of a spiritualist named Mrs Eurydice Spragg, and she and her husband Absalom moved in. Nothing would convince him that they were frauds.

Near to death, Clode called Petherick to draw up a new will, leaving the bulk of his estate to the Spraggs. Clode wrote it out himself and two of the servants witnessed it. Petherick put the signed will in the pocket of his coat, which was taken from him by George Clode when he had tea. Later Mrs Spragg also had access to it.

Then Mr Spragg turned up at Petherick's office where the will was lying on the table. After he left, Petherick sealed the will and put it in the safe.

Two months later, when Simon Clode died, Petherick opened the will to find nothing but a sheet of blank paper.

Miss Marple writes the solution to the mystery on a piece of paper and hands it to the lawyer.

'The Thumb Mark of St Peter'
First published in issue 355 of the Royal Magazine, *May 1928; in the US, Volume 102, Number 4 of* Detective Story *magazine, 7 July 1928*
Now it is the turn of Miss Marple herself. Her story concerns her niece, Mabel. She had been married to a man

named Denman who had a violent temper and a history of insanity in his family. Denman died and there were rumours that she had poisoned him.

Miss Marple went to visit Mabel, finding her living alone with the servants and her father-in-law 'who was not quite right in the head'. She questioned the staff who said that Denman died with the words 'a heap of fish', or something like that, on his lips.

The next morning she was walking along the high street when she saw in the window of a fishmonger's shop some fresh haddock. They had on them black spots that are thought, by tradition, to be the marks of St Peter's thumbs.

Miss Marple then cross-questioned the staff once more about the fish Mr Denman had spoken of as he died. As a result, and using her knowledge of pharmacology, she worked out how Denman had been killed and who had done it.

'The Thumb Mark of St Peter' is scheduled to be filmed in the *Marple* TV series alongside 'Greenshaw's Folly'.

'The Blue Geranium'
First published in issue 272 of the Story-Teller *magazine, December 1929*

A year after the first Tuesday Night Club had run its course, Sir Henry Clithering is staying with Colonel and Mrs Bantry near St Mary Mead. Miss Marple comes to dinner and Colonel Bantry tells a story. It concerns George Pritchard and his wife, an irascible semi-invalid; only Nurse Copling could put up with her tantrums.

One day, when both Mr Pritchard and Nurse Copling were out, Mrs Pritchard was visited by the psychic Zarida who tells her to avoid blue flowers – a blue primrose is a warning, a blue hollyhock means danger and a blue geranium means death.

Soon after, one of the pink primroses on her bedroom

wallpaper turned blue. At the next full moon, one of the hollyhocks turned blue, even though the bedroom door was locked. A month later, the geraniums on the wallpaper had turned blue and Mrs Pritchard was found dead in bed with smelling salts by her hand.

Although she seemed to have died of natural causes, there were some suspicious circumstances. Zarida had completely disappeared and the nurse who was supposed to have recommended her knew nothing of her.

Miss Marple then deduced that Mrs Pritchard had been murdered, who had done it and why the flowers had changed colour.

This appeared in the *Marple* TV series in 2010.

'The Companion'
First published in issue 274 of the Story-Teller *magazine, February 1930, as 'The Resurrection of Amy Durrant'*
Dr Lloyd was out on the Canary Islands where his story is set. Two English ladies, Mary Barton and her companion Amy Durrant, were also holidaying there. On their first day, they went swimming. One drowned; the other was saved. However, an eyewitness said that she had seen Miss Barton holding Miss Durrant's head under water.

Back in England, Miss Barton was staying in Cornwall when she went missing, leaving a note confessing to the murder of Miss Durrant and saying that now she must drown in the sea too. Her clothes were found on the beach. No body was discovered, however she was presumed dead. She had been a rich woman, but she died intestate and her fortune passed to her cousins in Australia.

From the fact that Miss Barton had put on weight, Miss Marple deduces why she had killed her companion and, seemingly, killed herself. Dr Lloyd confirms that she is right.

'The Four Suspects'
First published in issue 276 of the Story-Teller *magazine, April 1930*
Sir Henry Clithering relates a mystery that Scotland
Yard has been unable to solve. It concerns the German
Schwartze Hand gang, a blackmail and terror outfit along
the lines of the *Camorra*. It had been broken up by a Dr
Rosen who, working for the secret service, had penetrated
the gang. In fear of his life, he hid out in a remote cottage
in Somerset.

One morning he was found dead at the bottom of the
stairs. There were four suspects – his servant of forty years
Gertrude, his niece Greta, the gardener Dobbs who had
never been out of the village, and his secretary Charles
Templeton, who was one of Clithering's own men. Somehow the *Schwartze* Hand must have communicated with
one of them, telling them to kill Rosen.

Among the mail that morning was a letter to Dr Rosen
from a 'Georgine', which mentioned a Dr Helmuth Spath,
Edgar Jackson and Amos Perry who had just got back from
Tsingtau. Miss Marple also notes that the word 'Honesty'
in the letter is written with a capital letter.

Dr Rosen did not know who 'Georgine' or 'Georgina'
was and showed the letter to Templeton. Later, when Greta,
who had developed feelings for Templeton, was returning
to Germany, she went to see Clithering to assure him that
Templeton was not guilty.

With her knowledge of gardening and German, Miss
Marple names the guilty party.

'A Christmas Tragedy'
First published in issue 273 of the Story-Teller *magazine, January*
1930, as 'The Hat and the Alibi'
Miss Marple was at Keston Spa Hydro when she first suspected that Mr Sanders intended to kill his wife. They were
on a tram when Mr Sanders, seemingly inadvertently, lost
his balance and knocked Mrs Sanders down the stairs.

However, she was saved by the conductor. There was another 'accident' when they were crossing the street. Miss Marple investigated and found that Mr Sanders would benefit from his wife's will.

Talk in the Hydro is of the porter who died of pneumonia and a housemaid who died of a septic finger. Later when Mr Sanders and Miss Marple go up to the Sanders' room, they find a body lying face down. 'My wife, my wife,' cried Sanders.

Suspicious, Miss Marple stopped him touching her and had the room locked until the police arrived. Sanders, in grief, went out into the grounds.

When the police eventually arrive, Miss Marple notes that a cheap felt hat lay just by Mrs Sanders' head. The hat cupboard was locked. Jewellery was missing and the police surmise that a thief had come in via the fire escape. Mrs Sanders had been playing bridge that evening, leaving at quarter past six after receiving a phone call. From six, Mr Sanders had been with two friends and his time was accounted for up until a quarter to seven when his wife must already have been dead.

It was only when Miss Marple asks the police to try the hat on the corpse to find it does not fit that Miss Marple discovers how the murder had been committed.

'The Herbs of Death'

First published in issue 275 of the Story-Teller *magazine, March 1930*

Mrs Bantry and her husband were staying with Sir Ambrose Bercy when foxglove leaves, picked with the sage, had been used to stuff the ducks they had for dinner. Everyone got ill. But only one, Sir Ambrose's ward Sylvia Keene, died, poisoned by digitalin, the active ingredient of digitalis.

The assembled company then try to figure out if this was a murder. And if so, who had done it?

Among the other guests at Sir Ambrose's table were Jerry Lorimer and Maud Wye. Lorimer had been engaged to

Sylvia for a year. Sir Ambrose opposed the match, but had recently given in. However, Mrs Bantry had seen Lorimer kissing Maud Wye.

When it transpires that Sir Ambrose suffered from a heart condition, Miss Marple solves the mystery and Mrs Bantry confirms that the killer named by Miss Marple later confessed.

'The Affair at the Bungalow'

First published in issue 277 of the Story-Teller *magazine, May 1930*

Actress Jane Helier relates her story, disguising the participants behind false names. She had been on tour when she was called to the police station. A young man had been arrested for burglary. His name was Leslie Faulkener, an unsuccessful playwright who had sent her a play to read. He claimed that he had a letter from her inviting him to visit her at The Bungalow, Riverby.

A parlour maid showed Faulkener in and he met a woman purporting to be Miss Helier. He drank a cocktail and later found himself lying in the road. Arrested, he was charged with stealing jewellery from a bungalow that a City knight had bought to house his mistress, a married actress named Miss Mary Kerr.

The police had been called by a woman calling herself Mary Kerr. She gave a description of a young man who had called at the bungalow that morning; it matched Faulkener. Her maid had refused him admittance, she said, but later they saw him climbing through a window.

The police found that the bungalow had indeed been ransacked, but when Mary Kerr returned she denied making the call to the police. Both she and her maid had been called away on false pretexts, leaving the house locked.

The letter Faulkener had received was not in Jane's handwriting. The jewellery was never recovered and, although the wealthy gent tried to hush things up, his wife got to hear about it. Faulkener was released due to lack of evidence.

Even Miss Marple seems stumped and Jane says that the mystery was never solved. However, as Miss Marple leaves she whispers something in Jane's ear that indicates that she knows the truth.

'Death by Drowning'
First published in issue 462 of Nash's Pall Mall Magazine, *November 1931*

Some time later Sir Henry Clithering is staying with the Bantrys again. A young woman from the village named Rose Emmot is said to have drowned herself after getting pregnant by architect Rex Sandford. Then Miss Marple turns up to tell Sir Henry that Rose had not drowned herself, but was murdered. She writes the name of the killer on a piece of paper and gives it to him.

Sir Henry visits the chief constable and Inspector Drewitt who is investigating the case. A doctor has spotted bruises on Rose's upper arms indicating that she was thrown in. Her screams were heard by twelve-year-old Jimmy Brown.

Rose had a note from Sandford, saying that he would meet her by the bridge. He had a fiancée in London and wanted to ditch her. Rose, too, had an admirer, a local lad named Joe Ellis.

Sandford admits writing the note, but says he did not go to meet Rose. However, he had been out for a walk at the time. The police think that they have enough evidence to get a warrant for his arrest, but Clithering persuades them to interview Ellis first.

He lodges with Mrs Bartlett, a local widow who takes in washing. She says he is good man who takes a pride in his work and never touches a drop of drink. However, he worships Rose, though Mrs Bartlett thought she was a bad lot.

Mrs Bartlett gives Ellis an alibi and Ellis insists that he would have married Rose despite her being pregnant. Then the police interview Jimmy Brown who says he heard someone whistling in the woods and thought it was Joe Ellis, but he was heading away from the bridge. In the dusk, he thought he saw two men with a wheelbarrow.

Sir Henry then consulted the note in his pocket and set off to see Miss Marple, whose local knowledge has ensnared the guilty party.

The Body in the Library

London: Collins, The Crime Club, 1942; New York: Dodd, Mead & Co., 1942

Agatha Christie said that she wrote The Body in the Library at the same time as N or M? 'to keep her fresh to the task'. While N or M? deals with the all-too-real threat of a Nazi invasion, The Body in the Library very consciously visits one of the clichés of detective fiction while Christie revives Miss Marple for the first time in some ten years.

Mrs Dolly Bantry from Thirteen Problems (The Tuesday Club Murders) is awoken one morning by her maid Mary telling her that there is a body in the library. Dolly's husband, Colonel Arthur Bantry, finds this hard to believe but when he goes to investigate he discovers that there is, indeed, a body in the library. While he summons the police to Gossington Hall, Dolly phones Miss Marple because she is 'very good at murders'. She pits her wits against Inspector Slack and Colonel Melchett from Murder in the Vicarage. Sir Henry Clithering makes an appearance and nine-year-old Peter Carmody, a fan of detective stories who has the autographs of Dorothy L. Sayers, Agatha Christie, etc, also collects clues.

The victim is a beautiful young blonde; she has been strangled. No one knows who she is or what she is doing there. However, Miss Marple knows of local resident Basil Blake's penchant for platinum blondes.

A second girl is murdered and Miss Marple sets a trap to catch the killer.

The BBC made a TV version in their *Miss Marple* series in 1984 and the tale also appeared in the *Marple* TV series in 2004.

The Moving Finger
New York: Dodd, Mead & Co., 1942 (also published in the US as The Case of the Moving Finger*); London: Collins, The Crime Club, 1943*

The book is narrated by Jerry Burton who, with his sister Joanna, received an anonymous letter one morning. They are living in Lymstock where Jerry is recovering from a flying accident.

The letter is made up of printed words cut out and stuck on to a sheet of paper. It says that they are not brother and sister, and she is some 'fancy tart'. Jerry tells Dr Griffiths about it on one of his regular visits. Griffiths says that other people have received similar letters. He has had one himself, accusing him of interfering with his lady patients. And solicitor Richard Symmington also had one, accusing him of illicit relations with his lady clerk.

Then Symmington's wife dies, seemingly having committed suicide after receiving a letter saying that one of her two sons was not Symmington's. She drank cyanide kept to kill wasps and a note was found saying: 'I can't go on.' The coroner rules that she killed herself while temporarily insane.

An Inspector Graves is sent from London to investigate. He thinks a middle-aged woman, probably unmarried, is responsible for sending the poison-pen letters. The only clue is that all the envelopes were written on same typewriter, an old device that Mr Symmington had donated to the Women's Institute, so plenty of people have access to it. The typist used only one finger to prevent anyone identifying an individual's distinctive 'touch'.

Symmington's maid Agnes Woddell calls the Burtons' house to speak to their maid, Partridge. Partridge

apologizes to the Burtons for the call, explaining that
Agnes was upset and asks if it is all right to invite her over
for tea. But Agnes does not turn up. Her body is found
in the cupboard under the stairs; she has been killed, it is
assumed, because she knew the identity of the writer of the
poison-pen letters. With the police getting nowhere, the
vicar's wife invites Miss Marple to stay.

The BBC made a TV version in their *Miss Marple* series in
1985, while BBC Radio 4 dramatized it in 2001. It appeared
in the *Marple* TV series in 2006.

A Murder is Announced

*London: Collins, The Crime Club, 1950; New York: Dodd, Mead
& Co., 1950*

On Friday, 29 October, in the personal columns of the *Chipping Cleghorn Gazette* an ad appeared saying: 'A murder is
announced and will take place on Friday, October 29th, at
Little Paddocks at 6.30pm. Friends please accept this, the
only intimation.' It is assumed that this is an invitation to
some sort of 'murder game' party. However, it seems a bit out
of character for Letitia Blacklock, owner of Little Paddocks.
Even Miss Blacklock claims no knowledge of it, dismissing
it as a joke, but she makes provision for guests anyway.

That evening, half the village turns up. At 6.30 p.m., the
lights go out. A door opens. A flashlight plays around the
room and a man's voice says: 'Stick 'em up.'

Then there are two shots. Thrill turns to horror. Someone screams. The figure in the doorway turns. A third shot
rings out and the victim crumples to the ground.

When the lights go back on, blood is pouring from Miss
Blacklock's ear and there is a dead man on the floor. Miss
Blacklock's companion Bunny recognizes him. He is from
the nearby Royal Spa Hotel and had asked Miss Blacklock
for money; she had refused.

Chief Constable Rydesdale thinks that the death is either
an accident or suicide. But Sir Henry Clithering takes

Detective-Inspector Dermot Craddock, who is in charge of the case, for lunch at the Royal Spa Hotel, where Miss Marple happens to be staying. After initially dismissing Miss Marple as 'ga-ga', Craddock is quickly impressed by her reasoning and Rydesdale lets her read the witness statements. She quickly draws different conclusions to those drawn up by everyone else and goes to stay at the vicarage in Chipping Cleghorn to investigate the series of murders that ensue.

A dramatized version of this story was performed live in the *Goodyear Television Playhouse* on NBC in 1956 and it was adapted for the stage, opening at the Vaudeville Theatre, London, in 1977. The BBC made a television version in their *Miss Marple* series in 1985, and BBC Radio 4 broadcast their dramatization in 1999. It appeared in the *Marple* TV series in 2005.

They Do It with Mirrors
London: Collins, The Crime Club, 1952; New York: published as Murder with Mirrors, Dodd, Mead & Co., 1952
Miss Marple is visiting Ruth Van Rydock. She had been at school in Italy with Ruth and her sister Carrie. Ruth had come over from America because she was worried about Carrie who, although she lived in England, Miss Marple had not seen for more than twenty years.

Carrie was an idealist. Her first husband had been wealthy philanthropist Eric Gulbrandsen, who died when she was thirty-two. Her second husband was a playboy who went off with another woman. Then Carrie married Lewis Serrocold, another humanitarian. Together they have turned the country estate Stonygates into a home for juvenile delinquents where, as part of their therapy, inmates write, produce and perform plays.

Miss Marple agrees to go to Stonygates to find out what's wrong. She is met from the train by Edgar Lawson, who she finds 'theatrical'. Later he claims to be

Winston Churchill's son – or the son of Field Marshall Montgomery.

Carrie's stepson Christian Gulbrandsen, who is principal trustee, arrives unexpectedly to inspect Stonygates and talk with Lewis Serrocold. After dinner, Gulbrandsen goes to write a letter. Edgar Lawson comes in distraught, claiming that Lewis Serrocold is conspiring against him. Serrocold takes him into his office. From behind the closed door, they hear Edgar claim that Lewis is his father. There is a row. Edgar says he has a revolver. They hear a shot, perhaps out in the park. Edgar then threatens to murder Lewis. Then they hear two more shots directly behind the locked office door. There is a thud and the sound of sobbing.

They try desperately to unlock the door. Eventually, the door is opened – not by Edgar but by Lewis Serrocold. Edgar lies sobbing. The revolver is on the floor. Then comes news that Christian Gulbrandsen has been shot dead.

This was adapted for the TV in 1985. A second version appeared in the BBC's *Miss Marple* series in 1991 and it appeared in the *Marple* TV series in 2010.

A Pocket Full of Rye
London: Collins, The Crime Club, 1953; New York: Dodd, Mead & Co., 1953

At the offices of Consolidated Investments Trust, glamorous blonde secretary Miss Grosvenor gives her boss Rex Fortescue a cup of tea. He promptly keels over and dies – poisoned with taxine, an alkaloid found in the berries and leaves of the yew tree. However, this is only effective three hours after it has been ingested. Curiously, Fortescue has a pocket full of the cereal rye.

Inspector Neele is intrigued to find that Fortescue lived in Yewtree Lodge in Baydon Heath, some twenty miles from London. He lived with his second wife, Adele, who is much younger than him, his daughter Elaine, his son

Percival, a partner in his father's firm, and Percival's wife, Jennifer, daughter of Rex's former partner in the Blackbird Mine in East Africa.

Adele is 'a sexy piece' and is said to have married Rex for his money. She plays tennis and golf with Mr Vivian Dubois – 'the type that specialized in the young wives of rich and elderly men' – and is an obvious suspect.

Rex Fortescue's younger son, Lance, the black sheep of the family, arrives unexpectedly from Africa with his wife Patricia. He had been summoned by his father who doubted Percival's competence in business. However, Fortescue has not changed his will, so Lance gets nothing.

Then Adele is found dead. She had been eating a scone with honey. Someone had put cyanide in her teacup. Parlour maid Gladys Martin is subsequently found strangled near the washing line with a clothes peg on her nose.

Miss Marple reads of the three murders and takes the train to Baydon Heath. She had trained Gladys in domestic service. She has also noticed that the murders are related to lines in the nursery rhyme 'Sing a Song of Sixpence'.

After the Russians produced a version whose title translates as *The Secret of Blackbirds*, the BBC made their own, using the original title, in their *Miss Marple* series in 1985. It also appeared in *Marple* TV series in 2009.

4.50 from Paddington
London: Collins, The Crime Club, 1957; New York: published as What Mrs McGillicuddy Saw!, Dodd, Mead & Co., 1957

On her way to visit Miss Marple, Mrs McGillicuddy sees a woman being strangled in a train running on an adjacent track. But, as no body is found, no one believes her – except Miss Marple. Together they travel back to London to return on the same train Mrs McGillicuddy travelled on, the 4.50 from Paddington, but to no avail.

Miss Marple's great-nephew David works for British Railways and identifies the only two trains that the murder could have taken place on. From a map and a gazetteer, Miss Marple identifies the only place a body could be removed from the train unobserved before it arrived at a station. It was on the estate of Rutherford Hall, which is owned by the elderly son of a manufacturer called Crackenthorpe. She then employs her old friend, bluestocking Lucy Eyelesbarrow to go to work as a domestic servant at Rutherford Hall, while she takes up residence nearby. Lucy is greeted by Emma Crackenthorpe, the spinster daughter of the owner and lady of the house. There is a big family in residence. Luther Crackenthorpe, now head of the family, thinks that one or other of his sons might bump him off to build on his land. Lucy uses the excuse of golf practice to search the grounds. In a barn she finds an antique sarcophagus. Inside she finds a woman's body. She calls Miss Marple, then the police.

Emma Crackenthorpe cannot identify the body and confides in Dr Quimper, the GP looking after her father. He, too, examines the corpse.

There is speculation that the body is that of Martine, a French girl that may have been married to Edmund Crackenthorpe who had, soon after, been killed in the war. When the police contact the Paris Prefecture, they mention that the particulars given also apply to Russian ballerina Anna Stravinska. Then someone debilitates the whole family with arsenic.

Family friend Lady Stoddart-West then reveals that she is Martine. Edmund died before he could marry her, so she married someone else.

As poison begins to scythe through the Crackenthorpe family. Miss Marple and Mrs McGillicuddy visit Rutherford Hall. The household is assembled for tea. Mrs McGillicuddy makes her excuses and goes to the loo. Meanwhile Miss Marple samples the fish-paste sandwiches. She begins to choke, complaining of a fishbone stuck in her throat. When Mrs McGillicuddy re-emerges, she identifies the person with their hands around Miss Marple's throat, ostensibly trying to help her, as the murderer on the train.

The novel was filmed in 1961 as *Murder She Said* and *Le Crime Est Notre Affaire* in 2008. The BBC broadcast a TV version as part of the *Miss Marple* series in 1987 and it appeared in the *Marple* TV series in 2004.

The Mirror Crack'd from Side to Side

London: Collins, The Crime Club, 1962; New York: published as The Mirror Crack'd, Dodd, Mead & Co., 1963

St Mary Mead has changed and there is a new housing estate called The Development. While taking a walk there, Miss Marple stumbles. Heather Badcock comes running out of her house, helps Miss Marple to her feet and takes her in for a cup of tea. The conversation, naturally, turns to murder and Gossington Hall, where the corpse was found in *The Body in the Library*. The Hall has now been bought by former movie star Marina Gregg and producer Jason Rudd, her fifth husband. Mrs Badcock is a big fan. Years before, Marina Gregg was opening a charity event; although she was ill, Heather put on a lot of make-up and went along. They talked for three minutes and Heather was thrilled to get her autograph.

Marina Gregg's career had faltered when she had a nervous breakdown. Now she is planning a comeback with a film being shot at the nearby studios at Hellingforth and she is hosting a fête for charity at the Hall. Mrs Badcock attends. She reminds Marina Gregg that they met before – at length. Marina's eyes glaze over and the look on her face is likened to the Lady of Shalott. She is looking over Heather's shoulder into the distance at a copy of a Bellini Madonna, where the Virgin Mary holds up the infant.

Mrs Badcock takes a drink and dies. She has been poisoned. Inspector Cornish discovers that Heather spilt her cocktail and Marina gave her hers.

The recently promoted Chief Inspector Dermot Craddock – last seen in *A Murder is Announced* – is called in. Naturally, the first thing he does is visit Miss Marple. He and Cornish soon draw a blank. As they can find no one who had a reason to kill Mrs Badcock, they soon come to the conclusion that the poison was meant for Marina Gregg who had far more enemies.

Although the aged Miss Marple is not even allowed the pleasure of gardening – beyond a little light pruning – she works out who the intended victim was, the motive for the murder and fingers the culprit, who then takes appropriate action, leaving Miss Marple to quote softly from Tennyson's 'The Lady of Shalott'.

A feature film was released in 1980. The BBC produced a TV version in the *Miss Marple* series in 1992 and it appeared in the *Marple* TV series in 2011.

A Caribbean Mystery

London: The Crime Club, 1964; New York: Dodd, Mead & Co., 1965
Following a bout of pneumonia, Miss Marple is convalescing in the Caribbean, courtesy of her nephew Raymond West. Everything is perfect, except that she has to humour ex-colonial bore Major Palgrave. In an attempt to interest her, he turns the topic to murder. Then he pulls out a small photographic print and asks: 'Like to see a picture of a murderer?' He is just about to hand it to her when other people arrive and he slips it back into his wallet and changes the subject.

The following morning Major Palgrave is found dead. Miss Marple is suspicious. She tells the doctor officiating that the major had a picture of hers and she would like it back. However, when he goes through the major's effects, he can't find it.

The major, it seems, had died from high blood pressure and a surfeit of Planter's Punch. A bottle of the blood-pressure medicine Serenite was found in his room. But the

maid, the Rodinesque Victoria Johnson, says that the pills
were not there before. They belong to another guest. She
has seen who put them in the major's bungalow, but before
she can tell anyone she, too, is found dead.

Another of the guests drowns in the creek. To prevent
another murder, Miss Marple co-opts a cantankerous old
millionaire named Rafiel into her investigation.

A US TV movie version was made in 1983. The BBC
produced their adaptation in the *Miss Marple* series and it
is being filmed for the *Marple* TV series.

At Bertram's Hotel

London: Collins, The Crime Club, 1965; New York: Dodd, Mead
& Co., 1966

Miss Marple goes to stay at Bertram's Hotel in the heart
of London's West End. In 1955, the hotel looks just as it
did in 1939. The clientele are much the same. Miss Marple
meets old friend Lady Selina Hazy who seems to recognize
everyone – though many were not the people she thought
they were.

One of the people she does identify correctly is the
famous adventuress Bess Sedgwick. Lady Sedgwick bumps
into Miss Marple as she is alighting from the elevator, takes
one look at the commissionaire, turns around and gets
back in. He had been opening the door for Mrs Carpenter and Elvira Blake who have come to stay with Colonel
Luscombe, Elvira's guardian. Elvira is going to come into a
large sum of money when she is twenty-one.

It transpires that Lady Sedgwick is Elvira's estranged
mother and she once had a romantic attachment in Ireland
with the commissionaire. Elvira pays a flying visit to Ireland, while Lady Sedgwick is having an affair with racing
driver Ladislaus Malinowski. His car is seen regularly
parked outside the hotel. Elvira also sets her cap at him.

Returning to his room, another guest, Canon Pennyfather, is knocked out. The Irish Mail train is held up and

robbed, and a dazed and confused Pennyfather is found near the scene. When he is reported missing from Bertram's Hotel, Chief Inspector Fred Davy takes an interest. He has been called in to tackle a recent spate of large-scale robberies; he investigates and discovers that Lady Sedgwick is a shareholder in Bertram's Hotel.

At the hotel, he recognizes Miss Marple who tells him that there is something wrong with the place. Some of the people aren't 'real'. While they are talking, the commissionaire is shot. Elvira Blake is found beside the body; the gun is Malinowski's. Davy and Miss Marple then join forces to unravel the mystery.

The BBC made a TV version for their *Miss Marple* series in 1987 and it appeared in the *Marple* TV series in 2007.

Nemesis
London: Collins, The Crime Club, 1971; New York: Dodd, Mead & Co., 1971

Miss Marple reads in *The Times* of the death of Jason Rafiel, who helped her out in *A Caribbean Mystery*. He has left her £20,000 if she investigates a 'certain crime' and mentions 'Nemesis', which was what Mr Rafiel called her in the Caribbean. With that, she receives a letter telling her that she will receive a communication from a travel bureau – she has been booked on a lengthy tour of the Famous Houses and Gardens of Great Britain.

On the bus is Elizabeth Temple, the retired headmistress of a school that was endowed by Mr Rafiel. One of her girls was engaged to his son Michael, though they did not marry. The girl died. After being injured in a fall of rocks, Elizabeth calls for Miss Marple and asks her to find out what happened to the girl whose name was Verity Hunt.

Mr Rafiel also wrote to Lavinia Glynne and her two sisters, Clotilde and Anthea Bradbury-Scott, asking them to put Miss Marple up for a couple of nights. It transpires that Clotilde had adopted the daughter of friends who were killed. The girl fell in love with the son of a rich man. This was, of course, Michael Rafiel. She was murdered and he was convicted. Clearly this is the crime that Mr Rafield wants Miss Marple to investigate.

The BBC filmed *Nemesis* in their *Miss Marple* series in 1987 and it appeared in the *Marple* TV series in 2007.

Sleeping Murder
London: The Collins Crime Club, 1976; New York: Dodd, Mead & Co., 1976

Agatha Christie wrote *Sleeping Murder* during the early 1940s, but it was not published until after her death.

Gwenda Reed arrives in Plymouth from New Zealand and finds a house in nearby Dillmouth for herself and her husband Giles who has been delayed on business. However, she momentarily feels an irrational terror on the stairs and fears that the house is haunted. Nevertheless, she goes ahead and buys the house.

She wants the nursery decorated with wallpaper with bunches of poppies and cornflowers and a path laid down through the rockery. It is then discovered that there had been a path there before. Several times she walked into a wall, expecting there to be a door there, only to discover there had indeed been a door there before, but that it had been plastered over. And in a cupboard that had been painted over, there is the exact same wallpaper she wanted for the nursery.

Spooked, she travels to London to visit Raymond West and his wife Joan, who are friends of her husband's. Along with their aunt, Miss Marple, they go to the theatre to see *The Duchess of Malfi*. In the closing scene, the line 'Cover her face; mine eye dazzle; she died young' sends Gwenda fleeing from the auditorium.

Later Gwenda tells Miss Marple that she believes she has heard this line before – said over the body of a woman who

had been strangled as she looked on through the bannis-
ters. The dead woman's name, she thinks, is Helen.

Gwenda tells Miss Marple of the other strange incidents
that have happened since she bought the house. Miss Marple
concludes that she had been there before as a child. Her
husband Giles loves detective stories and when he arrives
in England he is determined to investigate. Miss Marple is
adamant: they should let sleeping murders lie. As it is plain
that the Reeds are not going to do this, Miss Marple heads
to Dillmouth to help investigate a murder that occurred
eighteen years earlier.

This appeared as a two-part episode in the BBC *Miss
Marple* TV series in 1987, a radio play on BBC Radio 4 in
2001 and in the *Marple* TV series in 2006.

Miss Marple's Final Cases and Two Other Stories
London: Collins, The Crime Club, 1979
These six short stories had all appeared previously in col-
lections in the US or in periodicals in the UK. 'Sanctuary'
appeared in *Double Sin* in the US in 1961. 'Strange Jest',
'Tape-Measure Murder', 'The Case of the Caretaker' and
The Case of the Perfect Maid' appeared in *Three Blind Mice*
in the US in 1950. 'Miss Marple Tells a Story' appeared in
The Regatta Mystery and Other Stories in the US in 1939.
The two other stories do not feature Miss Marple. They are
'The Dressmaker's Doll' which appeared in *Double Sin* in
the US in 1961 and 'In a Glass Darkly' which appeared in
The Regatta Mystery and Other Stories.

'Sanctuary'
First published in This Week *magazine in two instalments, 12–19
November 1954*
In Chipping Cleghorn, the vicar's wife 'Bunch' Harmon is
arranging the church flowers when she finds a dying man
who whispers the word: 'Sanctuary'. Then he looks up at

the stained-glass window and murmurs something that sounds like 'Julian' – which is her husband's name.

The doctor has him moved into the vicarage while an ambulance and the police are called. The injured man had been shot. Looking at Bunch, he says 'please – please' and dies.

A Mr and Mrs Eccles phone the police station, saying the dead man is Mrs Eccles' brother. His name is Sandbourne. He had been ill and was in a low state when he walked out of the house, taking a revolver with him.

Mr and Mrs Eccles then turn up at the vicarage. They ask to take the dead man's coat and ask whether he had any letters with him.

While his death is generally considered a suicide, Bunch is not so sure and consults her godmother, Miss Marple. There are too many unanswered questions. Why would a man thinking of committing suicide take a bus out to Chipping Cleghorn to do it? Why would he then drag himself into a church and claim sanctuary? On his watch, there was the inscription: 'To Walter from his father.' But the Eccles called him William. This was a case of murder, Bunch decided, and the two of them set about investigating.

'Strange Jest'

First published as 'A Case of Buried Treasure' in This Week *magazine, 2 November 1941; in the UK, in* Strand Magazine, *1944*

Miss Marple is called in by former Tuesday Night Club member Jane Helier to help her friends Charmain Stroud and Edward Rossiter find some buried treasure. Their Uncle Matthew died recently leaving everything to be divided between them. They thought that he had bought gold bullion and buried it. They have searched everywhere.

With the aid of a hairpin, Miss Marple finds a recipe and some old love letters – as well as the missing treasure.

'Tape-Measure Murder'

First published in This Week *magazine, 16 November 1941*

When Miss Politt brings a new dress to Mrs Spenlow's house for a fitting, she gets no answer. Miss Hartnell, who is passing by, looks through the window and sees Mrs Spenlow is dead. She has been strangled. The police suspect Mr Spenlow as he shows no emotion and is set to inherit. His alibi is that he received a telephone call from Miss Marple summoning him to her house. When he arrived, she was not there. Miss Marple denies making the call, nevertheless she intervenes in the investigation. Again she has to contend with Colonel Melchett and Inspector Slack. But the solution is easy to a woman's eye.

'The Case of the Caretaker'

First published in the Chicago Sunday Tribune, *5 July 1942*

Miss Marple is suffering from post-flu depression, so Dr Haydock gives her the manuscript of a detective story he has been writing. The story is about a young scapegrace named Harry Laxton who got entangled with the tobacconist's daughter and was sent to Africa.

When he returned, he had married an Anglo-French girl named Louise who has money. He has Kingsdean Hall pulled down and a new house built for his bride. However, they are plagued by old Mrs Murgatroyd, caretaker at the old house. To get rid of her, Harry says that he will pay for her to join her son in America. Before she goes, she spooks the horse his wife is riding. Louise Laxton is thrown and killed.

The manuscript stops there, but Miss Marple deduces the ending.

'The Case of the Perfect Maid'

First published in the Chicago Sunday Tribune, *13 September 1942*

The maid Gladys has been sacked after a brooch goes missing, though it was returned as soon as the police were

mentioned. Miss Marple, who believes in the girl's honesty, agrees to have a word with her employers, Emily and
Lavinia Skinner. Emily is bed-bound with some unknown
complaint and Lavinia is one of the few who believe anything is wrong with her.

A visit to the Skinners' did not bear fruit. Gladys is
sacked and replaced by Mary. More jewellery goes missing
and Mary disappears. Miss Marple then reveals the identity
of the real thief, and helpfully supplies the police with their
fingerprints.

'Miss Marple Tells a Story'

*Originally commissioned as a radio play for the BBC, read on air by
Agatha Christie on 11 May 1934*

This is a first-person narrative told by Miss Marple to her
nephew Raymond West and his wife Joan. It concerns
a Mr Rhodes who believes he is about to be arrested for
a murder. His wife has been stabbed to death in a hotel
in nearby Barnchester where they had been occupying
adjoining rooms. When Mr Rhodes looked in on his wife,
a hypochondriac, he found her lying on the bed, stabbed
through the heart. She had been dead for at least an hour.
No one, except Mr Rhodes and the chambermaid, had
entered his wife's room. The chambermaid had no motive
and not one jury would convict. But Miss Marple, without
stirring from her fireside, comes up with another solution.

'The Dressmaker's Doll'

First published in Volume 33, Number 6 of Ellery Queen's Mystery
Magazine, *June 1959*

Dressmakers Sybil Fox and Alicia Coombe have a doll in
their salon which begins to give both the customers and
staff the creeps. They can't remember how long they have
had it, or where it came from. When left on its own, it
moves around by itself. Eventually it seems to want to take
over, and they employ drastic measures to get rid of it.

'In A Glass Darkly'

First published in Volume 94, Number 4 of Collier's Weekly, *28 July 1934*

A house guest at Badgeworthy has a vision of a fair-haired woman being strangled by a man who has a scar down the left side of his face. The woman concerned is another guest in the house who is about to get married. The narrator tells the woman of his vision. She breaks off her engagement and marries the narrator. The jilted fiancé is killed in the First World War. Only later does the narrator discover that he was not the man who he saw in the vision strangling the woman.

7

TOMMY AND TUPPENCE

Tommy and Tuppence Beresford appear in four novels and fourteen short stories between 1922 and 1973. This covers practically their entire adult life, from being young and hopeful after then First World War to being grandparents retiring to the coast long after the Second World War. They are not an attractive couple. When we first meet him, Tommy has red hair, which is slicked back, and a 'pleasantly ugly' face – 'nondescript, yet unmistakably the face of a gentleman and a sportsman'. His redeeming quality is his well-cut suit.

Tuppence, Christie says, has no claim to beauty, even as a youngster. However, there was 'character and charm in the elfin lines of her little face'. Her chin was 'determined', her eyes grey and misty, her eyebrows black and straight. When she first appears, her black hair is bobbed, her skirt short, though shabby, revealing a pair of uncommonly dainty ankles. All in all, Christie says, 'her appearance presented a valiant attempt at smartness'. In action, Tommy is plodding. In the estimation of an adversary: 'He is not very clever, but it is hard to blind his eyes to fact . . .' Tuppence, by contrast, is impetuous. She is always taking off on her own investigations. Although she is frequently wrong, she makes things happen. And while initially down at heel, they are undeniably the 'bright young things' of the 1920s.

The Secret Adversary
London: The Bodley Head, 1922; New York: Dodd, Mead & Co., 1922

Childhood friends Tommy Beresford and Prudence Crowley – aka 'Tuppence' – meet up in London just after the First World War. Now unemployed they decide to become the 'Young Adventurers', taking on any assignment provided the pay is good. A man overhearing their conversation offers Tuppence £100, plus expenses, to go to Paris where she is to pose as an American. However, when she uses the alias Jane Finn – a name Tommy said he overheard the day before – her would-be employer takes fright. The Young Adventurers are taken on by a Mr Carter from the Secret Service. He tells them that Jane Finn was an American, last seen on the *Lusitania* when it was torpedoed in 1915. She was in possession of a draft treaty which, if published, could spark a revolution. Variously aided and hindered by Julius P. Hersheimmer, the millionaire cousin of Jane Finn, and Sir James Peel Eagerton KC, a famous barrister tipped as a future prime minister, they find themselves pitted against a criminal organization headed by a mysterious Mr Brown, who no one has seen, but everyone fears. They are aided by a small lift-boy named Albert, who continues to appear in varying roles in forthcoming Tommy and Tuppence titles.

The Secret Adversary was made into the German silent movie *Die Abenteuer GmbH* (*Adventure Inc*) in 1928. London Weekend Television adapted it for television in 1983 as an introduction to their *Partners in Crime* series.

Partners in Crime
London: Collins, 1929: New York: Dodd, Mead & Co., 1929
This series of short stories feature Tommy Beresford and
Tuppence Crowley from *The Secret Adversary*.

'A Fairy in the Flat'
First published in issue 1652 of the Sketch, *24 September 1924, as*
'Publicity'
Six years on and Tommy and Tuppence are now married.
Mr Carter asks them to take over the International Detective Agency whose manager Theodore Blunt has been
arrested. They are to look out for a letter bearing a Russian
stamp with the number 16 written underneath it. Albert
the lift-boy who helped them in *The Secret Adversary* also
joins the staff.

'A Pot of Tea'
First published in issue 1652 of the Sketch, *24 September 1924, as*
'Publicity'
Tommy and Tuppence jump at the chance to run a detective agency. Both claim to have 'every detective novel that
has been published in the last ten years'. This gives Christie the chance to tackle each case in the style of a different
fictional detective. While fastidious about divorce cases,
Tuppence contrives a way to pull off a successful missing-
person's inquiry for a swain named Lawrence St Vincent,
doing a little matchmaking in the process.

'The Affair of the Pink Pearl'
First published in issue 1653 of the Sketch, *1 October 1924*
Tommy is manhandling a pile of detective novels, saying
that he intends to try different styles and compare the
results. That day he intends to be a 'Thorndyke', after
forensic scientist Dr John Evelyn Thorndyke, the detective
in the work of R. Austin Freeman (1862–1943). However,
as science is not his strong point, he has bought a camera.

A client arrives saying that a precious pink pearl has been stolen from their house guest in Wimbledon. They head for the house. Searching it they find that the bathroom door won't open, giving them a clue to the whereabouts of the pearl. A photograph and fingerprints on the glass plates from Tommy's camera confirm the culprit.

The first three stories appeared as *The Affair of the Pink Pearl*, part of the *Partners in Crime* series made by London Weekend Television in 1983. The series later aired in the US.

'The Adventure of the Sinister Stranger'
First published in issue 1656 of the Sketch, *22 October 1924, as 'The Case of the Sinister Stranger'*

A letter from Russia eventually turns up but, before they can check whether there is a '16' under the stamp, the club-footed Dr Charles Bower arrives. He complains that he has repeatedly been called away from his office by hoax calls, only to return to find his desk has been ransacked. The perpetrator may be looking for his notes on 'certain obscure alkaloids'. Tommy and Tuppence decide to tackle the case in the manner of Francis and Desmond Okewood from *The Man with the Clubfoot* by Valentine Williams (1883–1946).

A Detective Inspector Dymchurch arrives to warn them that Dr Bower might not be what he seems. Tommy is chloroformed and threatened with torture, but tips off Tuppence with a letter signed 'Francis' and she turns up with their old friend Inspector Marriot.

'Finessing the King'
First published in issue 1654 of the Sketch, *8 October 1924*

Bored, Tuppence surveys the personal columns in the newspaper and finds one that reads: 'I should go three hearts. 12 tricks. Ace of Spades. Necessary to finesse the King.' She deduces that this refers to the Three Arts Ball which takes place the following night, '12 tricks' means twelve o'clock midnight and the 'Ace of Spades' refers to a fashionable Bohemian café where people usually go afterwards. But she does not know what 'Necessary to finesse the King' means. They decide to find out, attending the Three Arts Ball in fancy dress – and adopting the guises of detectives Tommy McCarty, an ex-cop, and Dennis Riordan, a former fireman, created by Isabel Ostrander (1885–1924). A woman is stabbed and they discover that 'finesse the king' means murder.

'The Gentleman Dressed in Newspaper'

First published in issue 1654 of the Sketch, *8 October 1924*

Tommy and Tuppence return home after the ball. In the morning, Inspector Marriot arrives with the murdered woman's husband. She had been killed by a man in a costume made out of newspaper. However, Tommy and Tuppence work out that there were two men wearing almost identical costumes and unmask the killer.

The two parts of the story appeared as *Finessing the King* as part of the *Partners in Crime* series made by London Weekend Television in 1983.

'The Case of the Missing Lady'

First published in issue 1655 of the Sketch, *15 October 1924*

The International Detective Agency is visited by famous explorer Gabriel Stavasson. He has just returned from the Arctic to find his fiancée has vanished, and hires Tommy and Tuppence to track her down. Tommy picks up a violin. 'If you must be Sherlock Holmes,' says Tuppence. 'I'll get you a nice little syringe and a bottle labelled cocaine, but for God's sake leave that violin alone.'

The couple trace Stavasson's missing fiancée to a dubious nursing home, where she is strapped to the bed, moaning and injected. But, Tuppence discovers, no crime has been committed.

It was adapted for TV in 1950 as part of the *Nash Airflyte Theater* on CBS. The BBC adapted it for radio in 1953. Then it appeared as part of the *Partners in Crime* TV series made by London Weekend Television in 1984.

'Blindman's Buff'
First published in issue 1661 of the Sketch, *19 November 1924*
Tommy imitates Thornley Colton, the blind detective created by Clinton Holland Stagg (1890–1936). He is then abducted from a restaurant where they are having lunch. But Tommy outsmarts his abductor who falls for the ruse that he really is blind.

'The Man in the Mist'
First published in issue 1662 of the Sketch, *3 December 1924*
Tommy adopts the clerical garb of G. K. Chesterton's Father Brown. The actress Gilda Glen – said to be the most beautiful woman in England and the stupidest – is taken in. She is rumoured to be engaged to Lord Leconbury (see *The Mystery of the Blue Train* above), but a pacifist poet who is enamoured of her threatens to kill her. Then she turns up dead. The murder is, perhaps, glimpsed through the mist.

This appeared as part of the *Partners in Crime* series made by London Weekend Television in 1983.

'The Crackler'
First published in issue 1660 of the Sketch, *19 November 1924, as* '*The Affair of the Forged Notes*'
Tommy and Tuppence are involved in an Edgar Wallace-type adventure, though they concede that to accommodate his oeuvre they will need a larger office. Inspector Marriot turns up and asks them to investigate the number of counterfeit bank notes that are in circulation on both sides of the Channel. The suspect is a Major Laidlaw, a gentleman who is interested in the turf and has a French wife. One of

their friends is Lawrence St Vincent, who the Beresfords know from 'A Pot of Tea'. Tommy calls the person who passes counterfeit notes 'the Crackler' because bank notes crackle.

Mrs Laidlaw is also a suspect. Among her trail of admirers is a wealthy gentleman from Alabama named Hank Ryder. He leads Tommy to the counterfeiters' den in Whitechapel. Tommy marks the entrance with a chalk cross on the door, only to discover that every door in the alley is marked with an identical cross. However, Tommy has also marked the door by spilling a bottle of valerian that attracts cats. This is also the signal that attracts Inspector Marriot.

The story appeared as part of the *Partners in Crime* series made by London Weekend Television in 1984.

'The Sunningdale Mystery'
First published in issue 1657 of the Sketch, *29 October 1924, as 'The Sunninghall Mystery'*
Tommy plays the unnamed old man from the *Old Man in the Corner* by Baroness Emmuska Orczy, who also wrote *The Scarlet Pimpernel*. This leaves Tuppence to play the narrator, journalist Polly Burton. Over lunch, they discuss the 'Sunningdale Mystery', a case that is then in the newspapers. Captain Sessle has been found dead on the links at Sunningdale. He has been stabbed through the heart with a hatpin. The previous day, during a round of golf with his business partner, Sessle had disappeared off the course briefly with a woman, returning alone. After that, it was remarked that his game went to pieces. The police arrested a girl called Doris Evans, who Sessle had picked up. But he had acted so strangely that she fled. Simply from the newspaper cuttings, Tommy and Tuppence work out who really did it.

The story appeared as part of the *Partners in Crime* series made by London Weekend Television in 1983.

'The House of Lurking Death'
First published in issue 1658 of the Sketch, *5 November 1924*
A lovely young woman turns up in the private office of Mr
Blunt. She is of the type that appeared in the books of Alfred
Edward Woodley Mason (1865–1948), so Tommy adopts the
role of Mason's detective, Inspector Gabriel Hanand of the
Sûreté. Her name is Lois Hargreaves and she lives at Thurnly Grange. A week earlier, a box of chocolates appeared in
the post. She did not like chocolate, but the rest of the household who ate them were ill. The doctor said that they contained a non-lethal dose of arsenic. He also said that this had
occurred at other households in the area.

Miss Hargeaves believes that the chocolates had been
sent by someone in the household. The wrapping paper
had been reused and she recognized it. She has inherited
Thurnly Grange from her aunt over nephew, Dennis Radclyffe, who thought he would inherit.

Before Tommy and Tuppence visit Thurnly Grange,
Miss Hargreaves and Captain Radclyffe are killed. This
time it is not arsenic that is responsible.

This appeared as part of the *Partners in Crime* series
made by London Weekend Television in 1983.

'The Unbreakable Alibi'
First published in Holly Leaves, the Christmas special of Illustrated
Sport and Dramatic News, *December 1928*
Mr Montgomery Jones has fallen for a capricious Australian named Una Drake. They have a bet that he cannot
crack two unimpeachable alibis proving that she was in
two different places at the same time. Conscious that he is
not very clever, he brings the case to Tommy, who decides
to crack it as Inspector Joseph French, the creation of Freeman Wills Crofts (1879–1957), who was known for breaking alibis.

According to one alibi, she dined in a restaurant in Soho
alone, went to the Duke's Theatre, and then had supper at

the Savoy with Peter le Marchant. But she was also staying at the Castle Hotel in Torquay, only returning to London on the following morning. Tommy and Tuppence interview witnesses who place Miss Drake both in London and Torquay that night. The Beresfords sleep on it and, in the morning, Tuppence sends a cable and cracks the case.

In the next case, they decide Tuppence will play the part of Roger Sheringham, the talkative detective created by Anthony Berkeley Cox (1893–1971).

The story appeared as part of the *Partners in Crime* series made by London Weekend Television in 1983.

'The Clergyman's Daughter'
First published in issue 226 of The Grand Magazine, *December 1924, as 'The First Wish'*
Monica Deane, the daughter of a deceased rector, arrives at the office. Her aunt has died, leaving her the house. However, there is no money. Rather than sell the building – and there are lucrative offers – she decides to run the place as a guesthouse with the help of her aunt's maid, Crockett, who agrees to stay on. However, paying guests are frightened off by what appears to be a poltergeist. Monica is then contacted by a Dr O'Neill from the Society for Physical Research who wants to buy the place to conduct experiments. But Monica suspects that he is the same man who made an offer previously, in disguise. The house in question is The Red House in Stourton in the Marsh.

'The Red House'
First published in issue 226 of The Grand Magazine, *December 1924, as 'The First Wish'*
Tommy and Tuppence head for Stourton in the Marsh, pretending to be potential buyers. They discover from the local bank that, before she died, Monica's aunt had withdrawn all her money. The bank manager also reveals that Crockett has a nephew. Tommy and Tuppence visit the Red

House where a jug and basin go flying. 'The ghost up to its tricks again,' says Tommy. By a close examination of clues in the aunt's papers, they solve the mystery.

These two stories appeared as *The Case of the Clergyman's Daughter*, part of the *Partners in Crime* series made by London Weekend Television in 1983.

'The Ambassador's Boots'

First published in issue 1659 of the Sketch, *12 November 1924, as* 'The Matter of the Ambassador's Boots'

Tommy is playing Dr Reggie Fortune and Tuppence is Superintendent Bell, the creations of H. C. Baily (1878–1961), when the American ambassador Randolph Wilmott comes to see them. On board ship, his kitbag had somehow got mixed up with that of Senator Ralph Westerham – they both had the same initials. The matter was sorted out when Wilmott's kitbag was sent around to the embassy and exchanged for Westerham's. But when Wilmott phoned Westerham, he denied any mix-up had taken place. Indeed, he had not travelled with a kitbag. However, nothing was missing from Wilmott's bag, which contained mainly boots.

Wilmott's valet confirms the story. However, while unpacking the other bag, before realizing his mistake, he had noticed a tin of bath salts. On board ship, a young lady named Eileen O'Hara had fainted outside Mr Wilmott's cabin and the valet had fetched a doctor. When the Beresfords advertise for her, Cicely March turns up, along with a man with a gun.

An extended version of the story appeared as part of the *Partners in Crime* series made by London Weekend Television in 1983.

'The Man Who Was No. 16'

First published in issue 1663 of the Sketch, *10 December 1924*

Mr Carter tells the Beresfords that the man who devised the No.16 code is on his way. He is the master of disguise.

Carter instructs them on the agent's passwords. They are confident they can handle the situation as they have done well so far using 'the little grey cells'. Back at the office they discover that, although it is only the eleventh, the leaves of the calendar have been torn off, revealing the sixteenth. This is the handiwork of a nurse who had been waiting for them and makes reference to *The Big Four* – Tommy is to be Hercule Poirot and Tuppence is Hastings.

A man calling himself Prince Vladiroffsky turns up. They exchange passwords. The prince says that he assumes Tuppence is the agent Marise and takes her to the Blitz for lunch. Tommy calls Carter; they follow Tuppence to the Blitz where Carter already has his men installed. Tuppence and the prince go up to his suite, but get off at the wrong floor and disappear into the suite of Mrs Cortlandt Van Snyder of Detroit. When Tommy and Carter discover this, they break in to find Mrs Van Snyder bound hand and foot, but there is no sign of Tuppence nor the prince. However, an invalid French lad and a nurse have been seen leaving the hotel.

Tommy goes to Green Park where he uses the little grey cells to work out where Tuppence is and have No.16 arrested.

N or M?

London: Collins, The Crime Club, 1941; New York: Dodd, Mead & Co., 1941

It is the spring of 1940 and Tommy and Tuppence Beresford are frustrated that they are considered too old to contribute to the war effort. A Mr Grant turns up; he has been sent by Mr Carter. Initially he pretends he has a desk job for Tommy but, when Tuppence makes herself scarce, Grant commissions Tommy to combat the Nazi Fifth Column because he is an amateur and not known to the enemy. Already one of their best agents has been killed with the words 'N or M, Song Susie' on his lips. N and M are known Nazi agents. The dead agent had a ticket for Leahampton in his pocket and one of the guesthouses there is called the 'Sans Souci'.

Tommy tells Tuppence that he has some clerical role in the wilds of Scotland. He takes a train to Aberdeen, then heads south again for Leahampton and the Sans Souci – only to find Tuppence already there, posing as a Mrs Blenkensop. She had overheard everything Grant had said. So, hand in hand, Tommy, Tuppence and Agatha Christie lend a shoulder to the war effort.

By the Pricking of My Thumbs
London: Collins, The Crime Club, 1968; New York: Dodd, Mead & Co., 1968

The Beresfords, who we have not met since *N or M?* in 1941, visit Tommy's Aunt Ada in Sunny Ridge old peoples' home. Leaving Tommy with her aunt, Tuppence meets an old lady who is sipping milk, saying: 'It's not poisoned today.'

Her name is Mrs Lancaster. She notices Tuppence looking at the fireplace and says: '. . . was that your poor child?' There is a child, she says, behind the fireplace.

Three weeks later Aunt Ada dies. When they go to collect her effects, Tuppence spots a picture of a pink house next to a canal above the mantelpiece. The picture had recently been given to her by Mrs Lancaster and Tuppence thinks they should give it back. But Mrs Lancaster has left. When Tuppence tries to track her down, she finds the old lady has disappeared completely.

The only clue she has is the picture. Tuppence thinks she has seen the house before and, yearning for adventure, sets off to find it. Eventually, she locates the house. The woman who lives there says that artists often came to paint it and she invites Tuppence in for tea.

The house has been divided and only one half is occupied

currently. A reclusive actress had lived there, but she has not been seen for two years. They hear scratching sounds and squawking – a jackdaw has got down the chimney in the empty half. They go in to find what they think are two dead birds in the fireplace, before Tuppence realizes that one is a child's doll.

Tuppence continues her investigation in the nearby village of Sutton Chancellor. She asks a lot of troubling questions and, when rooting around in the graveyard looking for clues, she is hit over the head. Tommy is then drawn into the investigation.

A French film version was made in 2005 called *Mon Petit Doigt M'a Dit* and the story was rewritten to include Miss Marple for the *Marple* TV series in 2006.

Postern of Fate
London: Collins, The Crime Club, 1973; New York: Dodd, Mead & Co., 1973

Tommy and Tuppence Beresford are moving into the Laurels, a large house in the resort town of Hollowquay. Along with the house comes a collection of books. One of them, *The Black Arrow* by Robert Louis Stevenson, had words in it underlined in red ink. Tuppence quickly works out that if you put together key letters from the words underlined you get: 'Mary Jordan did not die naturaly [sic]. It was one of us.' According to a childish script on the flyleaf, the book has belonged to one Alexander Parkinson.

There is no grave with the name Jordan on it in the local graveyard and no one remembers anyone of that name. Eventually Tuppence finds someone who remembers her grandmother talking about Mary Jordan. She lived in the house with the Parkinsons during the First World War and was involved, in some way, with naval secrets concerning a new submarine. Afterwards, they suspected that Mary Jordan was not her real name.

Tuppence asks aged handyman Isaac Bodlicott about Mary Jordan. He says: 'You mean that German spy girl, don't you?'

Isaac is subsequently murdered and Tuppence leads the investigation into the secrets of the Beresfords' new home.

8

THE OTHER CRIMES OF AGATHA CHRISTIE

Under her own name, Agatha Christie wrote another sixteen novels, numerous short stories and plays, some based on her stories, others later novelized. They feature a number of recurring characters.

Colonel Race appears in four novels. In *The Man in the Brown Suit*, the good-looking ex-soldier is working for MI5, Britain's counterintelligence service. In *Cards on the Table*, he meets Poirot and assists in unmasking the murderer of Mr Shaitana. They meet again in Egypt in *Death on the Nile*. Then he takes over from Poirot as the sleuth in *Sparkling Cyanide*.

Superintendent Battle appears in five novels. He works for Scotland Yard and in *The Secret of Chimneys* and *The Seven Dials Mystery* finds himself embroiled in cases involving international espionage. Battle joins Poirot, Race and Ariadne Oliver in *Cards on the Table*. He makes a cameo appearance at the end of *Murder is Easy* and joins his nephew Inspector James Leach to investigate the murder in *Towards Zero*. He has a wife named Mary and five children. Agatha Christe said she thought that Colin Lamb, Special Branch officer in *The Clocks*, was Battle's son. Poirot thinks that the good superintendent has retired to write his memoirs.

Parker Pyne appears in three collections of short stories. He is not a detective, rather a retired civil servant who hires himself out to solve people's problems.

'I am, if you like to put it that way, a heart specialist,' he says in *Death on the Nile* where he appears alongside Poirot. He also employs Ariadne Oliver and others in his schemes.

Harley Quin appears alongside his old friend Mr Satterthwaite in a series of short stories. Clearly based on the character Harlequin, he mysteriously turns up at key moments to nudge Satterthwaite in the right direction. Various devices are used to make Mr Quin appear dressed in a colourful Harlequin costume, while Satterthwaite is a man of independent means who has no family ties. Satterthwaite also appears alongside Poirot in *Three Act Tragedy* and 'Dead Man's Mirror'. Other books are completely stand-alone and use none of Christie's stock characters.

The Man in the Brown Suit
London: The Bodley Head, 1924; New York: Dodd, Mead & Co., 1924

In a prologue, there is a conversation about a super-criminal called 'the Colonel'. Then the feisty young heroine Anne Beddingfield witnesses the death of a man who falls on the track at Hyde Park Corner Underground station. A man purporting to be a doctor who examines him drops a mysterious note that mentions the *Kilmorden Castle* – a ship, she discovers, that is bound for South Africa. The death in the Underground station is linked to the murder of a beautiful young woman in the country home of Sir

Eustace Pedler. A man wearing a brown suit followed her to the house and returned alone. Deciding to investigate, Anne gets a newspaper magnate to hire her. She then heads for South Africa on the *Kilmorden Castle*. On board is Sir Eustace Pedlar with his sinister secretary, a handsome man with a scar on his face, and Colonel Race. The voyage is not without incident: a man staggers into her cabin, stabbed, and someone tries to throw her overboard.

Outside Cape Town, she is captured by the Colonel's cohorts, but manages to escape. At a hotel near Victoria Falls, she is chased over a cliff, only to be rescued by the man of her dreams. She survives a gunfight, a swim across a crocodile-infested river and an insurrection in Johannesburg before 'the Colonel' is eventually unmasked. According to the *New Statesman*, *The Man in the Brown Suit* was 'remarkable especially for a brand new device for concealing the villain's identity to the very end'.

A TV adaptation was made by Warner Brothers in 1988 and a graphic novel was published by HarperCollins in 2007.

The Secret of Chimneys
London: The Bodley Head, 1925; New York: Dodd, Mead & Co., 1925

Chimneys is a country house near Market Basing where negotiations are going on about British support for the return of the monarchy to the central European country of Herzoslovakia in exchange for certain oil concessions.

In Bulawayo, a posh drifter named Anthony Cade agrees to take the manuscript of the memoirs of the recently deceased former Prime Minister of Herzoslovakia, Count Stylptitch, to London where he is to collect £1,000. He also agrees to return some compromising letters written to a Captain O'Neil by one Virginia Revel.

Mrs Revel, the charming widow of the former British ambassador to Herzoslovakia, is invited to Chimneys.

Meanwhile, Anthony Cade arrives in London where various Herzoslovakian political factions try to deprive him of the memoirs, which are thought to contain embarrassing secrets damaging to the Herzoslovakian monarchy. In one attempt, a waiter named Giuseppe steals the letters instead. He attempts to blackmail Mrs Revel, but the letters, she says, are not hers. Giuseppe is then found dead in Mrs Revel's home; Cade disposes of the body.

When Mrs Revel goes to Chimneys, Cade follows, arriving just at the moment that the heir to the Herzoslovakian throne, Prince Michael Obolovitch, is assassinated. The next in line is Prince Nicholas Obolovitch who has gone missing in the Congo.

Superintendent Battle arrives from Scotland Yard to investigate. He is joined by Monsieur Lemoine of the Sûreté who is on the trail of King Victor, a famous jewel thief. King Victor was in cahoots with the last queen of Herzoslovakia, former Parisian actress Angèle Mory, to steal the crown jewels. It is also thought that a missing jewel – possibly the Kohinoor – is hidden at Chimneys and a clue to its whereabouts might be found in Count Stylptich's memoirs – or, indeed, the letters to Captain O'Neill.

The new king of Herzoslovakia is unmasked and the missing jewel – possibly – found.

Christie adapted the novel for the stage in 1931. A performance at the time was cancelled and it did not appear on stage until 2003 when it premiered in Canada. It appeared as a graphic novel published by HarperCollins in 2007, and numerous changes were made – including the addition of Miss Marple – when it was adapted for the *Marple* TV series in 2010.

The Seven Dials Mystery
London: Collins, 1929; New York: Dodd, Mead & Co., 1929
Chimneys has been rented by Sir Oswald Coote and his wife Lady Maria. One of their young house guests, Gerald

Wade, is a notorious late riser. So the other guests buy eight alarm clocks that are set in his room after he has gone to sleep. They all go off, but fail to wake him. He is dead due to an overdose of chloral. But why would Wade, of all people, need a sleeping draught? Then it is found that there are only seven clocks on the mantelpiece, not eight.

In an unfinished letter to his half-sister Loraine, Gerald Wade tells her to 'forget what I said about the Seven Dials business'.

Returning, Lord Caterham, owner of Chimneys, says he considers Wade's death 'very inconsiderate'. His daughter Lady Eileen Brent, aka Bundle who had also appeared in *The Secret of Chimneys*, finds another man dying. As he expires, he says: 'Seven Dials . . . Tell Jimmy Thesiger.'

With the help of Superintendent Battle, Bill Eversleight and others from *The Secret of Chimneys*, Bundle uncovers the secret of the Seven Dials.

The novel was adapted for TV by London Weekend Television in 1981 and aired in the US as part of the Mobil Showcase the same year.

The Mysterious Mr Quin
London: Collins, 1930; New York: Dodd, Mead & Co., 1930
This book contains twelve short stories featuring Harley Quin, the self-appointed patron saint of lovers, and the sixty-two-year-old Mr Satterthwaite – 'a little bent, dried-up man with a peering face oddly elflike, and an intense and inordinate interest in other people's lives'. The tales were written in the 1920s, however Agatha Christie later wrote two more Mr Quin stories. 'The Harlequin Tea Set' was written in the 1950s and published in *Winter Tales 3*, an anthology published in 1971. And 'The Love Detectives', originally published in *Flynn's Magazine* in the UK in 1926, was published in the *Three Blind Mice* collection in the US in 1950. Both then appeared in *Problem in Pollensa Bay* in the UK in 1991. 'The Harlequin Tea Set' was

included in *The Harlequin Tea Set* published in the US in 1997. The Quin stories all have a supernatural bent.

'The Coming of Mr Quin'

First published in issue 229 of The Grand Magazine *in March 1924 as 'The Passing of Mr Quin'; the first of a six-part series entitled 'The Magic of Mr Quin'. The seventh part 'At the Crossroads' appeared in issue 236 in December 1926 and was later renamed 'The Love Detectives'. First US publication was in* Muncey *magazine of March 1925 as 'Mr Quinn Passes By'.*

Mr Satterthwaite is at a New Year's Eve party at Royston. Also present are Alex Portal and his unconvincing Australian wife who has dyed her fair hair black. The conversation turns to Derek Capel, the previous owner of the house who shot himself.

A dark man appears at the front door, although the stained glass above the door makes him appear as if he is dressed in every colour of the rainbow. His car has broken down and he is invited in. He introduces himself as Harley Quin, who always seems to turn up when trouble is brewing or there is a problem to be solved. He had known Mr Chapel, and his skilful questioning of the guests reveals why Chapel had killed himself, to the evident relief of two of the guests.

The story was made into the British movie *The Passing of Mr Quin*.

'The Shadow on the Glass'

First published in issue 236 of The Grand Magazine, *October 1924*

Mr Satterthwaite goes to a party at a house that is supposed to be haunted by a cavalier who was killed by his wife's roundhead lover. As the guilty couple fled, they looked back to see the dead husband watching them from an upstairs window. His face now appears as a flaw in the glass, no matter how many times the window is replaced.

Other house guests include big-game hunter Richard

Scott, his young wife, his former lover Mrs Staverton and Captain Allenson. Allenson and Mrs Scott are found shot dead in the garden under the ghostly window. Beside them Mrs Staverton is found holding a gun. Mr Quin turns up. He notices a spot of blood on Mrs Scott's ear, as if her earring had been torn out. Mr Quin's deft questioning leads to a startling conclusion.

'At the Bells and Motley'

First published in issue 249 of The Grand Magazine, *November 1925, as 'A Man of Magic'; first UK publication in* Flynn's Weekly, *17 July 1926*

Mr Satterthwaite's car breaks down in the village of Kirtlington Mallet and he seeks refuge in the local pub, the Bells and Motley. (This curious pub name comes up throughout Christie's canon.) Mr Quin is there. Kirtlington Mallet is the centre of a mystery. Eleanor Le Couteau, a French-Canadian collector of relics and antiques, has bought nearby Ashley Grange. She had fallen for Captain Richard Harwell and they married. They returned from their honeymoon and, the following morning, Captain Harwell disappeared.

While no body was found, it was thought he had been murdered. Suspects include Stephen Grant, who had tended Harwell's horse, and the rheumatic gardener John Mathias. The police could uncover no antecedents for Harwell and assumed he was an impostor, but he had not taken a penny of his wife's money. Mrs Harwell then sold Ashley Grange with all its contents and Mathias and his wife moved on. This leaves Satterthwaite and Quin to unravel the mystery.

'The Sign in the Sky'

First published in issue 249 of The Grand Magazine, *November 1925, as 'A Sign in the Sky'*

Mr Satterthwaite attends the trial of Martin Wylde for the murder of Lady Vivien Barnaby at her home Deering Hill.

He is found guilty. Satterthwaite then runs into Mr Quin whose perceptive questions cast doubt on the verdict. All the witness testimonies at the trial are consistent, although one housemaid who testified has since gone to Canada. Quin also notes that the telephone was out of order. Satterthwaite remains convinced that Wylde is guilty, but is persuaded to go to Canada to track down the maid. When he finds her, she has no doubt that Wylde is guilty. White smoke from a passing train made an ominous sign in the sky. When he tells this to Quin back in London, Quin shows Satterthwaite that it is the evidence that proves Wylde is innocent.

'The Soul of the Croupier'

First published in issue 237 of the Story-Teller *magazine, January 1927; first UK publication in* Flynn's Magazine, *13 November 1926*
In Monte Carlo, Satterthwaite finds himself in the middle of a love triangle between the sophisticated, but ageing Countess Czarnova, young American Franklin Rudge and the ingénue Elizabeth Martin. Quin arrives. At the casino, they witness the Countess Czarnova stun rivals by arriving wearing no jewels. She then bets on six, while Satterthwaite puts his last stake on five.

Five wins, but the croupier hands Satterthwaite's winnings to the countess; Satterthwaite is too much of a gentleman to protest. Later, at a supper hosted by Quin, Rudge turns up with the countess, followed by the croupier. At Satterthwaite's prompting, the croupier tells his life story and the love triangle is broken.

'The World's End'

First published in issue 238 of the Story-Teller *magazine, February 1927, as 'World's End'; first UK publication in* Flynn's Magazine, *20 November 1926*
Mr Satterthwaite is on Corsica with the Duchess of Leith. They meet the duchess's first cousin, artist Naomi Carlton Smith. She had been involved with a writer who had

been jailed for stealing someone's jewels. They head off on a tour of the island. Naomi takes them to Côte Chiaveeri, which she calls 'the World's End'. Here, sitting on a boulder, is Mr Quin.

It starts to snow and they take shelter in a snack bar where they meet the famous actress Rosina Nunn. She is absent-minded and, once, almost lost her pearls. But they were insured, unlike an opal that she says was stolen by playwright Alec Gerard. Satterthwaite and Quin find the opal and Naomi reveals that Gerard is her fiancé.

'The Voice in the Dark'

First published in issue 239 of the Story-Teller *magazine, March 1927; first UK publication in* Flynn's Magazine, *4 December 1926*

In Cannes, Lady Stranleigh tells Mr Satterthwaite that she is worried about her daughter, Margery, who had been seeing, or rather hearing, ghosts in the family home at Abbot's Mede. She asks Satterthwaite, who is returning to England, to investigate. On the train home, he meets Mr Quin. They discuss the case. Apparently Lady Stranleigh had only inherited the title and the family fortune because her sister, Beatrice, drowned sometime before when the *Uralia* sank. Quin says he will not join Satterthwaite on the case, but he will be nearby in the Bells and Motley.

At Abbot's Mede, Margery says that at night, she hears the words: 'Give back what is not yours. Give back what you have stolen.' But when she switches on the lights, there is no one there. She became so frightened that she got her mother's maid, Clayton, to sleep on a sofa in her room. Clayton had also been on board the *Uralia* when it sank and had been hit on the head by a spar.

Lady Stranleigh then receives a poisoned box of chocolates, ostensibly from Margery, though she denies sending them. A medium is called in who contacts Beatrice. Satterthwaite asks her a question only the two of them will know the answer to. The spirit voice gets the answer right.

Another house guest, Roley Vavasour, who would inherit if Margery and her mother died, has asked Margery to marry him. She declines.

Satterthwaite leaves Abbot's Mede and Lady Stranleigh returns, only to drown in her bath. Satterthwaite immediately consults Mr Quin at the Bells and Motley. Hearing the details, he refuses to help, saying that Satterthwaite can solve the case himself.

'The Face of Helen'

First published in issue 240 of the Story-Teller *magazine, April 1927;*
first UK publication in Detective Story Magazine, *6 August 1927*

Mr Satterthwaite attends a performance of *Pagliacci* at Covent Garden where he meets Mr Quin. They see a girl beautiful enough to be compared with Helen of Troy. Afterwards Quin declines a lift and Satterthwaite alone rescues the girl when two suitors come to blows in the street. The following Sunday, he sees her with one of her beaux. They have just become engaged.

At tea with the girl, Satterthwaite finds that the other suitor has given her a wireless and a beautiful glass ball as wedding presents. By chance, Satterthwaite meets the rejected lover and they discuss what he did in the war. Consulting the radio schedule in the newspaper, Satterthwaite suddenly realizes that the girl is in terrible danger.

'The Dead Harlequin'

First published in the UK in Volume 42, Number 3 of Detective Fiction Weekly, *22 June 1929*

Mr Satterthwaite buys a painting called 'The Dead Harlequin'. It depicts a dead Harlequin with a second one looking at him through the window. Both look like Mr Quin and the setting appears to be the Terrace Room at Charnley, the home of Lord Charnley who shot himself fourteen years earlier.

Satterthwaite invites the artist Frank Bristow to dinner. His other guest is Colonel Monckton, though a fourth place has been laid. Monckton says that the ghost of Charles I walks up and down the terrace, followed by a weeping woman with a silver ewer. Monckton was there the night Lord Charnley died – it was a fancy-dress ball thrown to celebrate his return from his honeymoon with his young bride Alix.

Monckton reveals that Charnley died, not in the Terrace Room where there was a red carpet on the floor, but in the Oak Parlour. There was a priest's hole there where Charles I was once supposed to have hidden. It was also a former duelling room with many bullets in the walls. Satterthwaite and Bristow begin to doubt that Lord Charnley's death was suicide, so Monckton relates the tale. Before Charnley died, a guest called out to him, but he took no notice. He then went into the Oak Parlour where he died. The door was locked and when he was discovered there was surprisingly little blood on the floor. No one benefited from his death, except Charnley's unborn child whose claim to the title trumped that of Charnley's brother Hugo. An actress named Aspasia Glen arrives at Satterthwaite's. She wants to buy the painting. Then Alix Charnley phones, also wanting the painting. Satterthwaite allows Alix to have it, pretending it is a gift. He then introduces Miss Glen to Harley Quin, who has now arrived, Frank Bristow and Colonel Monckton. When Lady Charnley arrives, Satterthwaite reveals that Lord Charnley had been murdered and the killers are unmasked.

'The Bird with the Broken Wing'
This was the first publication of this story.
Satterthwaite has refused an invitation to a house party at the home of David Keeley, an uncharismatic mathematician. But at a séance, the words QUIN and LAIDELL are spelt out, and he changes his mind. At dinner at the

Keeleys', he meets a woman he immediately thinks of as 'the bird with the broken wing'. This is Mabelle Annesley whose life has been dogged by tragedy.

Later Satterthwaite sees a figure in the moonlight playing the ukulele. When he approaches it is Mabelle. She says that she thought she saw a man who looked like a harlequin in the woods. Her husband then calls Mabelle inside to play for the guests.

When everyone is turning in, Mabelle goes back downstairs to get her ukulele. In the morning, she is found hanged. Inspector Winkfield turns up to investigate. Satterthwaite is convinced that Mabelle's death was not suicide, but murder – because he had received a message from Mr Quin. The clue to the murderer is found in the ukulele, which is no longer in tune.

'The Man From the Sea'

First published in Volume 1, Number 6 of Britannia and Eve *magazine, October 1929*

Now sixty-nine, Satterthwaite is holidaying on a sunny island. Near a lonely villa he meets a young man who says that, the previous evening, he had encountered someone dressed as a Harlequin there. He had appeared almost instantaneously, as if he had risen from the sea. This was impossible as they were on the top of a sheer cliff. The man's name was Anthony Cosden. He had been told that he had six months to live. He had visited the island years before as a youngster and he had returned to kill himself there – only to be thwarted the previous evening by the Harlequin, then again that day by Satterthwaite.

Visiting the nearby villa, Satterthwaite finds it occupied by an English woman. Over tea, she says that she is a widow. Long ago her abusive husband had drowned at the foot of the cliffs. In her grief, she had a brief affair with a young Englishman. She had a baby nine months later. Her grown-up son is now about to marry. Now he and his fiancée's parents want to know about his father. The truth would ruin his life, so she has decided to kill herself.

Satterthwaite asks her to stay her hand for twenty-four hours and to leave her shutters open that night. When Satterthwaite meets Cosden again, he expresses an interest in the villa. Satterthwaite tells him to go there that night and try the shutters. The following morning, Satterthwaite visits the villa to find the lady and Cosden together. They are to marry. At the clifftop, Satterthwaite finds Quin, who disappears the way he has come.

'Harlequin's Lane'

First published in issue 241 of the Story-Teller *magazine, May 1927; first UK publication in* Detective Fiction Weekly, *22 June 1929*

Mr Satterthwaite goes to stay with the Denmans. Mr Denman had been in Russia during the Bolshevik revolution and escaped with a penniless refugee, whom he then married. Their house is in Harlequin's Lane and Satterthwaite is not surprised to find Mr Quin there. He says that the locals call Harlequin's Lane, Lover's Lane. It ends in a rubbish heap.

The Denmans are rehearsing for a Harlequinade with locals playing the parts, though two professional dancers had been employed to play Harlequin and Columbine. Mrs Denman had been a dancer before she was married and the conversation turns to Kharsanova, a dancer who was 'destroyed ignorantly and wantonly in the first days of the Revolution'. The professional dancers were being brought by Prince Oranoff, who Mrs Denham knew in Russia. However, he has a car accident on the way and the two dancers are injured. So Mrs Denman takes the part of Columbine. From her dancing, Satterthwaite recognizes that Mrs Denman is Kharsanova. She had given up dancing at the insistence of her husband. Now she intends to elope with Prince Oranoff, but is found dead on the rubbish heap.

The Sittaford Mystery
London: Collins, The Crime Club, 1931; New York: published as
Murder at Hazelmoor, Dodd, Mead & Co., 1932

The snow lies deep on Dartmoor. In the remote village of
Sittaford, Major Burnaby braves the weather to visit Mrs
Willet and her daughter Violet at the house they are renting
from Captain Joseph Trevelyan RN, who himself is renting a small house six miles away in Exhampton. Burnaby
and Trevelyan are old friends, both keen sportsmen. They
tackle newspaper competitions together and walk the
twelve miles from Sittaford to Exhampton and back to visit
each other.

Others turn up and they have a séance. Trevelyan is
absent and a message comes through for Major Burnaby,
saying 'Trevelyan is dead', then 'murder'. It is 5.25 p.m.

Although a declared sceptic, Major Burnaby decides to
walk to Trevelyan's as there is no phone. Two-and-a-half
hours later, Burnaby arrives at the door of 'Hazelmoor',
the house Trevelyan is renting. He does not answer the
door, so Burnaby fetches the police. When they return to
Hazelmoor, they find Trevelyan has been bludgeoned to
death with a sandbag. The doctor confirms that he was
killed around 5.25 p.m.

Inspector Narracott investigates the killing. There are
a number of beneficiaries of the will, including Trevelyan's nephew John Pearson, who was in Exhampton on
the night of the murder. Narracott is also puzzled why
Mrs Willett and her daughter, who are from South Africa,
are renting the house on Dartmoor in the middle of the
winter.

Charles Enderby of the *Daily Wire* arrives to give Burnaby a cheque for £5,000 for winning the newspaper's foot-
ball competition. He decides to cover the case.

Narracott tracks down Pearson in London and he is
later arrested. But his fiancée is Emily Trefusis and she
joins Enderby on his investigations. Things look black

for Pearson when it is discovered that he used his firm's money to speculate. Then it is discovered he travelled to Devonshire to ask for help from his uncle, who refused him. But when Emily finds a pair of ski boots hidden in the chimney at Hazelmoor and two pairs of skis of different sizes, she solves the mystery and uncovers the real killer.

This story was adapted to accommodate Miss Marple and appeared in the *Marple* TV series in 2006.

The Hound of Death and Other Stories
London: Odhams Press, 1933
This collection of twelve Agatha Christie stories was not sold in the shops. Instead it could be purchased with coupons collected from the *Passing Show* magazine, issues 81–83, 7–21 October 1933, as a promotion for the relaunch of the publication.

'The Hound of Death'
This was the first publication of this tale.
A young Englishman named Anstruther is having dinner with William P. Ryan, an American war correspondent who had been in Belgium during the First World War. When the Germans arrived and entered a convent, the building blew up, though they did not seem to have high explosives with them. The blast left a black powder mark the shape of a terrifying hound which the local peasants called the Hound of Death.

Anstruther goes to visit his sister in Cornwall. During the war she had taken in Belgian refugees. A Belgian nun named Sister Marie Angelique is still in the vicinity. She has hallucinations and is being studied by the wolf-like Dr Rose. When Anstruther meets her, she seems to confirm that she came from the convent that was destroyed. But then she talks of the 'City of Circles' and the 'House of Crystal'. He then becomes suspicious of Dr Rose's

interest in the nun. She talks of the power of destruction
and associates the word 'hound' with 'death'. Later a letter
comes from Marie Angelique, saying that Dr Rose is 'of
the Brotherhood'. Then Anstruther gets a letter from his
sister telling him that Dr Rose's cliff-top cottage has been
swept away by a landslide, killing both him and Sister
Marie Angelique. The debris, from a distance, looks like a
giant hound.

'The Red Signal'

First published in issue 232 of The Grand Magazine, *June 1924*
Jack and Claire Trent are having a dinner party. Among
the guests are the psychiatrist Sir Alington West and his
nephew Dermot. Sir Alington dismisses the idea of pre-
monitions, while Dermot insists that one saved his life in
Mesopotamia. It was an example of what he called 'the red
signal'. What he does not reveal is that he is having a red
signal that night.

The danger lies, he thinks, in the fact that he is in love
with Claire Trent, while her husband Jack is his best friend.

After dinner, a medium arrives to hold a séance. Her
spirit guide warns one of the gentlemen not to go home. Sir
Alington has a private word with Dermot and warns him
off Mrs Trent who may be a homicidal maniac. Their alter-
cation is overheard. Dermot then goes to the Grafton Gal-
leries where he meets up with Claire again. She confesses
that she cares for him, but wants him to go away.

Returning to his flat he is overwhelmed by the red signal
again and finds a revolver in his drawer. The police arrive
to arrest him for the murder of Sir Alington, who had been
shot dead. Dermot pretends to be his own manservant and
escapes, but immediately bumps into Jack Trent who takes
him home – where Dermot discovers that the warning at
the séance was not just for Sir Alington and himself, but
for Jack Trent too.

'The Fourth Man'
First published in issue 250 of The Grand Magazine, *December 1925*
Four men occupy the same compartment on a train. Three
of them – a canon, a lawyer and a psychiatrist – fall into
conversation. The fourth man appears to be asleep. They
discuss the case of Felicie Bault, an orphan from Brittany
who, at the age of twenty-two, developed three or four
separate personalities. One morning she was found dead.
The marks around her neck proved she had strangled
herself.

The fourth man then awakes and explains everything,
before mysteriously disappearing.

'The Gipsy'
This was the first publication of this story.
Dickie Carpenter has a life-long aversion to gipsies. In his
nightmares, he sees a gipsy woman with a red handkerchief over her head. At dinner at the Lawes', he meets Mrs
Haworth who wears a red scarf. In the garden, she warns
him not to go back into the house. When he does, he is
immediately smitten with young Esther Lawes; they get
engaged.

Next time he sees Mrs Haworth, she is wearing a red
tam-o'-shanter. Again she warns him not to go back into
the house. When he does, Esther tells him that she does not
care for him.

Carpenter relates this to his friend Macfarlane. Now he
is going to have an operation. Mrs Haworth has warned
him not to.

Macfarlane goes in search of Mrs Haworth who lives on
the moors. He tells her that Carpenter had died during the
operation. She denies giving Carpenter the warning. She
then demonstrates that Macfarlane has the gift of second
sight. Her husband, she says, has it too.

Returning to the house the following day, Macfarlane is
told that Mrs Haworth is dead, accidentally poisoned by

her husband. Later he is told that the sailor and the gipsy who lived on the moor were only ghosts.

'The Lamp'
This was the first publication of this tale.
Mrs Lancaster takes a house in a cathedral town. The rent is low because it is supposed to be haunted. The ghost is that of a child who starved to death after his father, who had told him not to speak to anyone when left in the house, was arrested.

Not believing in ghosts, Mrs Lancaster moves in with her father, Mr Winburn, and her young son Geoff. They begin to hear footsteps and Winburn has bad dreams. The housemaid says she thought she heard Master Geoffrey crying, though he appears perfectly happy.

Geoff then asks his mother whether he can play with the little boy he has seen sitting on the floor in the attic crying. Mrs Lancaster says that there is no little boy. However, Windburn encourages him. Geoffrey then falls ill and talks of the little boy in his delirium.

With his dying breath, Geoffrey says: 'I'm coming.'

Mrs Lancaster hears laughter and two sets of footsteps.

'Wireless'
First published in Sunday Chronicle Annual, *December 1926*
Mrs Harter is ill with a heart condition. Her doctor says that she will survive if she avoids exertion. To keep her amused, her nephew Charles Ridgeway provides a radio set. She gets to like it and has her will altered in Charles' favour.

After three months though, she begins to hear the voice of her dead husband Patrick. He tells her he is coming for her. Eventually he gives a time and a date. She was found dead an hour later. However, as she died, her will had slipped from her hand into the open fire, so Charles gets nothing.

'The Witness for the Prosecution'
First published in the US in Volume 4, Number 2 of Flynn's Weekly,
31 January 1925, as 'The Traitor Hands'
A solicitor named Mayherne is talking to his client Leonard
Vole, who has been charged with murder. Vole had met an
old lady named Emily French in Oxford Street when she
had dropped some parcels and he had picked them up. They
became friends and he gave her financial advice. He went on
to become the principal beneficiary in her will. And while
he claimed he knew nothing of it, the maid said he did.

At half past nine on the night of the murder, the maid
heard voices in the sitting room – Miss French's and a
man's. Vole says he is saved. At half past nine he was at
home with his wife Romaine, an actress from Austria. It
transpires that Miss French had been killed by a blow from
a crowbar. The maid also said that Vole had pretended to
be single and Miss French intended to marry him.

When Mayherne visits Romaine Vole, she refuses to support her husband's alibi. She says she hates him and wants
to see him hanged. When told that she cannot be forced to
give evidence against her husband, she says that back in
Vienna she has a husband in a madhouse so she and Vole
could not marry. She intends to appear as a witness for the
prosecution.

On the eve of the trial, Mayherne receives a scrawled
note saying that, if he wants to paint Romaine as a lying
hussy, he should visit a Mrs Mogson at an address in Stepney with £200. There an old hag gives him bundle of love
letters from Romaine to another man, one from the date of
Leonard's arrest.

In court, the letters are used to undermine Romaine's
damning testimony. But Mayherne notices that she had a
habit of clenching and unclenching her hand, exactly like
the hag in Stepney. Then there are more twists and turns.

Christie changed the ending for the stage version which
opened at the Winter Garden Theatre, London, in 1953,

and the Henry Miller Theater, New York, in 1954. It was filmed in 1957. There were TV versions in 1949 and 1982.

'The Mystery of the Blue Jar'

First published in issue 233 of The Grand Magazine, *July 1924*

A keen golfer, Jack Hartington is staying at a small hotel near Stourton Heath links. He is out practising when he hears a woman's voice crying: 'Murder. Help! Murder!'

At a cottage easily within earshot, a girl denies hearing the cry. She asks whether he is suffering from shell-shock.

The following day, Hartington hears the same cry. Again the girl denies hearing it. On the third day, he hears the cry again coming from somewhere near the cottage.

Hartington then comes across a Harley Street specialist named Lavington, who he invites to join him in a round of golf. Again Jack hears the cry of murder, but Lavington does not react. He says Hartington may be suffering from acute stress, but agrees to check out the cottage, reporting back later that some mystery surrounds it.

Then the girl turns up at his hotel. She says that she has heard the same cry of 'Murder. Help! Murder!' but in a dream. It came from a woman holding a blue jar. From the girl's sketch, Lavington identifies it as of Chinese origin. Hartington's uncle, a collector, has recently acquired such a jar.

While Hartington's uncle is away, the girl persuades Hartington to bring the jar to the cottage to spend the night there. Jack awakes the following afternoon in a copse nearby. His uncle turns up and says that the blue jar is a priceless Ming. A note left by Lavington at the hotel explains the mystery.

'The Strange Case of Sir Arthur Carmichael'

This was the first publication of this story.

Dr Edward Carstairs is called to attend the case of Sir Arthur Carmichael, the son of Sir William Carmichael's first marriage, who has inherited his father's estates at Wolden. Sir William's second wife is half Asiatic and also has a son.

Sir Arthur has recently got engaged to Phyllis Patterson. When Carstairs arrives at Wolden he sees Miss Patterson with a Persian cat at her feet. However, the mention of the cat at tea unsettles the second Lady Carmichael, who Carstairs surmises possesses occult powers.

Examining Sir Arthur, Carstairs finds that he exhibits all the characteristics of a cat. That night, Carstairs hears a cat outside his bedroom door, but when he opens the door there is nothing there.

When he asks about it in the morning, Lady Carmichael says that they never had a cat. But when Carstairs asks a footman he says that there had been a cat, but it had been destroyed. Lady Carmichael had killed it herself and had buried it in the garden. That night the mewing takes on a more menacing tone, scaring all the residents of Wolden, except for Arthur. In the library, a book is missing. Meanwhile, asleep in bed, in a locked room, Lady Carmichael is attacked.

Carstairs decides to dig up the cat's body and finds it had been killed with Prussic acid.

As soon as Lady Carmichael is well enough, she is to be removed from Wolden. Before she goes, Sir Arthur falls in the lake. Although he was a good swimmer, he was found drowned. Then, miraculously, he revives. He is his old self but remembers nothing of the past few weeks. However, Lady Carmichael is dead. The key to the mystery lies in the missing volume from the library.

'The Call of Wings'

This was the first publication of this story.

Silas Hamer and Richard Borrow are having dinner with nerve-specialist Bernard Seldon. Hamer, Borrow decides, is happy because he has made himself rich, while Borrow himself is happy because he is a poor East-End parson. On his way home, Hamer sees a drunken derelict run over by a bus. Further on he notices a legless musician playing a strange tune on the flute, unlike anything Hamer had ever heard before. He got the impression that the music was carrying him upwards.

That night, after talking to the crippled man, Hamer hears the music again. It seems to have wings – although as it raised him up something else seemed to be pulling him down. Hamer asks Seldon's advice about the visions he is having. Seldon advises Hamer to find the cripple and talk to him again. It transpires that the man is a street artist as well as a musician. He draws a man with the legs of a goat, but says he is evil. Hamer flees, but has more visions.

He goes to Borrow and gives him every penny he has got for the relief of the poor. On the tube, he sees a drunk stumble off the platform in front of an oncoming train. Hamer leaps to his rescue, sacrificing his own life.

'The Last Séance'
First published in issue 87 of the Sovereign Magazine, *March 1927, as 'The Stolen Ghost'; in the US, in Ghost Stories, November 1926, as 'The Woman Who Stole a Ghost'*
Raoul Daubreuil loves the beautiful Simone who is exhausted by her work as a medium. Before she gives it up, she is holding one last séance for Madame Exe who grieves for a lost child that Simone can make materialize. When she does this one last time, Madame Exe wants to hold her lost child. She grabs the manifestation and runs off with it. Simone screams and dies.

'SOS'
First published in issue 252 of The Grand Magazine, *February 1926*
Charlotte Dinsmead claims the remote house the family are staying in is haunted. Her father dismisses the idea.

There is a knock on the door. Mrs Dinsmead cries out in fright. Charlotte's says it is a miracle.

Mortimer Cleveland's car has broken down. With the rain driving down, he seeks refuge. Cleveland is a member of the Psychical Research Society. Knocking on the door of a cottage, he finds it opened by a fifteen-year-old boy. The scene inside is reminiscent of a Dutch painting. He is invited inside by his host who introduces himself as Dinsmead, and presents his wife and two daughters. The boy, Johnnie, shuts the door.

Mrs Dinsmead makes Cleveland a fresh cup of tea and Cleveland accepts a bed for the night, but written in the dust on a table beside the bed are the letters 'SOS'.

The following morning he attempts to find out who had written the letters. Charlotte is in the garden and Cleveland spells out SOS in the soil with a twig. She denies writing them on the table, but says she easily might have. She is frightened, insisting that the house is haunted because a murder had been committed there. Over breakfast, Cleveland mentions Johnnie's evident interest in chemistry and Mrs Dinsmead drops a cup.

Mr Dinsmead tells Cleveland that his daughter Magdalen was adopted and, according to a small ad in the paper, stands to inherit £60,000. Magdalen follows Cleveland when he leaves. She too thinks there is something wrong with the house and is afraid. It was she who wrote SOS.

Cleveland returns the following night having worked out that the solution to the mystery concerns tea and poison.

The Listerdale Mystery
London: Collins, The Crime Club, 1934

Another collection of twelve short stories, *The Listerdale Mystery* was not published in the US. However, all the stories, except for 'Sing a Song of Sixpence' were anthologized there. 'Accident', 'Philomel Cottage' and 'Mr Eastwood's Adventure' – renamed 'The Mystery of the Spanish Shawl' – were published in *Witness for the Prosecution* (1948), all the rest in *The Golden Ball* (1965).

'The Listerdale Mystery'

First published in issue 250 of The Grand Magazine, *December 1925*
Reduced to poverty by her late husband's lack of business acumen, Mrs St Vincent and her two children are living in cheap lodgings where they can no longer entertain people of their class. Her daughter Barbara dare not bring home a suitor and her son Rupert has had to get a job. In the *Morning Post*, Mrs St Vincent sees a small house in Westminster for rent at a nominal sum. It is a Queen Anne house in perfect condition, complete with a butler named Quentin. The house belonged to Lord Listerdale who has disappeared. Although they don't understand why the rent is so low, they move in, only to find that flowers and food are sent up from Lord Listerdale's country seat. Convinced that Lord Listerdale has been murdered, Rupert pays a visit to the estate. He finds Lord Listerdale's real butler Quentin living in a cottage there and solves the mystery – to his mother's satisfaction.

'Philomel Cottage'

First published in issue 237 of The Grand Magazine, *November 1924*
Short-hand typist Alix Martin has a romance, of sorts, with fellow clerk Dick Windyford, but they cannot afford to marry. A cousin dies and Alix comes into some money. She has a whirlwind romance with Gerald Martin and marries him, though Dick warns her that he is a perfect stranger to her.

The newlyweds move into a country cottage and Alix has dreams that her husband is dead with Dick standing over the body. Then Dick phones from a local inn, but Alix puts off seeing him.

The gardener has gained the impression from Gerald that she is going to London and is not sure when she would be back. He also reveals that her husband had lied about the purchase price of the cottage. Alix becomes convinced that her husband is going to murder her, but she outsmarts him and it is Gerald who dies.

The story was adapted for the stage as *Love from a Stranger* at the New Theatre, London, in 1936, and filmed as *A Night of Terror* the following year. Another version was made in 1947 and released in the UK as *A Stranger Walked In*. It was adapted three times for the radio in the US – in 1942, 1943 and 1946 – and once for BBC Radio 4 in the UK in 2002. And it was adapted for TV in Germany in 1967 under the title *Ein Fremder Klopft*.

'The Girl on the Train'
First published in issue 228 of The Grand Magazine, *February 1924*
Cast adrift by his uncle for his dissolute ways, George Rowland takes a train to a hamlet called Rowland's Castle to try his luck. At Waterloo, a girl jumps into his carriage and begs him to hide her. Then a foreign man insists that Rowland return his niece. But Rowland had a trueborn Briton's prejudice against foreigners and calls the guard, complaining of harassment with 'that air of authority which the lower classes so adore'.

When the girl gets off, she asks George to keep an eye on a man with a beard who is getting on and she gives Rowland a package to guard. At Portsmouth, Rowland books into the same hotel as the bearded man. A ginger-haired man also takes an interest.

While Rowland is out, two foreign gentlemen call; they address him as 'Lord Rowland' and ask him about the Grand Duchess Anastasia of Catonia, a small kingdom in the Balkans, who Rowland takes to be the girl on the train. Through a crack in the door, he sees the bearded man hiding something behind the skirting board in the bathroom, then discovers that the package the girl has asked him to guard has gone. The bearded man disappears and Rowland finds the package has been returned. Inside is a wedding ring.

The ginger-haired man then introduces himself and solves one mystery. After that, a story in the newspaper and the reappearance of the girl on his train back to London solves another.

The story was adapted for the Thames TV series *The Agatha Christie Hour* in 1982.

'Sing a Song of Sixpence'
First published in Holly Leaves, *the Christmas special of* Illustrated Sport and Dramatic News, *December 1929*
Retired criminal barrister Sir Edward Palliser KC is visited by Magdalen Vaughan who he had met some years before on a trip home from America. She wants his help. Her aunt, Miss Crabtree, has been murdered. The police believe that one of the four family members – who all live in her Chelsea home, were supported by her and would benefit equally from her will – is responsible. Sir Edward visits the house to investigate. The only other member of the household, apart from the family, is Martha, the elderly servant who has been in service with Miss Crabtree since she was a girl. Though Miss Crabtree left a considerable sum, she was notoriously careful with money. In her last conversation with Martha, she complained of a bad sixpence in her change – though, in fact, it was a new one with an oak-leaf design.

After seeing a restaurant called 'The Four and Twenty Blackbirds', Sir Edward remembers the old nursery rhyme and realizes that the sixpence is the clue. He confronts Martha and she names the murderer.

'The Manhood of Edward Robinson'
First published in issue 238 of The Grand Magazine, *December 1924*
Edward Robinson longs to be the sort of he-man he reads about in novels. He is a clerk and loves the very

sensible Maud who won't marry him until his prospects improve.

But Edward wins £500 in a competition and blows it on a two-seater car. He takes a drive out into the countryside. Stopping at the Devil's Punch Bowl, he takes a walk in the moonlight. Taking to the road again, he looks for his muffler in the side pocket of the car. Instead he finds a diamond necklace and concludes that he has got into the wrong car. He also finds a note giving details of a meeting.

Keeping the assignation, he meets a girl who mistakes him for someone named Gerald. She is delighted that he has brought the necklace and takes the wheel. They head for a posh nightclub in London named Ritson's. They dance and the girl dons the diamond necklace.

She is Lady Noreen Eliot, a celebrated beauty known for her daring. She then explains why she and her wealthy boyfriend, Captain James Folliet, VC, of the Household Cavalry, go about stealing jewellery.

The story appeared in the Thames TV series *The Agatha Christie Hour* in 1982.

'Accident'
First published in the Sunday Dispatch, *22 September 1929, as 'The Uncrossed Path'*

In a country village, ex-inspector Evans, late of the CID, recognizes Mrs Anthony who was acquitted of poisoning her husband some nine years earlier. When she was eighteen, her stepfather had fallen from a cliff to his death. Evans is concerned there may be another 'accident'.

She is now married to Professor George Merrowdene who had just taken out life insurance in favour of his wife. Mr Anthony's life had similarly been insured. When Merrowdene visits a fortune teller, she predicts that he will soon be engaged in a matter of life or death.

Evans seeks to intervene and greets Mrs Merrowdene as 'Mrs Anthony'. She invites him home for tea. Producing

Chinese tea, she accuses her husband of conducting his chemistry experiments, involving potassium cyanide, in the bowls they are drinking from.

'One of these days, you'll poison us all,' she says.

Though Evans switches bowls, the Chinese tea does result in a third 'accidental' death.

'Jane in Search of a Job'
First published in issue 234 of The Grand Magazine, *August 1924*
Jane Cleveland sees a job advertisement in the *Daily Leader.* The applicant needs to be a good mimic and be able to speak French. Ahead of numerous other applicants, Jane gets the job. She is told she is to imitate Grand Duchess Pauline of Ostrova who, after a Communist revolution in her country, is a target for assassination.

Wearing a striking red dress, Jane is to be driven to a bazaar in aid of Ostrovian refugees. A hundred society women have donated one pearl each from their necklaces. These are to be auctioned. If there is any threat of assassination, Jane is to swap dresses with the Grand Duchess and take her place. All goes as planned, but on the way home the chauffeur pulls a gun.

She is locked in a remote house. After drinking some soup, Jane feels sleepy. When she awakes, she finds a newspaper reporting that a girl in a red dress had held up the charity bazaar. She had been set up, but her salvation lies in a handsome young man she finds knocked out outside.

The story appeared in the Thames TV series *The Agatha Christie Hour* in 1982.

'A Fruitful Sunday'
First published in the Daily Mail, *11 August 1928*
Dorothy Pratt is out for a Sunday drive with Edward Palgrove in the fourth-hand Baby Austin he bought for £20. She dreams of diamonds from Bond Street while wearing Woolworths pearls.

They buy a basket of cherries from a fruit seller who says they are getting 'more than their money's worth'. Stopping by a stream, they read in the newspaper of the theft of a ruby necklace worth £50,000 and find in the bottom of the basket 'a long glittering chain of blood-red stones'.

Edward is fearful that they will be sent to prison and wants to hand them in at a police station, but Dorothy sees this as an opportunity and wants to take them to a fence. Though he has no idea how to find a fence, Edward finally agrees.

However, the next day, Dorothy has second thoughts. That evening, in the paper, there is more news about the jewel robbery. Alongside it, there is another paragraph about an advertising stunt. Imitation necklaces had been put in one in every fifty baskets in an 'eat more fruit' campaign.

'Mr Eastwood's Adventure'

First published in The Novel Magazine, *August 1924, as 'The Mystery of the Second Cucumber'*

Anthony Eastwood is trying to write a story he has titled 'The Mystery of the Second Cucumber', but he has writer's block. The phone rings. It is a woman with a foreign accent who calls him 'beloved' and says: 'Come at once. It is death for me if you don't come.' She gives an address and a password: 'Cucumber.'

He goes to the address, gives the code word and is ushered in to meet the exotic creature who kisses him. Then she draws away, afraid he was followed.

Two men in plain clothes turn up and arrest him for the murder of Anna Rosenburg under the impression that he is Conrad Fleckman. To establish his identify, he takes them back to his flat. While one of then searches the apartment, Eastwood asks the other about the murder and is told a complicated story involving a Spanish shawl, known as the 'Shawl of a Thousand Flowers'.

When the men are gone, Eastwood learns that he has

made a costly mistake. However, he renames his story
'The Mystery of the Spanish Shawl' and his writer's block
is gone.

'The Golden Ball'

First published in the Daily Mail, *5 August 1929, as 'Playing the
Innocent'*

George Dundas is sacked from his job in the City by his
uncle for taking too much time off and not grasping 'the
golden ball of opportunity'.

George is standing in the City considering the possibilities when an expensive car pulls up. It is driven by society
girl Mary Montresor. When she invites him to get in, he
does not hesitate.

Heading westwards, she asks him to marry her. He
accepts, though the newspaper hoardings say that she is
going to marry the Duke of Edgehill. Nevertheless she
insists that they look for a marital home. Somewhere
beyond Kingston, she sees a house she likes so they stop to
take a proper look. When a butler answers the door, Mary
asks whether Mrs Pardonstenger is in. They are shown into
the drawing room. A couple come in – the man brandish-
ing a revolver. He forces them upstairs, but on the staircase
George kicks the man in the stomach. He and Mary then
make their escape, taking the gun with them. In the car, he
finds it is not loaded. He has, it seems, grasped the golden
ball.

'The Rajah's Emerald'

First published in issue 420 of Red Magazine, *30 July 1926*

James Bond (twenty-seven years before Ian Fleming's creation) is on holiday at Kimpton-on-Sea with his ladyfriend
Grace. But while she stays in the Esplanade Hotel on the
seafront, he is relegated to an obscure boarding house. This
causes bad blood.

They go swimming. James nips into a private beach hut

to change. Afterwards, he lunches alone in a cheap café and finds in his pocket an enormous green emerald and recognizes it as one belonging to the Rajah of Maraputna. He realizes that he picked up the wrong pair of trousers in the bathing hut. He then notices the hoarding for the local evening paper that announces: 'The Rajah's emerald stolen.'

Buying the paper, he discovers that the Rajah was staying nearby with Lord Edward Campion. The beach hut he used, he discovers, belonged to Lord Campion. He returns to change his trousers, but is apprehended by a man introducing himself as Detective Inspector Merrilees of the Yard. Playing for time, James says the emerald is in his lodgings. On the way there, they pass the police station. James cries out 'Help! Thief!' He claims he has had his pocket picked. The police search Merrilees and find the emerald.

'Swan Song'
First published in issue 259 of The Grand Magazine, *September 1926*
The singer Paula Nazorkoff is booked to sing at Covent Garden. She has also been invited to make a private performance of *Madame Butterfly* at Rustonbury Castle. She agrees to take the engagement, but only if she can sing *Tosca*. However, the Italian baritone Roscari who is to sing the part of the police chief Scarpia falls ill. The great French baritone Edouart Bréon lives near Rustonbury Castle. She has seen a picture of his house in *Country Homes*. Lady Rustonbury hires Bréon instead. He does not remember Nazorkoff, but she sat at his feet when she was an unknown.

However, he does remember a young singer in Milan named Bianca Capelli singing Tosca, but she was involved with a member of the Camorra who was to be executed. She had begged Bréon to use his influence to save her lover, but the Camorrista was put to death and the young singer disappeared.

During that night's performance at Rustonbury Castle,
Bréon plays Scarpia without mercy, while Nazorkoff –
instead of pretending to stab him – does it for real.

This story was adapted for radio by BBC Radio 4 in 1982.

Why Didn't They Ask Evans?

London: Collins, The Crime Club, 1934; New York: published as
The Boomerang Clue, *Dodd, Mead & Co., 1935*

Local vicar's son Bobby Jones is playing golf at Marchbolt,
a small seaside town in Wales. He slices the ball over a cliff.
At the bottom, he finds a man whose dying words are:
'Why didn't they ask Evans?'

When Bobby pulls a handkerchief from the dead man's
pocket to cover his face, the picture of a beautiful young
woman falls out. While his golf partner goes to get help, a
stranger turns up who introduces himself as Bassington-
ffrench. Bobby has to play the organ for his father at six
and so leaves the stranger with the body.

On a train back from London, Bobby meets Lady Frances
'Frankie' Derwent who shows him the paper. The dead
man had been identified as Alex Pritchard from the photograph in his pocket which is said to be of his sister Mrs
Cayman. Frankie speculates that Pritchard was pushed
over the cliff because it makes it 'much more exciting'.

When Mrs Cayman takes the stand at the inquest, Bobby
does not recognize her as the beauty from the photograph,
but assumes it was taken a long time ago. Afterwards, Mrs
Cayman and her husband visit Bobby and ask whether
her brother left dying words. Bobby said he didn't. Later
he recalls that the dying man said: 'Why didn't they ask
Evans?' and he writes to Mr Cayman.

Bobby has a job lined up in a friend's garage. Suddenly,
out of the blue, he is offered a lucrative job in Buenos Aires.
But, loyal to his friend, he refuses it.

Then there is an attempt to murder him by lacing
his beer with a lethal dose of morphia, but he survives.

Convalescing, Bobby opens an old newspaper and sees a reproduction of the picture found in the dead man's pocket – only it is not the one that Bobby saw. Bassington-ffrench must have switched it. Bobby and Frankie decide to track down Bassington-ffrench and get to the bottom of the mystery.

They follow a complex and dangerous trail that eventually leads them back to Marchbolt – hence 'The Boomerang Clue'.

This story was adapted by London Weekend Television in 1980 and appeared in the *Marple* TV series in 2009.

Parker Pyne Investigates
London: Collins, The Crime Club, 1934; New York: published as Mr Parker Pyne Detective, *Dodd, Mead & Co., 1934*

The first six short stories in this collection feature cases that retired civil servant James Parker Pyne has solicited with an advertisement in *The Times* that reads: 'Are you happy? If not, consult Mr Parker Pyne, 17 Richmond Street.' His secretary Felicity Lemon later works for Hercule Poirot.

The remaining six stories concern cases that Parker Pyne comes across on his travels.

'The Case of the Middle-Aged Wife'
This was the first publication of this story.

The long-married Mrs Packington answers Mr Pyne's advertisement. She is unhappy with her husband. After thirty-five years of compiling statistics in a government office, Pyne surmises that Mr Packington is seeing a young lady from his office though, apparently, he claims there is no harm in it. Pyne charges two hundred guineas, and arranges appointments with beauty specialists and a dressmaker for Mrs Packington. At lunch in the Ritz, he introduces her to handsome thirty-year-old Claude Luttrell who takes her dancing. Inevitably, they run across her husband and his girlfriend. He is furious and jealous.

Claude admits to being a gigolo and husband and wife are reconciled, but not without consequences for Claude.

This story was adapted for TV for Thames Television's *The Agatha Christie Hour* in 1982.

'The Case of the Discontented Soldier'
First published in issue 554 of Cosmopolitan, *August 1932; in the UK in issue 614 of* Woman's Pictorial, *15 October 1932*
Recently returned from East Africa, Major Wilbraham visits Parker Pyne, who diagnoses that he is missing the element of danger. He sends the major on a date with Madeleine de Sara, who the major thinks is a vamp. However, before scaring him off, she had determined what the major's taste in ladies is.

After consulting Mrs Oliver, the novelist, Parker Pyne sends the major to an address in Hampstead. There he finds a young woman named Freda Clegg, another client of Pyne's, being attacked by two men. Wilbraham rescues her. She is embroiled in some legal imbroglio involving papers, which the major finds hidden in the lining of her father's old sea chest. They are written in Swahili and reveal the hiding place of a cache of ivory. When the girl goes missing, Wilbraham is lured back to Hampstead, where he is knocked out. He awakes to find himself imprisoned with her in a cellar. Water pours in; fearing they are going to be drowned, the pair make their escape and marry, never realizing that their predicament had been contrived.

The story was adapted for TV for Thames Television's *The Agatha Christie Hour* in 1982.

'The Case of the Distressed Lady'
First published in issue 554 of Cosmopolitan, *August 1932; in the UK in issue 615 of* Woman's Pictorial, *22 October 1932*
Daphne St John wants Parker Pyne to return a diamond ring that she had stolen from a friend, Lady Naomi Dortheimer, who she has since fallen out with. Pyne sends

Claude Luttrell and Madeleine de Sara as exhibition dancers to a ball given by Lady Dortheimer. As Claude is dancing with Lady Dortheimer, her ring slips from her finger, the lights go out and Claude replaces it. But Miss St John is not what she seems and Pyne refuses his fee since he has not made his client happy as promised in his advertisement.

'The Case of the Discontented Husband'
First published in issue 554 of Cosmopolitan, *August 1932; in the UK in issue 616 of* Woman's Pictorial, *29 October 1932*
Sportsman Reginald Wade's wife Iris wants to divorce him and marry fellow intellectual Sinclair Jordan. Again Parker Pyne thinks jealousy will do the trick. He sends Madeleine de Sara to stay at the Wade's. Iris sees them kissing and invites her own beau along. He naturally falls for Madeleine, though she mocks him. Iris rekindles her love for her husband, but he has fallen in love with Madeleine too. Parker Pyne writes 'failure' on the file.

'The Case of the City Clerk'
First published in issue 554 of Cosmopolitan, *August 1932; in the UK in issue 503 the* Strand Magazine, *November 1932, as 'The £10 Adventure'*
Mr Roberts, a forty-eight-year-old city clerk, is respectably married with two children. But he wants to 'live gloriously for ten minutes' before returning to his rut. A Professor Peterfield has been murdered and plans in his care have to be taken to the League of Nations in Geneva. Pyne volunteers Roberts for the assignment, telling him that he is carrying details of the hiding place of the Russian crown jewels. Roberts, who has never been abroad before, is told to watch out for Bolshevik agents.

He carries off the mission without spotting a Bolshevist. However, in Geneva he is approached by a Russian who gives him fresh instructions as well as a gun, and he finds himself drawn into the world of espionage.

'The Case of the Rich Woman'
First published in issue 554 of Cosmopolitan, *August 1932*
Former farm girl Mrs Abner Rymer married a poor man
who was clever and worked hard and became rich. She is
now a widow and unhappy with her life. Plucked from her
social class, she has no friends. People either want money
from her or laugh at her behind her back. Pyne charges her
£2,000.

When Mrs Rymer returns to Pyne's office, Nurse de Sara
takes her to see Dr Constantine. Mrs Rymer is drugged;
when she wakes up, she is addressed as Hannah. Looking
out of the window, she sees a farmyard and is told that she
has lived there for the past five years. Glimpsing a newspaper, she discovers that she has only been there for three
days, but the paper also reports that Mrs Abner Rymer has
been confined to a mental home under the delusion that she
is a servant girl named Hannah Moorhouse. Another story
in the paper concerns Dr Constantine who claims that it is
possible to transfer a soul between two bodies. She curses
Parker Pyne for what he has done to her, but she eventually accepts that she must return to menial work to save up
the money to return to London and beard him in his den.
However, happiness intervenes.

'Have You Got Everything You Want?'
First published in issue 562 of Cosmopolitan, *April 1933; in the UK
in issue 481 of* Nash's Pall Mall Magazine, *June 1933, as 'On the
Orient Express'*
Elsie Jefferies meets Parker Pyne on the Orient Express.
She is to meet her husband in Constantinople. However,
she has seen, on a piece of blotting paper in his study, in
his handwriting, the words 'just before Venice is the best
time'.

As they were crossing the rail bridge to Venice, a woman
points out smoke pouring from a compartment. Parker
Pyne and Elsie run along the corridor, but the conductor

assures them that the fire is being brought under control. It turns out to have been a smoke bomb. Returning to her compartment, Elsie finds that her jewellery is missing, and it is nowhere to be found on the train.

Pyne sends a telegram from Trieste and, at Istanbul, her husband returns her jewels to her.

'The Gate of Baghdad'
First published in issue 562 of Cosmopolitan, *April 1933; in the UK in issue 481 of* Nash's Pall Mall Magazine, *June 1933, as 'At the Gate of Baghdad'*

Parker Pyne is in Damascus. He reads in a local paper that embezzling financier Samuel Long is thought to have fled to South America, though other speculation suggests that the old Etonian could be in disguise anywhere in the world.

The six-wheeler Pullman coach Pyne is taking to the Gate of Baghdad gets stuck in the mud. Most of the men get out to help, but Captain Smethurst, an old Etonian, stays on board; he is found to be dead. Squadron Leader Loftus, a doctor in the RAF, concludes that, as there is no mark on him, he must have hit his head on the roof when they went over a bump. When Pyne queries this, Loftus concedes that the injury to the head could have been caused by a sandbag. Another RAF officer named Hensley admits to always carrying a spare pair of socks. Loftus gets them – one sock contains wet sand.

On examining the body, Pyne notices that Smethurst has been stabbed with a something sharp like a stiletto. This leads him to the murderer and the rogue financier.

'The House at Shiraz'
First published in issue 562 of Cosmopolitan, *April 1933; in the UK in issue 481 of* Nash's Pall Mall Magazine, *June 1933*

In Persia, Parker Pyne dines with Herr Schlagal, his pilot. He tells Pyne of his first passengers, two English ladies.

One was Lady Esther Carr, who Schlagal says is mad and now lives as a recluse in Shiraz. The other, who Schlagal had fallen for, was dead and he suspects that Lady Esther killed her.

Speaking with the consul, Pyne discovers that Lady Esther will see no one British since her companion had fallen from a balcony. Nevertheless, Pyne writes to Lady Esther, enclosing his advertisement from *The Times*. She agrees to see him. He finds her quite sane and discovers why she had become a recluse. She then consents to have Herr Schlagal fly her to Baghdad.

'The Pearl of Price'

First published in issue 482 of Nash's Pall Mall Magazine, *July 1933, as 'The Pearl'*

At Petra, Parker Pyne listens to famous archaeologist Dr Carver talk of the Nabataeans, a band of thieves, who had lived there. One of Carol Blundell's pearl earrings falls out. Her father, an American magnate, complains that they cost him $80,000 and she screws them in so loosely that they fall out. Dr Carver says he does not covet pearls and shows them something he says is more interesting. He has a small cylinder of black hematite that, when rolled across a piece of plasticine he has in his pocket, reveals a scene of celebration.

The following day, they are out sightseeing when Carol drops her earring again. This time it cannot be found. It can't be far, she says, because Dr Carver had just pointed out it was loose and screwed it in again. All those present are searched. Carol then employs Parker Pyne to find the missing pearl because she is in love with her father's secretary, Jim Hurst. Hurst is a former thief; her father does not approve of the match and is sure to accuse him.

That afternoon, Pyne finds the pearl and unmasks the thief.

'Death on the Nile'

First published in issue 562 of Cosmopolitan, *April 1933; in the UK in issue 482 of* Nash's Pall Mall Magazine, *June 1933*

Parker Pyne in on board the SS *Fayoum* with Lady Gayle and her husband Sir George who married her for her money. With them are his private secretary Basil West, her nurse Miss MacNaughton and their niece Pamela, who says her aunt is not really ill but is always complaining.

While the others are ashore, Lady Gayle consults Pyne, telling him she suspects her husband is poisoning her. Miss MacNaughton also thinks Lady Gayle is being poisoned as her condition improves when her husband is away. She thinks arsenic or antimony is being used.

Lady Gayle then dies of strychnine poisoning. Pyne finds a clue in the form of a scrap of a burnt letter in an ashtray. Strychnine is then found in Sir George's cabin and in his dinner jacket. Miss MacNaughton carried strychnine for Lady Gayle's heart condition. Pamela thinks that Lady Gayle took it and committed suicide. Pyne then confronts the real killer, though he later admits he hasn't a shred of evidence.

'The Oracle at Delphi'

First published in issue 562 of Cosmopolitan, *April 1933; in the UK in issue 482 of* Nash's Pall Mall Magazine, *June 1933*

Mrs Peters and her eighteen-year-old son Willard are visiting Delphi. Her son is kidnapped. She is afraid to contact the police, but a note comes from another guest containing Parker Pyne's advertisement from *The Times*. They meet discreetly.

The kidnappers want a diamond necklace she carries as a ransom. Pyne and Mrs Peters cook up a plan to have a jeweller in Athens make up a copy. This is to be given to the kidnappers. But it is a ruse. The next day, Willard is returned, along with the diamonds, by a man named Thompson who turns out to be the real Parker Pyne.

Murder Is Easy

London: Collins, The Crime Club, 1939; New York: published as Easy to Kill, Dodd, Mead & Co., 1939

Returning from the colonies, ex-policeman Luke Fitzwilliam meets an old lady from the village of Wychwood under Ashe on the train. She says she is on her way to Scotland Yard to report three murders – and her suspicions that a fourth, that of Dr Humblebly, is about to take place. Her name is Lavinia Pinkerton (changed to Fullerton in the US).

The following morning, Luke reads in the paper that she has been killed in a hit-and-run. Over a week later, he reads that Dr Humbleby is also dead. Luke goes to Wychwood under Ashe to investigate, posing as a researcher into witchcraft. Fortunately, his friend Jimmy Lorrimer has a cousin there. Her name is Bridget Conway and she is secretary to, and fiancée of, local bigwig Lord Easterfield.

Luke and Bridget begin investigating the series of deaths together. However, they seem unrelated, although the victims are all disapproved of by Lord Easterfield. A friend of Miss Pinkerton's named Honoria Waynflete says she knows who Miss Pinkerton suspected. She also mentions, in passing, that she was once engaged to Lord Easterfield.

Luke and Miss Waynflete overhear a row between Lord Easterfield and his chauffeur, who is later found dead. Bridget chucks Easterfield for Luke. This is as well, as Easterfield is thrilled by the death of his argumentative chauffeur. Providence, it seems, is clearing a path for him.

Travelling to Scotland Yard, Luke finds out from old colleagues that the registration number given for the car that ran down Miss Pinkerton was that of Lord Easterfield's Rolls-Royce. Back in Wychwood, Miss Waynflete confesses that she feared Lord Easterfield was the murderer. Both Luke and Bridget are now in danger. For her protection, Bridget goes to stay with Miss Waynflete. It is only then that Bridget discovers the truth. Thankfully Superintendent Battle is on hand to put together the final pieces.

This was adapted for the stage in 1993 and for TV by CBS in 1982. It appeared in the *Marple* TV series in 2008.

Ten Little Niggers

London: Collins, The Crime Club, 1939; New York: published as And Then There Were None, Dodd, Mead & Co., 1940

Eight people are invited to a house on Nigger Island (Indian Island and Soldier Island in later editions). They are attended by a newly hired butler and his wife, making ten in all. In the bedrooms is hung the old nursery rhyme 'Ten Little Niggers' ('Indians', 'Soldiers'). There is no sign of their host.

After dinner, a disembodied voice accuses each of them of murder. It comes from an old-fashioned gramophone. Each is then killed in a manner outlined in a couplet from the nursery rhyme. Meanwhile, ten small china figures disappear one by one. When there are only two left, each suspects the other. Out of fear, one shoots the other then, prompted by a noose hanging from the ceiling, hangs themself.

The police are baffled. They piece together some of what happened from the diaries and notes left by the victims. Then the master of a fishing trawler finds a message in a bottle that explains how the murders were done. It is signed by the killer.

Christie adapted the story for the stage, changing the ending so that two characters survive. It appeared as *Ten Little Niggers* at the St James's Theatre, London, in 1943, and as *Ten Little Indians* at the Broadhurst Theater, New York, in 1944. It was filmed as *And Then There Were None* the following year. A second version was filmed in England as *Ten Little Indians* in 1965, with a third interpretation using the same title in 1974; a fourth version was made in 1989. A Russian version, *Desyat'Negrityat*, was made in 1987.

TV versions were made in the UK in 1949 and 1959, and versions have been made in Germany, France, Cuba and the Lebanon.

The Regatta Mystery and Other Stories
New York: Dodd, Mead & Co., 1939

For the first time, one of Agatha Christie's books was published in the US without an equivalent publication in the UK. However, the stories it contained appeared in later UK collections. 'The Regatta Mystery', 'Problem at Pollensa Bay' and 'Yellow Iris' appear in *Problem at Pollensa Bay and Other Stories* in 1991. An extended version of 'The Mystery of the Baghdad Chest' appears as 'The Mystery of the Spanish Chest' in *The Adventure of the Christmas Pudding and a Selection of Entrées* in 1960, along with 'The Dream'. 'How Does Your Garden Grow?' appears in *Poirot's Early Cases* in 1974. 'Miss Marple Tells a Story' and 'In a Glass Darkly' appear in *Miss Marple's Final Cases and Two Other Stories* in 1979. And 'Problem at Sea' appears in *Poirot's Early Cases* in 1974.

'The Regatta Mystery'
First published as a Poirot story in the Hartford Courant, *3 May 1936*

Diamond merchant Isaac Pointz and a party from his yacht *Mermaid* come ashore at Dartmouth to dine at the Royal George. Guest Eve Leathern bets she can steal the Morning Star, a big diamond Pointz always carries with him. Seemingly by accident, she drops it. She is searched but the diamond cannot be found. Eve was not seen to swallow it and the room is searched. She has won the bet, but when she reveals her hiding place, the diamond is gone. Fortunately, Parker Pyne is on hand to solve the mystery.

'Problem at Pollensa Bay'
First published in Volume 12, Number 36 of Liberty *magazine, 5 September 1936, as 'Siren Business'*
Parker Pyne is holidaying on Majorca. A fellow guest at the Piños d'Oro hotel, Mrs Adela Chester, wants his help to save her son Basil from marrying an unsuitable woman who lives in the local artists' colony. Pyne solves the problem by introducing someone even more unsuitable.

'Yellow Iris'
First published in issue 559 of the Strand Magazine, *July 1937; in the US in the* Hartford Courant, *10 October 1937, as 'The Case of the Yellow Iris'*
Poirot gets a phone call from a woman saying she is in great danger. He is to come to the Jardin des Cygnes restaurant, to the table with yellow irises. The party is in honour of Iris Russell who died four years earlier. The same guests have been invited. At the initial dinner Mrs Russell had been poisoned with cyanide. The verdict returned was suicide, but her husband believes that she was murdered by someone now sitting at the table. When another guest is murdered, Poroit has a fresh mystery to solve.

This story was altered and extended to make the novel *Sparkling Cyanide* (*Remember Death*) with Colonel Race substituted for Hercule Poirot.

Towards Zero
London: Collins, The Crime Club, 1944; New York: Dodd, Mead & Co., 1944
In a prologue, lawyers are discussing cases when one points out that detective stories start in the wrong place – with the murder. The murder is actually the end and the story begins a long time before that, with things 'converging towards zero'.

First we meet Angus MacWhirter, who is in hospital after a failed suicide attempt. He lost his own job after refusing to lie for his boss. Soon he was penniless and his wife left him for another man.

A month later, someone is writing a detailed plan for a murder. Three weeks after that Superintendent Battle receives a letter saying that his daughter, Sylvia, has been caught stealing at school. When he visits the headmistress, he decides she is a fool and withdraws his daughter.

The following month, tennis player Nevile Strange is having breakfast with his wife Kay. They discuss a forthcoming visit to the widow of his guardian, Lady Camilla Tressilian, at Gull's Point, where she lives with her companion Mary Aldin. Nevile's ex-wife Audrey will be there too. For added tension, Malayan planter Thomas Royde, a former suitor of Audrey's who wants to try his luck again now she is divorced, will also be present. Assorted staff and guests converge.

Nevile wants to divorce Kay and remarry Audrey. There is a confrontation. Lady Tressilian disapproves. She and Nevile have a row. The following morning she is found dead with her head beaten in.

Superintendent Battle is holidaying with his nephew Inspector James Leach who is called in on the case. Together, they investigate. The murder weapon appears to have been one of Nevile Strange's golf clubs. His fingerprints are found on it. There is a blood stain on the cuff of his suit and water on the floor by the washbasin in his room, as if he had been trying to wash the blood of himself hurriedly. However, Leach and Battle decided that this is all too pat and someone is trying to frame Nevile Strange.

Christie adapted the story for the stage. It opened at the St James's Theatre, London, in 1956, and appeared as a movie as *Innocent Lies* in 1995, with a French version *L'Heure Zéro* in 2007. It appeared in the *Marple* TV series in 2007 and was adapted for radio by BBC Radio 4 in 2010.

Death Comes as the End
New York: Dodd, Mead & Co., 1944; London: Collins, The Crime Club, 1945

The action is set in ancient Egypt around 2000 BC. It begins with the return of the recently widowed Renisenb to the house of her father Imhotep. He is away and returns with a beautiful young concubine called Nofret. The family are told to welcome her, but her presence causes tension.

This comes to a head with Imhotep threatening to disinherit his sons and their families. Nofret is then found dead at the foot of a cliff. This could have been an accident, but then one of Imhotep's daughters-in-law falls to her death in the same place. The family believe that Nofret has come back from the dead to avenge herself on them. But, as more die, it becomes clear that a living murderer is among them.

Sparkling Cyanide
London: Collins, The Crime Club, 1945; New York: published as Remembered Death, Dodd, Mead & Co., 1945

This is an expansion of the Hercule Poirot short story 'Yellow Iris', published in 1937, with the names of the guilty parties changed and Colonel Race substituted for Poirot. Again it uses the 'murder in retrospect' plot device.

A year after the death of Rosemary Barton, six people are thinking of her. They are her younger sister Iris, Iris's boyfriend Anthony Browne who had once been infatuated with Rosemary, the MP Stephen Farraday who risked his marriage and career over an affair with Rosemary, his wife Alexandra, Iris's husband George Barton and his devoted secretary Ruth Lessing. They were all present at Rosemary Barton's birthday party when she suddenly died after drinking champagne laced with cyanide. More cyanide was found in her evening bag and her death was considered suicide.

George receives anonymous letters saying that his wife has been murdered. He shows the letters to Colonel Race,

then invites the same guests to an anniversary dinner at the
same restaurant, the Luxembourg. This time George dies,
leaving Colonel Race to find the killer.

A TV version was made by CBS in 1983. Another TV
adaptation was made in the UK in 2003. BBC Radio 4
broadcast their adaptation in 2012.

Witness for the Prosecution
New York: Dodd, Mead & Co., 1948
This collection of short stories was only published in the
US. In the UK, they had all been published in earlier collec-
tions. 'The Witness for the Prosecution', 'The Red Signal',
'The Fourth Man', 'SOS', 'Where There's a Will' (as 'Wire-
less') and 'The Mystery of the Blue Jar' had all appeared
in *The Hound of Death and Other Stories*; 'Sing a Song
of Sixpence', 'The Mystery of the Spanish Shawl' (as 'Mr
Eastwood's Adventure'), 'Philomel Cottage' and 'Acci-
dent' in *The Listerdale Mystery*; and 'The Second Gong' in
Murder in the Mews.

Crooked House
*London: Collins, The Crime Club, 1949; New York: Dodd, Mead
& Co., 1949*
Initially published in a condensed version in *Cosmopolitan* magazine in October 1948 and as a serial in *John Bull*
in seven weekly instalments in 1949, this is another Christie book that takes its title from a nursery rhyme. The
narrator is Charles Hayward who meets Sophia Leonides in Egypt towards the end of the war and falls in love.
Back in England, Sophia says she has a large family that
'all lived together in a little crooked house' – or rather a
gabled mansion in the fictional London suburb of Swinly
Dean.

When Hayward returns to England two years later, he
arranges a date with Sophia, only to learn from the newspaper that her grandfather, Aristide, has recently died.

He has been murdered and Hayward's father, an assistant commissioner at Scotland Yard, was on the case.

Aristide Leonides was a wealthy Greek restaurateur. He lived with his sons Roger and Philip, their two wives, and Philip's three children, Sophia, Eustace and Josephine, who reads lots of detective stories. Completing the household are the sister of Aristides' first wife Edith de Haviland and his second wife Brenda, who was some fifty years younger than her husband. She used to inject him with insulin for his diabetes, but someone substituted eserine, an alkaloid found in eyedrops, which killed him.

All the family members had the opportunity and a motive because of the large inheritance involved. Charles's father persuades him to go to stay at the house to gather evidence. Of course, Brenda Leonides is the obvious suspect. She is arrested after love letters are found written by her to Laurence Brown, a conscientious objector during the war who became a tutor to the children. However, the nanny is then poisoned with digitalin, and then Edith de Haviland drives into a quarry with Josephine. Both are killed. It turns out that the murders are child's play. A radio adaptation was broadcast by BBC Radio 4 as a four-part series and a film version is planned.

Three Blind Mice and Other Stories
New York: Dodd, Mead & Co., 1950 (later published by Dell as The Mousetrap and Other Stories)

All the stories appear in later collections in the UK, except for 'Three Blind Mice', a prose version on Christie's half-hour radio play broadcast on the BBC Light Programme on 30 May 1947. As it is then adapted into her long-running play *The Mousetrap*, she did not want to give the ending away. 'Strange Jest', 'Tape-Measure Murder', 'The Case of the Perfect Maid' and 'The Case of the Caretaker' are in *Miss Marple's Final Cases and Two Other Stories* in 1979. 'The Third-Floor Flat' and 'The Adventure of Johnnie

Waverley' appear in *Poirot's Early Cases* in 1974. 'Four and Twenty Blackbirds' appears in *The Adventure of the Christmas Pudding and a Selection of Entrées* in 1960. And 'The Love Detectives' appears in *Problem at Pollensa Bay and Other Stories* in 1991.

'Three Blind Mice'

First published in Volume 124, Number 5 of Cosmopolitan *magazine, May 1948*

Husband and wife Giles and Molly are opening Monkswell Manor Guesthouse. They have to do all the work themselves as they can't get servants. Advertisements in *The Times* and local papers attract a disparate selection of guests. They get snowed in. However, one of the party is a killer.

The story had started as a play written for the BBC in 1947. It later became *The Mousetrap*, which has been running on the London stage since 1952.

'The Love Detectives'

First published as 'At the Crossroads' in issue 236 of the Story-Teller *magazine, December 1926*

Mr Satterthwaite is visiting Colonel Melrose, a chief constable, who receives a call saying that Sir James Dwighton has been found murdered in his library. Melrose invites Satterthwaite to accompany him. Sir James' pompous and brusque manner may have made him enemies. In particular there was Paul Delangua, who Sir James had thrown out after finding him making love to Lady Dwighton.

On the way to the murder scene, Melrose has a minor accident. The other driver is Mr Quin who joins the investigation. Sir James had been struck on the head with a bronze statuette of Venus. Two people confess to the crime. Another is suspected. Mr Quin steers Satterthwaite and Melrose to the right conclusion, sparing another pair of lovers.

They Came to Baghdad
London: Collins, The Crime Club, 1951; New York: Dodd, Mead & Co., 1951

In Baghdad, two agents – Crosbie and Dakin – discuss an important meeting that is about to take place there. They think that 'Uncle Joe' – Joseph Stalin – means to be there. The implication is that he intends to meet the US president to come to some understanding in the midst of the rapidly escalating Cold War. Dakin draws a spider's web of all those coming to Baghdad. In the middle, he writes the name Anna Scheele.

Scheele is secretary to New York banker Otto Morganthal. She asks for three weeks' leave of absence to visit her sister in London. Morganthal knows about the president's visit to the conference in Baghdad.

In London, shorthand-typist Victoria Jones has just been fired. Sitting in FitzJames Gardens, she meets a man named Edward, who mentions he is on his way to Baghdad. He works for a Dr Rathbone who opens bookshops in remote places, though Edward thinks there is something fishy about the operation. After he leaves, she realizes that she is in love with Edward and decides to follow him to Baghdad.

Anna Scheele is followed. While she enjoys a quiet shopping trip around the West End, her luggage is searched at the Savoy.

At an employment agency, Victoria asks about a job in Baghdad. She is offered the post as assistant to Mrs Hamilton Clipp. When Mr Clipp is ushering her up to their suite in Savoy, he recognizes Anna Scheele. Asked why she wants to go to Iraq, Victoria says that her uncle is Dr Pauncefoot Jones, an archaeologist whose name she has seen in the newspaper.

Also on his way to Baghdad is British agent Henry Carmichael. Dressed as an Arab, he is carrying some secret and people were trying to kill him. He seeks refuge in the British consulate in Basrah.

On the plane to Baghdad, Victoria sees famous travel writer Sir Rupert Crofton Lee. They find they are both staying at the same hotel in Baghdad, run by Marcus Tio.

Back in London, those following Anna Scheele have lost her. They fear that she is on her way to Baghdad where Sir Rupert lets slip her name.

Not knowing Edward's surname, Victoria asks after Dr Rathbone and discovers that he runs an organization called Olive Branch. The following day, by chance, she finds it. She blusters her way in to see Dr Rathbone who tells her that Edward is in Basrah and does not know when he will be back. Back at the hotel she meets Mr Dakin and Captain Crosbie. They are there to see Crofton Lee – and to await Carmichael.

A man slips into Victoria's room and begs her to hide him. Stabbed through the heart, he dies, saying: 'Lucifer – Basrah . . .' then a name she thinks is 'Lefarge'. She tells Dakin this. He brings in Marcus Tio to get rid of the body.

Short of money, Victoria has to take a job with Dakin. He asks her to join the fight against a Fifth Column that is profiting from the Cold War . . .

Destination Unknown

London: Collins, The Crime Club, 1954; New York: published as So Many Steps to Death, *Dodd, Mead & Co., 1955*

Brilliant scientist Thomas Betterton is missing. He is one of many scientists with suspected left-wing sympathies who have disappeared. The security services have contacted his wife Olive. She is unhelpful, but agent Jessop thinks she knows something. A Polish-American, Major Boris Glydr, turns up. He is a cousin of Betterton's first wife, who died. He asks whether Betterton has gone behind the Iron Curtain.

Betterton's wife Olive takes a trip abroad. Meanwhile,

Hilary Craven is heading for Casablanca. She is depressed – her husband has left her and her child has died. When she hears that the plane ahead has crashed, she wishes she had been on it.

In Casablanca, she buys sleeping pills and plans to commit suicide. She is just about to take them when Jessop comes into her room. He had seen her buying the pills. Instead of killing herself, he offers her a dangerous assignment. Olive Betterton had been on the plane that crashed. Hilary looks like her. Jessop wants her to take Mrs Betterton's place. The odds are not good as Olive's last words were: 'Boris – dangerous.'

Checking into the Hotel St Louis with Mrs Betterton's passport, Hilary finds that she has tickets and reservations for six days in Fez and five days in Marrakesh, and follows her fateful itinerary . . .

Spider's Web
London: Savoy Theatre, 1954; New York: Lolly's Theater Club, 1974

Written for Margaret Lockwood, the play takes place in Copplestone Court in Kent, where Clarissa, second wife of diplomat Henry Hailsham-Brown, is entertaining guests. Oliver Costello, the new husband of Henry's first wife Miranda, turns up, insisting that Clarissa's stepdaughter Pippa be returned to her mother. Clarissa promises to fight this tooth and nail, and Pippa is fearful. She hates Oliver, saying he is 'wicked, wicked, wicked'. Later, returning alone in the room through the French windows, Costello is clubbed by an unseen hand. Pippa confesses to killing him, so Clarissa tries to conceal the body. Then the police turn up . . .

It was made into a movie in 1960. The BBC made a TV version in 1982 and the play was novelized by Charles Osborne, published by HarperCollins in the UK and St Martin's Press in the US in 2000.

Verdict

London: Strand Theatre, 1958

Professor Karl Hendryk and his invalid wife Anya have fled to London to escape persecution. Anya's cousin Lisa Koletzky acts as their housekeeper, though she is a trained physicist. The professor only takes on poor pupils who he thinks will profit from private tuition and refuses Helen Rollander, a former debutante and daughter of a rich man. Lisa spots that Helen is in love with the professor, though Lisa plainly has feelings for Hendryk herself.

When Helen's father, Sir William Rollander, offers to arrange a new cure from America for Anya, Hendryk agrees to take Helen on as a pupil. Then Helen is left with Mrs Hendryk, who persuades her to give her some medicine. Helen complies and Mrs Hendryk dies. After recovering from shock, Helen wipes her fingerprints off the medicine bottle, presses it into Anya's hand and flees . . .

The Unexpected Guest

London: Duchess Theatre, 1958

After running his car into a ditch on a foggy night, Michael Starkwedder makes his way to a nearby house. Entering through the French windows, he finds a man dead. Richard Warwick has been shot through the head. His wife, Laura, is standing nearby, holding a gun. Starkwedder is the unexpected guest. Laura admits to the murder and asks him to call the police, but first Starkwedder wants her to tell him why she shot her husband.

The story was adapted for the radio by the BBC in 1981 and novelized by Charles Osborne in 1999.

Ordeal by Innocence

London: Collins, The Crime Club, 1958; New York: Dodd, Mead & Co., 1959

Arthur Calgary turns up at Sunny Point with what he thinks is good news for the Argyle family. Calgary had been away on an expedition and had only just returned to England after two years. During that time, Jacko Argyle, the son of the family, has been convicted of murdering his foster mother, Mrs Rachel Argyle, after being overheard being threatening and abusive. She was found bludgeoned with a poker and money had been stolen.

Though he was picked up with the money on him, Jacko protested his innocence, saying he had an alibi. He had hitched a lift in a car to nearby Drymouth at the time. As the driver could not be found, Jacko was convicted and died of pneumonia in prison. Though the family believe that he is guilty, Calgary insists that Jacko was innocent. He was the driver who gave Jacko the lift that night.

Calgary had not come forward at the time because, shortly afterwards, he had been knocked down by a lorry and suffered temporary amnesia. Soon after he was on his way to Antarctica – it was only when he got back that he found out what had happened and went to the police.

The family are far from delighted by the news. Seeing him out, the housekeeper Kirsten Lindstrom says: 'It's not the guilty who matter. It's the innocent . . . Don't you see what you've done to us all?'

The problem for the family is, if Jacko was not guilty, then one of the others must be the murderer. Or perhaps Jacko is not as innocent as Dr Calgary believes him to be.

This was one of Agatha Christie's favourite books because there is no intrusion by a Poirot or a Marple to solve the mystery.

Ordeal by Innocence was filmed in 1985. It appeared in the *Marple* TV series in 2007. That same year, a dramatized version appeared on the stage in the New York State Theater Institute in Troy, New York, and it appeared as a graphic novel published by HarperCollins in 2008.

The Pale Horse
London: Collins, The Crime Club, 1961; New York: Dodd, Mead & Co., 1962

The narrator is Mark Eastbrook who lives in Chelsea. One evening, he visits a Bohemian coffee bar where a catfight takes place. One girl tears out tufts of the other girl's red hair. The redhead's name is Thomasina Tuckerton. About a week later, *The Times* carries her death notice.

Easterbrook visits his friend Ariadne Oliver. He mentions the encounter in Chelsea after Ariadne remarks how difficult it is to tear hair out by the roots. His cousin Rhoda Despard wants Mrs Oliver to open a fête at the village of Much Deeping. She refuses – she won't organize another 'murder hunt' after what happened last time (see *Dead Man's Folly*). Easterbook calms her fears, saying that she will only have to sit in a tent and sign her books – at five shillings (25p) a time.

The action then moves to a presbytery where Father Gorman is asked to come and give a woman her last rites. She is agitated and talks of 'wickedness', saying 'it must be stopped'. Walking home in the fog, Gorman is killed with a cosh. A list of names is found on a piece of paper in his shoe. One of the names on the list is Tuckerton. Another name on the list is Hesketh-Dubois. The police phone Lady Hesketh-Dubois to discover that she died five months before, seemingly of natural causes.

After seeing *Macbeth* at the Old Vic, Easterbrook is introduced to a girl called Poppy. The conversation, not unnaturally, turns to witches, then murder and how easy or difficult it would be to organize. In this context, Poppy mentions 'the Pale Horse', but when questioned grows flushed and drops the subject. (The pale horse is a reference to the Four Horsemen of the Apocalypse in the *Book of Revelation*; it is the mount of the fourth horseman who represents pestilence and death.)

The following morning, Mrs Oliver phones, saying that she will open the fête, but mentions a local pub she won't go near called the Pale Horse. Easterbook is then called by the solicitor of Lady Hesketh-Dubois, reminding him that, under her will, he is entitled to three of her pictures. Going to her home, he meets the police surgeon Dr Corrigan. They had been at Oxford together. Over lunch, Corrigan tells Easterbrook about Father Gorman's list.

At the fête Easterbrook discovers that the Pale Horse is no longer a pub. It is now a private house that belongs to Thyrza Grey, known for spiritualism, trances and magic. She lives there with the medium Sybil Stamfordis and Bella the cook, who, it is said, is also a witch.

Easterbrook takes tea at the Pale Horse where the conversation turns from magic to murder. Thyrza Grey talks of the ability to induce death at a distance. Mrs Oliver mentions that she has to attend the funeral the next day of Mary Delafontaine – another of the names on the list. Easterbrook now sets out to discover whether the three witches of Much Deeping are silly old women or part of sinister organization bent on murder.

The novel was adapted as a TV movie in 1996, then appeared in the *Marple* TV series in 2010.

Double Sin

New York: Dodd, Mead & Co., 1961

This collection of eight short stories was not published in the UK. However, 'The Last Séance' appeared in *The Hound of Death* in 1933. 'The Theft of the Royal Ruby' appears as 'The Adventure of the Christmas Pudding' in *The Adventure of the Christmas Pudding and a Selection of Entrées* in 1960, along with 'Greenshaw's Folly'. 'Double Sin', 'Wasp's Nest' and 'The Double Clue' appear in *Poirot's Early Cases* in 1974. And 'The Dressmaker's Doll' and 'Sanctuary' appear in *Miss Marple's Final Cases and Two Other Stories* in 1979.

Rule Of Three
London: Duchess Theatre, 1962

Christie wrote three one-action plays. In *The Rats* Sandra and her lover David arrive for a non-existent party to find themselves locked in with the body of Sandra's husband while a knife they have handled has been dropped over the balcony. *Afternoon at the Seaside* concerns a siren in a bikini who turns men's heads and makes women jealous. She turns out to be a policewoman out to solve a jewellery theft. And in *The Patient* Mrs Winfield has fallen over a balcony, but was it an accident, a failed suicide or an attempted murder? Only the apparatus set up by Dr Ginsberg can reveal the truth.

Endless Night
London: Collins, The Crime Club, 1967; New York: Dodd, Mead & Co., 1968

The narrator Michael Rogers has plans for a dream house, cooked up with his architect friend Rudolf Santonix, where he will live with a girl that he loved. It was a fantasy, something he knows he would never have.

Then one day he is strolling around Kingston Bishop, when he notices that a Victorian pile called 'The Towers' is for sale. While he hates the house, he is taken by the grounds which are called 'Gipsy's Acre'. The locals say that there are accidents there because it was cursed by the gipsies who have since been moved on. Mrs Lee, a fortune-teller with gipsy blood, warns him to stay away.

After the auction of the property, Roger walks along the road to Gipsy's Acre. He sees a young woman, Ellie, standing by a fir tree. She asks whether the property was sold; it had not reached its reserve. He admits that he could not afford to buy it, but outlines his plans if he did. Ellie is impressed. On the way back to the village, Mrs Lee warns them off again.

Michael and Ellie meet up again in London. Ellie is rich,

while Michael is a chauffeur – after a long line of menial jobs. They fall in love and Ellie buys Gipsy Acre. She has already been to see Santonix who is going to build the dream house for them.

They marry secretly in Plymouth, avoiding the press. While they honeymoon, building work starts. Mr Lippincott, Ellie's guardian and trustee, comes over from the US to check out Michael, who lets slip the story of the curse. Apparently, a man shot his wife and her lover on Gipsy's Acre, before turning the gun on himself.

Finally, the house is finished. They are having their first meal there – with Santonix – when a stone smashes through the window, injuring Ellie.

One morning they find a dead bird skewered on a knife with a note telling them to leave. Ellie sprains her ankle and Greta, an au pair who has been with Ellie since she was seventeen, moves in. Then there is a mysterious death . . .

The novel was filmed in 1972. BBC Radio 4 broadcast a radio adaptation in 2008. It is being filmed for the *Marple* TV series and a graphic novel was published by Harper-Collins in 2008.

Passenger to Frankfurt

London: Collins, The Crime Club, 1970; New York: Dodd, Mead & Co., 1970

Unfulfilled British diplomat Sir Stafford Nye, known largely for his brash sartorial style, is approached by a young woman in the transit lounge at Frankfurt Airport. She is in fear of being murdered. She wants to borrow his flamboyant cloak, his passport and his boarding pass so she can get to London safely – she is going to cut off her hair and pass herself off as him. All he has to do is swallow a sleeping draught and pretend to have been robbed. Out of boredom, Sir Stafford goes along with her plan.

Back in London, he is told that the woman who took

his passport was Miss Daphne Theodofanous, aka Mary Ann. She is a spy and Nye had indeed saved her life. Then he finds his flat has been searched and a car tries to run him down. Assuming that this has something to do with the girl, he puts a personal ad in the newspaper saying: 'Passenger to Frankfurt. November 3rd. Please communicate with fellow traveller to London.' Another attempt is made on his life and someone is plainly following him.

A reply to his ad suggests a rendezvous on Hungerford Bridge. On the bridge, a woman slips a ticket to the Festival Hall into his hand. Wagner's *Siefried* is playing. In the next seat is the girl he met at Frankfurt airport. She pencils some musical notation in his programme which he can't decipher.

At a dinner at the American Embassy, he meets the girl from Frankfurt again. She is introduced as Countess Renata Zerkowski. She offers him a lift home. Instead she takes him out to a house in Surrey. The assembled bigwigs there recruit Nye to investigate the cause of the unrest that is wracking the world. Their first stop is the Bayreuth Festival.

The Golden Ball and Other Stories
New York: Dodd, Mead & Co., 1971
This collection was not published in the UK. However, most of the stories had already appeared in anthologies in Britain – 'The Listerdale Mystery', 'The Girl in the Train', 'The Manhood of Edward Robinson', 'Jane in Search of a Job', 'A Fruitful Sunday', 'The Golden Ball', 'The Rajah's Emerald' and 'Swan Song' in *The Listerdale Mystery*, and 'The Hound of Death', 'The Gipsy', 'The Lamp', 'The Strange Case of Sir Arthur Carmichael' and 'The Call of Wings in *The Hound of Death and Other Stories*. There were also two stories that had not been published in book form before.

'Magnolia Blossom'
First published in issue 329 of the Royal Magazine, *March 1926*
Vincent Easton is waiting under the clock at Victoria Station for Theodora Darrell, the beautiful wife of Richard Darrell. They had first kissed under a magnolia tree. The pair are running way to South Africa together and take a train to Dover on the first leg of their journey.

Having tea in their hotel room there, Vincent reads that Hobson, Jekyll and Lucas have collapsed. This is Richard Darrell's firm. Theodora decides that she has to return to her husband, but this is not without its complications – Darrell faces jail if his wife does not retrieve papers that are in Easton's possession.

'Next to a Dog'
First published in issue 295 of The Grand Magazine, *September 1929*
Young widow Joyce Lambert is looking for a job, but she cannot leave her elderly, half-blind terrier, a present from her husband who had gambled all their money away. Consequently, she accepts the proposal of a wealthy man, although she does not love him. However, an accident takes her on a new path.

Fiddlers Three
Guildford: Yvonne Arnaud Theatre, 1972
Agatha Christie originally wrote the play *Fiddlers Five*, which toured the British provinces in 1971. The following year it opened in Guildford, but failed to transfer to the West End.

Akhnaton
London: Collins, 1973; New York: Dodd, Mead & Co., 1973
Agatha Christie wrote the play *Akhnaton* in 1937. It was not produced at the time. However, following the popularity of the 'Treasures of Tutankhamun' exhibition at the British Museum in 1972, it was published.

The story concerns the Egyptian Pharaoh Akhnaton, his wife Nefertiti and his son and successor Tutankhamun, and Aknaton's doomed attempt to set up a new religion.

Problem At Pollensa Bay and Other Stories
London: HarperCollins, 1991

The eight stories in this volume were published elsewhere in collections in the US. 'Problem at Pollensa Bay', 'Yellow Iris' and 'The Regatta Mystery' appeared in *The Regatta Mysteries and Other Stories* in 1939. 'The Second Gong' appeared as 'Dead Man's Mirror' in *Murder in the Mews* in 1937. 'The Love Detectives' appeared in *Three Blind Mice and Other Stories* in 1950. 'Next to a Dog' and 'Magnolia Blossom' appear in *The Golden Ball and Other Stories* in 1971. And 'The Harlequin Tea Set' appears in *The Harlequin Tea Set* in 1997.

'The Harlequin Tea Set'
First published in Winter's Crimes #3, Macmillan, 1971

Mr Satterthwaite's car has broken down again. While it is being fixed he walks to the Harlequin Café, thinking that he might find Harley Quin, who has not been seen for some years. Indeed, Mr Quin does appear, but he won't be persuaded to accompany Mr Satterthwaite who is visiting his old friend Tom Addison; instead he leaves Satterthwaite with one word: 'Daltonism.'

He recalls what the word means when he sees Tom wearing one red slipper and one green one. (Daltonism is another name for colour blindness.) Tom also had a scarecrow he calls Harley Barley which looks like Mr Quin in a certain light. Colour blindness runs in the family and, alerted to this, Mr Satterthwaite prevents a murder. Then the scarecrow catches fire.

The Harlequin Tea Set
New York: GP Putnam, 1997; London: published as While the Light Lasts and Other Stories, *HarperCollins, 1997*

There are nine short stories in each collection, but in the UK edition 'A Christmas Adventure' replaces 'The Harlequin Tea Set', which was published in *Problem at Pollensa Bay and Other Stories* in the UK in 1991; and 'The Mystery of the Baghdad Chest', published in *The Regatta Mystery and Other Stories* in the US in 1939, replaces 'The Mystery of the Spanish Chest', published in *The Adventure of the Christmas Pudding and a Selection of Entrées* in the UK in 1960.

'The Edge'
First published in issue 374 of Pearson's Magazine, *February 1927*

Thirty-two-year-old parish worker Clare Halliwell had been a childhood friend of Sir Gerald Lee and had hoped, one day, to marry him. Then he suddenly marries the beautiful Vivien Harper, who takes no interest in village matters. When Clare discovers that Vivien is having an affair, she finds that her emotions conflict with her conscience and discovers that she was not the person she thought she was at all.

'The Actress'
First published in issue 218 of The Novel Magazine, *May 1923, as 'A Trap for the Unwary'*

Blackmailer Jake Levitt is at the theatre and recognizes the star Olga Stormer as Nancy Taylor. However, when he tries to extort money from her, he walks right into a trap.

'While the Light Lasts'
First published in issue 229 of The Novel Magazine, *April 1924*

This story provided the plot for *Giant's Bread* (1930), the first novel Christie wrote under the pseudonym Mary Westmacott.

George Crozier is driving through Africa with his wife Deirdre and realizes that she is thinking of her first husband, Tim Nugent, who was killed in that part of Africa during the First World War. Although she loved him, she has now been fatally seduced by the wealthy lifestyle Crozier can offer her.

'The House of Dreams'

First published in issue 74 of the Sovereign Magazine, *January 1926*
This is a reworking of a story that Agatha Christie wrote in her teens called 'The House of Beauty'.

John Segrave came from a decayed landowning family that was on its last legs. He lives in a dingy bedsit, but dreams repeatedly of a beautiful house. The daughter of a wealthy businessman fancies him, but he falls for her beautiful friend who turns his dream into a nightmare.

'The Lonely God'

First published in issue 333 of the Royal Magazine, *July 1926 (originally 'The Little Lonely God')*
Frank Oliver has returned from years abroad to find life in London lonely. In the British Museum, he sees a little stone figure of a god. It looks lost and he fancies himself a worshipper. A second worshipper turns up in the form of a young woman. They become friends, but she is determined to remain mysterious.

'Manx Gold'

First published in the Daily Despatch, *23–28 May 1930, as clues in a treasure hunt to promote the Isle of Man*
The story concerns Juan Faraker and Fenella Mylecharane whose eccentric Uncle Myles has hidden four treasure chests on the island. Although cousins, if they find the treasure they can marry. They are pitted against two other members of the family. Clues to the treasure's location are given in the story, but after the first chest is found, the

house is broken into and the next set of clues are taken. There is, of couse, a murder.

'Within a Wall'

First published in issue 324 of the Royal Magazine, *October 1925*

Modernist painter Alan Everard has taken to portraiture with some acclaim. Then he unveils a portrait of his wife, society girl Isobel Loring, which the critics condemn as lifeless, whereas an unfinished portrait of Jane Haworth is full of life. It is only after Jane is dead that Alan understands why.

'Christmas Adventure'

First published in issue 1611 of the Sketch, *11 December 1923*

Later extended as 'The Adventure of the Christmas Pudding' (see *The Adventure of the Christmas Pudding and a Selection of Entrées*).

FURTHER READING

Bargainnier, Earl, *The Gentle Art of Murder: The Detective Fiction of Agatha Christie* (Bowling Green, Ohio: Bowling Green University Popular Press, 1980)

Bayard, Pierre, *Who Killed Roger Ackroyd? The Mystery Behind the Agatha Christie Mystery* (New York: The New Press, 2000)

Christie, Agatha, *4.50 from Paddington* (London: HarperCollins, 2002)

Christie, Agatha, *The ABC Murders: A Hercule Poirot Mystery* (Glasgow: Collins, 1962)

Christie, Agatha, *The Adventure of the Christmas Pudding and a selection of Entrées* (London: HarperCollins, 2002)

Christie, Agatha, *Afternoon at the Seaside* (London: Samuel French, 1963)

Christie, Agatha, *After the Funeral* (Glasgow: Collins, 1963)

Christie, Agatha, *An Autobiography* (London: William Collins, Sons & Co, 1977)

Christie, Agatha, *And Then There Were None* (London: Harper Collins, 1999)

Christie, Agatha, *Appointment with Death* (London: Pan Books, 1957)

Christie, Agatha, *At Bertram's Hotel* (London: HarperCollins, 2008)

Christie, Agatha, *The Best of Poirot* (London: Collins, 1980)

Christie, Agatha, *The Big Four* (London: William Collins, Sons & Co, 1931)

Christie, Agatha, *The Body in the Library* (Glasgow: Collins, 1962)

Christie, Agatha, *By the Pricking of My Thumbs* (London: Harper Collins, 1994)

Christie, Agatha, *A Caribbean Mystery* (London: HarperCollins, 2002)

Christie, Agatha, *Cat Among the Pigeons* (Glasgow: Collins, 1964)

Christie, Agatha, *The Clocks* (London: HarperCollins, 2002)

Christie, Agatha, *The Complete Ariadne Oliver* (London: Harper Collins, 2005)

Christie, Agatha, *Complete Short Stories of Miss Marple* (London: HarperCollins, 1997)

Christie, Agatha, *Crooked House* (London: Collins, 1967)

Christie, Agatha, *Curtain: Poirot's Last Case* (London: Harper Collins, 2002)

Christie, Agatha, *Death Comes as the End* (London: HarperCollins, 2001)

Christie, Agatha, *Death in the Clouds* (London: Pan Books, 1964)

Christie, Agatha, *Death on the Nile* (London: Harper, 2007)

Christie, Agatha, *Destination Unknown* (Glasgow: Collins, 1958)

Christie, Agatha, *Elephants Can Remember* (London: HarperCollins, 2002)

Christie, Agatha, *Endless Night* (London: HarperCollins, 2002)

Christie, Agatha, *Evil Under the Sun* (London: HarperCollins, 1999)

Christie, Agatha, *Five Little Pigs* (London: HarperCollins, 2000)

Christie, Agatha, *Hallowe'en Party* (London: HarperCollins, 2001)

Christie, Agatha, *The Harlequin Tea Set and Other Stories* (New York: William Morrow & Company, 2012)

Christie, Agatha, *Hercule Poirot's Casebook* (London: Fontana, 1989)

Christie, Agatha, *Hercule Poirot's Christmas* (London: HarperCollins, 2001)

Christie, Agatha, *Hercule Poirot's Early Cases* (London: HarperCollins, 2002)

Christie, Agatha, *Hickory Dickory Dock* (London: Pan Books, 1967)

Christie, Agatha, *The Hound of Death* (London: HarperCollins, 2003)

Christie, Agatha, *The Labours of Hercules* (London: Collins, 1980)

Christie, Agatha, *The Listerdale Mystery* (London: Harper Collins, 2003)

Christie, Agatha, *Lord Edgware Dies* (London: HarperCollins, 1997)

Christie, Agatha, *The Man in the Brown Suit* (London: Harper-Collins, 2002)

Christie, Agatha, *The Mirror Crack'd from Side to Side* (London: HarperCollins, 2002)

Christie, Agatha, *The Mousetrap and Selected Plays* (London: HarperCollins, 2011)

Christie, Agatha, *The Moving Finger* (London: Pan Books, 1948)

Christie, Agatha, *Mrs McGinty's Dead* (Glasgow: Collins, 1964)

Christie, Agatha, *Murder in Mesopotamia* (London: Harper Collins, 2001)

Christie, Agatha, *A Murder is Announced* (London: Pan Books, 1958)

Christie, Agatha, *Murder is Easy* (London: HarperCollins, 2002)

Christie, Agatha, *The Murder of Roger Ackroyd* (London: Harper, 2007)

Christie, Agatha, *Murder on the Links* (London: HarperCollins, 2007)

Christie, Agatha, *Murder on the Orient Express* (London: Harper Collins, 2001)

Christie, Agatha, *Murders to Die For* (London: HarperCollins, 2005)

Christie, Agatha, *The Mysterious Affair at Styles* (London: Harper Collins, 1997)

Christie, Agatha, *The Mysterious Mr Quin* (London: Harper Collins, 2003)

Christie, Agatha, *The Mystery of the Blue Train* (London: Collins, 1977)

Christie, Agatha, *N or M?* (London: Pan Books, 1959)

Christie, Agatha, *Nemesis* (London: HarperCollins, 2003)

Christie, Agatha, *One, Two, Buckle My Shoe* (London: Collins, 1959)

Christie, Agatha, *Ordeal by Innocence* (London: HarperCollins, 2003)

Christie, Agatha, *The Patient* (London: Samuel French, 1963)

Christie, Agatha, *The Pale Horse* (London: HarperCollins, 2002)

Christie, Agatha, *Parker Pyne Investigates* (London: Harper Collins, 2003)

Christie, Agatha, *Partners in Crime* (London: HarperCollins, 1997)

Christie, Agatha, *Peril at End House* (London: HarperCollins, 1997)

Christie, Agatha, *A Pocket Full of Rye* (London: HarperCollins, 2011)

Christie, Agatha, *Poirot Investigates* (London: HarperCollins, 2001)

Christie, Agatha, *Poirot Loses a Client* (New York: Dell, 1965)

Christie, Agatha, *Postern of Fate* (London: HarperCollins, 2003)

Christie, Agatha, *Problem at Pollensa Bay and Other Stories* (London: HarperCollins, 1991)

Christie, Agatha, *The Rats* (London: Samuel French, 1963)

Christie, Agatha, *The Regatta Mystery and Other Stories* (London: HarperCollins, 2003)

Christie, Agatha, *Sad Cypress* (Glasgow: Fontana, 1966)

Christie, Agatha, *Secret Adversary* (London: Fontana, 1991)

Christie, Agatha, *The Secret of Chimneys* (London: Harper Collins, 2001)

Christie, Agatha, *The Seven Dials Mystery* (Harmondsworth: Penguin Books, 1948)

Christie, Agatha, *The Sittaford Mystery* (Harmondsworth: Penguin Books, 1948)

Christie, Agatha, *Sleeping Murder* (London: HarperCollins, 2003)

Christie, Agatha, *Sparkling Cyanide* (London: Collins, 1960)

Christie, Agatha, *Spider's Web* (London: HarperCollins, 2001)

Christie, Agatha, *Taken at the Flood* (London: Pan Books, 1965)

Christie, Agatha, *They Came to Baghdad* (London: Harper Collins, 2001)

Christie, Agatha, *They Do it With Mirrors* (London: Harper Collins, 2001)

Christie, Agatha, *Three Act Tragedy* (London: HarperCollins, 2002)

Christie, Agatha, *Three Blind Mice* (New York: Macmillan, 1965)

Christie, Agatha, *Towards Zero* (London: Collins, 1973)

Christie, Agatha, *The Unexpected Guest* (London: Samuel French, 1958)

Christie, Agatha, *Verdict* (New York: Samuel French, 1958)

Christie, Agatha, *While the Light Lasts* (London: HarperCollins, 2003)

Christie, Agatha, *Why Didn't They Ask Evans?* (Glasgow: Collins, 1966)

Cresswell, James, *Miss Marple and All Her Characters* (Great Britain: James Cresswell, 2006)

Curran, John, *Agatha Christie's Secret Notebooks: Fifty Years of Mysteries in the Making* (London: HarperCollins, 2009)

Fido, Martin, *The World of Agatha Christie: The Facts and Fiction Behind the World's Greatest Crime Writer* (London: Carlton Books, 1999)

Gill, Gillian, *Agatha Christie: The Woman and Her Mysteries* (London: Robson, 1991)

Hack, Richard, *Duchess of Death* (Los Angeles: Phoenix Books, 2009)

Haining, Peter, *Agatha Christie's Poirot: A Celebration of the Great Detective* (London: Boxtree, 1995)

Hart, Anne, *The Life and Times of Hercule Poirot* (London: Sphere, 1990)

Holgate, Mike, *Stranger than Fiction: Agatha Christie's True Crime Inspirations* (Stroud, Gloucestershire: The History Press, 2010)

Keating H. R. F. (ed), *Agatha Christie: First Lady of Crime* (London: Weidenfeld and Nicolson, 1977)

Maida, Patricia, and Spornick, Nicholas, *Murder She Wrote: A Study of Agatha Christie's Detective Fiction* (Bowling Green, Ohio: Bowling Green State University, 1982)

Morgan, Janet, *Agatha Christie: A Biography* (London: Fontana, 1985)

Murdoch, Derrick, *The Agatha Christie Mystery* (Toronto, Ontario: Pagurian Press, 1976)

Norman, Andrew, *Agatha Christie: The Finished Portrait* (Stroud, Gloucestershire: Tempus Publishing, 2006)

Osborne, Charles, *Agatha Christie – Murder in Three Stages* (London: HarperCollins, 2007)

Robyns, Gwen, *The Mystery of Agatha Christie* (Garden City, New York: Doubleday & Company, Inc., 1978)

Sanders, Dennis, and Lovallo, Len, *The Agatha Christie Companion* (New York: Berkley Books, 1989)

Thompson, Laura, *Agatha Christie: An English Mystery* (London: Headline, 2007)

Toye, Randall, *The Agatha Christie Who's Who* (London: Federick Muller, 1980)

York, R. A., *Agatha Christie: Power and Illusion* (New York: Palgrave Macmillan, 2007)

Wagstaff, Vanessa, and Poole, Stephen, *Agatha Christie: A Reader's Companion* (London: Aurum Press, 2004)

Westmacott, Mary, *Absent in the Spring* (London: HarperCollins, 1997)

Westmacott, Mary, *The Burden* (London: HarperCollins, 1997)

Westmacott, Mary, *A Daughter's Daughter* (London: Harper Collins, 1997)

Westmacott, Mary, *Giant's Bread* (London: Fontana, 1975)

Westmacott, Mary, *The Rose and the Yew* (Glasgow: Fontana, 1974)

Westmacott, Mary, *Unfinished Portrait* (London: Collins, 1974)

Zemboy, James, *The Detective Novels of Agatha Christie: A Reader's Guide* (Jefferson, North Carolina: McFarland & Company, 2008)

INDEX